SOUTH AMERICA

ENCHANTMENT

BY THE SAME AUTHOR

NON-FICTION

MY JOURNEY TO AFRICA

RUSSIA AND THE SILK ROADS

SOUTH AMERICA EXPLORATION

FICTION

THE RED CARPET COLLECTION

THE RIVER OF LIFE

POEM COLLECTIONS

SONGS OF HONOUR

THE COLORS OF LIFE

THE BEST POEMS AND POETS OF 2005

SOUTH AMERICA

ENCHANTMENT

robert f. edwards

Cover Design/Artwork by: Robert F. Edwards

Photography by: Robert F. Edwards

Order this book online at www.trafford.com/07-2122
or email orders@trafford.com

Most Trafford titles are also available at major online book retailers.

Note for Librarians: A cataloguing record for this book is available from Library
and Archives Canada at www.collectionscanada.ca/amicus/index-e.html

Printed in Victoria, BC, Canada.

ISBN: 978-1-4251-4902-4

*We at Trafford believe that it is the responsibility of us all, as both individuals
and corporations, to make choices that are environmentally and socially sound.
You, in turn, are supporting this responsible conduct each time you purchase a
Trafford book, or make use of our publishing services. To find out how you are
helping, please visit www.trafford.com/responsiblepublishing.html*

*Our mission is to efficiently provide the world's finest, most comprehensive
book publishing service, enabling every author to experience success.
To find out how to publish your book, your way, and have it available
worldwide, visit us online at www.trafford.com/10510*

 www.trafford.com

North America & international
toll-free: 1 888 232 4444 (USA & Canada)
phone: 250 383 6864 ♦ fax: 250 383 6804 ♦ email: info@trafford.com

The United Kingdom & Europe
phone: +44 (0)1865 722 113 ♦ local rate: 0845 230 9601
facsimile: +44 (0)1865 722 868 ♦ email: info.uk@trafford.com

10 9 8 7 6 5 4 3

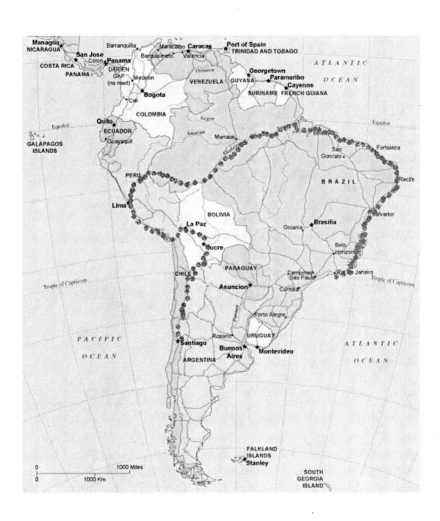

Table of Contents

continued ....

Table of Contents

Artist's Profile

Robert F. Edwards

Burnaby, British Columbia, Canada

Robert F. Edwards is presently living in Burnaby, Canada
with his wife, daughter and grandson. He is a world traveler
and has been on every continent. He enjoys sailing, trekking,
and mountain climbing. He does fencing with all three weapons, twice a week. He also writes poems, and fictional stories.
He pursues the arts in acrylic and water-color painting, and
clay sculpturing, along with photography.

His Credo;
The difficult is done at once, the impossible takes a little
longer.
If a job is worth doing, it is worth doing right.
Don't abuse your friendships, and you will always have
friends.

INTRODUCTION

My wish list on this particular journey of 2002 was to visit Robinson Crusoe Island, which unfortunately with time, the situation did not arise and I had to forfeit this dream. My next dream was to see Machu Picchu, which I did accomplish, and with far more reverence than I had ever hoped. I was able to do the Inca Trails, on a five day trek to Machu Picchu, which was as breathtaking and fulfilling as a moment of reflection when I saw for the first time, with my own eyes, Machu Picchu, and the surrounding mountains. There are moments that we say 'it takes your breath away'; this was one of those moments.

My third wish was to travel from the tributary all the way down through the Amazon River, to its mouth at Belém. I was able to accomplish this. This mighty river that holds second place in the world for length and first place for width, only broadened my imagination beyond anything I had ever experienced before. The vast jungles of the Amazon basin were Mother Nature's reassurance that there is a garden of paradise, that all things are available, within our reach.

So like many opportunities that appear in my life, this one was bountiful, and the rewards are irreplaceable. My journey took me from Lake Titicaca to the Nazca Lines, to Cuzcu and Iquitos in Peru, to the breathtaking landscapes of the high plateaus of Bolivia, to the jungle hamlets along the mighty Amazon. I experienced the Carnivals in Salvador, and the magic of religion that blends itself with the orthodox and the cultures of taboo and felt the pure love of life; of people and their lifestyles, in this region of the world.

I have taken more than one journey, but this one left me giddy and happy with pure merriment of the people that surrounded my days along this journey. I found myself towards the end, being so exuberant and full of life, and the sheer enjoyment of existence, that I told young people that I was Peter Pan, and that I never wanted to grow up, and always wanted to be a child at heart. God bless all of you that have given me this time of enchantment.

January 8, Tuesday

Vancouver, B.C.

No, it didn't start off as a normal morning! I had slept very poorly throughout the previous night, mentally preparing for the day ahead which would start at 4:00 a.m. After a quick shower I got dressed and my good wife drove me to the airport in Vancouver, Canada. I was on my way, starting my second adventure in South America. Once again, I had prepared myself with the equipment that I felt would be necessary for this adventure, everything from a backpack, with a mini-pack attached for trekking, my Gore-Tex outfit for altitude climbing, and the strongest insect repellant available for the jungles of the Amazon.

This adventure, I was hoping, would consist of landing in Chile, working my way into Peru or Bolivia, and then over to Ecuador and possibly Colombia, and finally working my way through the endless tributaries down the mighty Amazon River to the mouth, and then to Rio de Janeiro, completing this adventure. These events may materialize or dissipate as mere dreams - only time will tell.

I had phoned the airport previously, to find how much time was needed under the new stringent requirements of security. To my surprise an hour and a half would suffice and I allowed an extra ten minutes to be on the safe side. Thank goodness I did, for by the time I cleared security I had less than ten minutes to board the plane. In fact, they had already made the first announcement of my name as missing the flight. Boarding the plane, I found to my displeasure, that I was at the very back of the plane - you might say the back of the bus. However, with all my rushing for the scheduled take off at 6:20 a.m., it was well after 7:00 a.m. before we left, due to intensified luggage security. Once airborne, we had a very modest breakfast. United Airlines will never go down as being generous or innovative with their catering.

Robert F. Edwards

I arrived in Chicago on time and the layover was six hours long. I checked with a few attendants, but I knew it would be foolish to venture downtown, only to get back to the airport and go through the horrendous security checks that they are imposing. George Bush now has military personnel at these security points. So with this in mind, I felt that it would be prudent to stay in the greater compound of the security site. Chicago airport is one of the more unique and innovative airports I have been in, and immaculately kept. It is more inspired to provide gifts, jewelry and expensive perfumes than food facilities. I couldn't believe myself when I finally broke down and had a MacDonald's quarter-pounder and French fries for my basic meal of the day, as I am not a great fan of 'Ronnie's'. The hours whittled away to my 6:20 p.m. departure. Unfortunately, this was not going to be a direct flight to Chile, as it had been reassigned to Miami.

I wish now that I had had something more substantial to eat, as it was nearly 11:00 p.m. before we arrived in Miami. On the same flight, I met a Chilean fellow now lives in Vancouver, on his way to visit his wife in Chile. In this modest airport facility we searched but with no success, to find anything other than small vending machines and, after scouring the limited surroundings, we returned to the waiting area to be boarded on a different plane at a different gate. Again, to my displeasure, I found myself at the back of this plane, but the stewardesses were pleasant.

We took off at 12:00 midnight and I was now exceptionally hungry. After filling forms more numerous than one would care to remember, including a survey by United Airlines, we finally got served the evening meal (or the morning meal from the night before). I was sitting beside a gentleman from Holland, probably in his mid-twenties, going down to visit his girlfriend in Chile. When 33,000 ft. was obtained, the pilot informed us that this was going to be our cruising altitude, and dinner was being served. The attendant gave us first choice, after I made a comment that if we were at the back of the bus, we'd be the last ones served. She laughed and said

2

SOUTH AMERICA
ENCHANTMENT

"You have a choice of chicken, roast beef, or pasta" and I chose the pasta. The meal was adequate and quite filling, and I enjoyed a glass of red wine and Heineken beer.

My Dutch friend and I hit it off and as the conversation brushed against many subjects and the dinner tray was removed, he had brought some Dutch chocolates, which we enjoyed and he shared with the stewardess as well. To fully enjoy these delicious treats, we each ordered two cognacs to go with our chocolates.

Planning ahead, I took a sleeping pill, hoping that I would be in full form to tackle the day once I arrived in Chile. However, the conversation was so enjoyable and without realizing it, we had missed the main movie of the evening and out of nowhere, like a genie out of a bottle, one of the stewardesses showed up with champagne and two glasses. She advised us that we were the only ones still awake, so we might as well enjoy further conversation with a bubbly, once again thanking us for the chocolates and telling us that they were appreciated. By the time we had finished off the bottle, it was 5:00 a.m. Miami time? Maybe it is Chicago time? But anyway, my time on the airplane. I said goodnight to my Dutch companion and the next thing I knew, it was shortly after 7:00 a.m. The window blinds had been pulled up, the sun was streaming in and breakfast was now being served.

I could no longer say that it was January 8th, so this must conclude the first day of being mobile. Good night, good morning, and I love you, my darling Marietta and my daughter Wendy.

Robert F. Edwards

January 9, Wednesday

Santiago, Chile

As breakfast was being served, I was still feeling the hazy effects of being up over 24 hours and having a liquid evening. The plane arrived in Santiago, Chile, on time and to my pleasant surprise, my entrance fee paid on my visit last year is still valid, so I am already $65.00 U.S. better off. My newly acquired Dutch friend asked me where I was staying and offered me accommodations at his girlfriend's place. I politely declined, and said that I would be just grateful if they could drop me off in the downtown core at a hotel that I had chosen.

After having an espresso and meeting his charming young lady, we say our good-byes, and two of their friends with a pick-up truck offer to take me to town. These gentlemen do not speak any English and of course I don't speak Spanish. They start to take some back roads and finally ended up in a small neighborhood. I have to admit I was becoming a bit apprehensive, as I always prefer to be in control of the situation. I was soon to find out that they didn't know where the hotel was, so they were going to their home to check the phone book for an address.

North Americans do have a large dose of paranoia, and I am glad to be in South America, where people do things just because they are the right things to do and kindness is a way of life. After driving around the downtown core of Santiago without much success, they had stopped at three or four different places trying to find directions; I encouraged them that just any cheap hotel at a certain zone that I have pointed out would suffice.

To my delight, they find a very nice hotel for US$23.00. I have my own washroom; it is quiet, very clean and comfortable. It also has a nice little patio, with table and chairs for eating. I made the gesture more than once to try and put some gas into these gentlemen's truck, and both of them re-

SOUTH AMERICA ENCHANTMENT

peated "no, no, no. It's our pleasure." It used to be people would give me their addresses; then as things progressed, it was phone numbers; today, the e-mail is the gesture in the communication of the world and there is no exception down here. After exchanging our e-mail addresses, I said my good-byes to these kind emissaries of South America.

After checking my luggage in, I began to feel the effects of the cramped conditions on the plane and the long flight. Without elaborating in any great depths on air travel, I would say United and other airlines that have copied their seat arrangement are catering to either midgets or children, anything but medium height and build. I find that the seats are barely endurable for short periods of time, excruciating for long periods, and the reclining position is mere inches, so that you cannot find any kind of rest. Enough said on that. I am here and I do rest for a few hours. After getting up, I decided to try and get e-mail off to the beloved little wife and my deed was successful.

It's very hot compared to what I've left behind in Vancouver. The temperatures are well in the 80 degrees Fahrenheit. But with all due respect to Vancouver, I can't help but feel both at ease and glad to be back in Santiago. It's a beautiful city and it's surprising how much I remember since my last visit here and find my way around relatively easily. I venture out for something to eat and end up with a hamburger. Oh my goodness, what a difference. If the Americans ever get hold of this one, it would put McDonald's out of business. The bun alone is delightful. The meat is, believe it or not, real meat and absolutely smothered in mozzarella cheese. The quarter pounder with cheese isn't even a distant poor relative to this humungous meal and, this meal I may add, is much cheaper. So, way to go, Chileans!

A leisurely stroll around the streets renews memories of my last visit. I enjoy the plazas, so numerous to be almost the entire core of the city. Other than in the main artery, cars are the ones out of favor rather than the pedestrians. In terms of both the weather and the layout of the city, it's such a delight to walk these long corridors with shops on both sides. North American cities will have the occasional bench to sit on, but here you can easily sit on either side of the boulevards and just rest as you are enjoying the shopping bonanza.

There is a great deal of activity going on with street vendors; anything from American cigarettes to little trinkets and the universal 'hand-made', every entrepreneur's dream of making it as a street vendor. The shoeshine vendors are alive and well, and very organized. They have small metal chairs for the patron to sit on and they do their deed. Most of these men look like they have had fairly hard lives and range from 40 years plus. In one group, the men are all dressed in black T-shirts with their names on them and of course their little carts have advertising on them, probably promoting some form of shoe polish. Others are dressed in green with much the same type of advertising, but are obviously different vendors with a higher fee for franchising. Why I'm going into such great lengths to describe the shoeshine vendors is because it would be very difficult in my city to find a shoe shiner if not in an exclusive hotel, then probably a shoe repair shop is the only other choice for the common resident. But here there is an abundance of them and they are utilized by the local residents, so it's something in vogue.

Another aspect of the culture that I admired (and took a picture of) was two police officers. One was male, the other was female, both was wearing khaki uniforms riding beautiful horses through this downtown core and overseeing the occupation of people that are in the region. I noticed in the short time that I had been watching that the locals have no problems asking the police officers for information. It is a nice flavor of law and order that Chile should be very proud to have.

One other unique thing, I think, is that the cars permitted to go through this zone of open malls. At the intersections are large domes and I watched a man drive his car up to an inconspicuous looking machine and place a card in. Then two cones collapse to ground level, permitting the car to exit the zone. I also appreciate the cleanliness of the city and the people's attitudes.   There is an abundance of trashcans in all

types and descriptions, and also street sweepers that also aid
and assist in cleaning up. I sincerely believe that the Chileans
take a sincere pride in keeping their city clean for their own
enjoyment.

This is their summer period, (and extremely warm I felt) and
Chileans seem to consume a large numbers of ice cream
cones from the many kiosks along the way.   Walking
O'Higgins Boulevard, one of the main arteries in Santiago,
brought back many fond memories. This boulevard is massive by North American standards. It would be equivalent in
width to a North America twelve-lane highway, with its luxurious lawns and trees and an abundance of benches to sit on,
to say nothing of the many statues displayed artistically
throughout the boulevard.

If I sound quite exuberant about the appearance of this
city, it warrants it, and it was my first choice of destination
before heading to the Islands off the coastline of Chile known
as Robinson Crusoe Islands. However fate has not dealt this
one in the cards for me and unfortunately it's not going to be
a feasible adventure, so I will be heading up north to start my
adventure though Bolivia and Peru.

Robert F. Edwards

Even with the disappointment of not being able to experience that particular part of this expedition, I am still grateful to start this new adventure in Santiago. In such a short time, it's already been a very rewarding homecoming to me. I've returned to the hotel, as my feet are sore and I'm quite fatigued, so I have another small rest and by this time it's getting towards seven o'clock in the evening so I once more venture out for something to eat.

As I'm walking around and enjoying myself, a voice says, "Hi, how are you doing?" and with that I turned around and there was a young man that I met on the plane. Wes, a fellow Canadian, was now living in Calgary. We make a bit of small talk, sharing our first day in South America. He was quite surprised that so few people speak any amount of English, and he found it somewhat challenging. Needless to say, I've always found it challenging communicating with anybody anywhere in the world, and sometimes when they speak the language that I have at my disposal, English, I find them still not being able to communicate very well. So, it was nothing new for me.

As we strolled through the area, we came to the plaza where the Marco Polo restaurant was. Tonight, my wish of the previous year came true. I sat and had a meal though it was modest, due to the fact that I wasn't very hungry at the Marco Polo restaurant. The weather here is great, like Goldilocks' porridge- not too hot, not too cold- the baby's porridge is just right. In the evenings, with a light breeze, it is just pleasant to be outside. Also, to my delight, there are no mosquitoes or flies to interrupt or demand attention. The insect world, for whatever reason, has not found this place, which only adds to the sheer enjoyment of eating outside. I had a soup with some salsa and bread and a beer, and Wes had French fries and a beer. He kept on mentioning how expensive it was and I do seem to recall the first few days I was in Chile I too found it expensive. Both in my case and his, we were naive in thinking that South America is a developing country with poor economies and lifestyles and therefore a bargain to us rich

SOUTH AMERICA
ENCHANTMENT

North Americans. On the contrary, there is a high standard of living, excellent living conditions with a quality that we have abandoned in our fast pace gratification.

Wes and I discussed some of the things that he liked to do and I made some recommendations to him on which areas of Chile and South America he would achieve some of these dreams in, and without noticing it, the clock and Mother Time had moved up again to eleven o'clock at night. Both of us expressed a certain amount of fatigue and with that, we said goodnight to each other and I walked back to my hotel, got ready for bed, and read a little bit of some of the things that I might be prepared to venture out on both for tomorrow and in the future of this adventure.

Goodnight my beautiful wife, my wonderful daughter, and my little grandson. This concludes this day.

Robert F. Edwards

Boy! I guess you could call it jetlag, or travel fatigue or acclimatization; who knows, and really who cares, including me. Even though I woke up throughout the night, I still slept very well. It was close to 9:30 a.m. before I really got mobile. Not my style at all. However, it's one of those free days, because the bus that I'm leaving on to go north is not going to depart until 6:00 p.m. and therefore, a lazy summer day for me in beautiful Santiago.

I got up and still felt a bit groggy, and to add to it, my feet were sore, as I've managed to achieve my first blister of this journey. Before heading out, I decided to try a new procedure with just my mini backpack, which seems to be more than accommodating to enjoy the sights for the day. One of the first things that I really would like to have is a cup of coffee and yes, as on my last trip, it is instant coffee. This always gives me a little twinge, thinking that the rest of the world enjoys both Colombian and Brazilian coffees and the natives are left with instant.

I ventured into a small café, with a staff of one, the cook, the waitress, and cashier all being the same person. I pull out my translation book, manage to get a coffee, and order some eggs. This nice lady, being very accommodating, prepares the meal, serves it and explains to me that it's salt that she's brought, which I have no problem comprehending. However, when I try to explain that I'd like pepper as well, she's quite baffled by what I'm trying to convey. After a few attempts, I'm quite prepared to give up because it's not a big thing in my life, but she's really persistent on finding out what I want. I finally come up with the idea of pointing to the saltshaker and saying "negro", meaning black, which results in success. This little anecdote is an example of not only the kindness, but

SOUTH AMERICA
ENCHANTMENT

also the sincere attitude that South Americans have to be helpful, and not to give up at the least point of difficulty.

The same thing was applicable when I bought my bus ticket the other day. I wanted to go to Bolivia, but they kept on saying, "no, none of the buses go to Bolivia, but they do go north", and the men were sincerely helpful. It wasn't a case of 'that's your problem I have no time for it'. I think that's the thing that I've discovered before, in many parts of the world, and even in the short time I've been down here, that North Americans have run out of time for themselves, let alone for anybody else, this attitude is a real loss to the people in North America. It's only when you leave that zone of hustle- bustle of rushing to achieve nothing and self gratification that you realize that these people enjoy life and have time for them-selves, for each other, and takes the time to be able to help strangers. I feel it's so important for my memory to recall in my later years the sheer enjoyment of being here with these people and watching them enjoy life.

The same can be said for the children. As I watch them in the streets with their parents, babes in arms to teenagers, they are well behaved and well dressed. Maybe it is just an old man's hoping that the world will turn on its heels and re-turn to another period, but when you see North American children dressed in the current style of sloppiness, it demon-strates little or no respect for appearance.

Children in North America have developed a trend towards obesity in a warped ideal of time that everything that's fast is good and faster is better than anything in the past, whether it be food or commercials or instant gratification of a sugar fix. I find that people here dress well, and their attire is appealing. The men still wear ties and white shirts, looking very dignified as well as businesslike. Women wear light cotton dresses, knee length. Yes, it is summer, and extremely hot here com-pared to normal weather conditions. However, I do see the locals perspiring as well, and this might be inducive to the slower pace.

Robert F. Edwards

Even in a large city such as this, with a population that matches anything in the larger cities of North America, the people have a more relaxed, balanced approach even to their traffic. There seems to be a much easier flow, and even though these huge boulevards extract a heavy flow of traffic, traffic just seems to move effortlessly.

I notice a lot more private entrepreneurship, whether it is vendors displaying videos, CD's of music, and costume jewelry, or small kiosks in larger areas, to small restaurants (consisting of probably not more than 600 sq. ft.). I think there's a true independence of spirit and self-sufficiency rather than an institutional way of life. Not to mislead, I've also seen a fair number of universities and government buildings, so every country owns a bureaucracy regardless what form of politics is in favor.

I have to confess that I have now reached the age of old men on a park bench. Fatigue and exhaustion have caught up with me, and it's time to find a park bench for a rest. All walks of life are here and these benches seem to inspire the romantic at heart. I've witnessed more than one young couple kissing and holding each other's hands in the traditional moments of embrace. I've sat and just enjoyed the movement of people before my eyes, walking rather than running or pushing and shoving. But the streets themselves are wide and this enables people to walk more at their leisure.

After having a short *siesta*, I watch the maintenance workers. A man (probably my age) is watering the grass and hosing down the tiles. The word "pride" comes to mind; proud of their culture, proud of their city, and proud of themselves – a nice combination to witness.

As the day has now drifted onward, I've pick up some supplies for the trip ahead at six o'clock from the bus station. It's nice to return to a city that I've experienced before. I remembered a little *groceteria* that I shopped at on my last trip, and picked up some of the traditional Chilean pastries, some bread, pop, water, and other essentials for the trip. One mistake I did make was purchasing a chocolate bar (rather ex-

SOUTH AMERICA
ENCHANTMENT

pensive, at nine hundred *pesos*), only to find out that when I was going to have a piece of it that it was one big gob of melted chocolate. Thank goodness it's still in the wrapper and maybe at some point in time in the high Andes it will harden back up to an eatable size.

I board the bus this is going to be one of those long arduous journeys. My destination is Antofagasta, a bus ride of seventeen to possibly twenty hours. Buses seem to leave on time, but arriving on time is more of a challenge. One thing I've learned about bus travel in South America is you can never predict what is actually going to transpire. Some buses provide meals, others stop in bus terminals. One thing is for sure they are totally unpredictable and unexpected. If I was able to converse in the language, I would be able to have the information and ask the appropriate questions. Without this luxury, I've chosen to err on the side of caution and bring food along. In this particular case, thank God I did. This bus did not stop, even for mans' needs and served nothing but the seat.

Buses have various interiors - the exteriors may be painted in vibrant colors to represent different companies but the interiors are unique to the bus itself. This one, at least, has a lot of leg room and I can stretch out, which I am grateful for as I'm going to be traveling idealistically from about six o'clock this evening to somewhere around noon tomorrow.

The terrain, as we leave the city, is blanketed with small farms and villages hugging the coastline, so it's quite pleasant to see. The first major city that we arrive at is La Serena. I've been there on my previous trip and just to make honorable mention of it; it's one of the cities where you're supposed to be able to go to a different beach everyday for two weeks, and then some. I think it's just a little early for summer holidays, so the beaches are still sparsely populated.

As we continually motor north, the mountain ranges hug the coastline and it becomes very arid and the vegetation is almost non-existent. It's quite warm and this particular bus does not have any air-conditioning, but with the aid of open

13

windows open, it's acceptable for traveling. The terrain itself remained constant.

It's rather unique that although this bus has made stops

throughout the night, they were not water stops. People get off, luggage is dispersed, new people get on, luggage is put in the containment bins below, and off we go. Even the driver does not have the chance to go to the washroom? As we get closer to Antofagasta, I can't help but think, "Thank goodness, I brought some food supplies." I've eaten my buns, yogurt and drunk all the pop that I brought with me.

The hours tick away and finally the night gives way to the day and morning starts to take place.

SOUTH AMERICA
ENCHANTMENT

January 11, Friday

Antofagasta, Chile

Nothing has been served yet but at the tone of eight o'clock in the morning, at last a cup of coffee! It's not ground coffee, it's instant again. However, something warm in my stomach is a welcome treat.

I really have no idea whether I'm getting old, getting out of shape, or just not feeling well, probably a combination of all three. I'm surprised that the blister on my foot is the size it is, as I take great preparations to make sure that I'm in good walking condition. My boots are the ones that I've used in other expeditions and the same with my socks. Why I've acquired this large blister on my left foot is amazing to me - maybe I haven't changed my socks often enough, and I had not taken my boots off on the long flight down. Along with this, and fatigue, I'm also feeling quite nauseated. As a traveler, I know that looking after one's health is vital.

To my amazement, we're arriving somewhat on time to Antofagasta. The population is about a quarter of a million. It's approximately 1,350 kilometers north of Santiago. It's a mining city - as you approach it; you can see some of the smeltering facilities. It has a large harbor to facilitate shipping massive amounts of ore products to other parts of the world. Nitrates and copper have dominated this area ever since the Spaniards discovered it.

As the bus approaches the inner core of the city, we pass the typical high-rises, financial areas and progressive shopping centers. The Holiday Inn and other modern chains have their representation here. However, most buildings are smaller one-storey structures, and 90% or more are constructed of cement. During the long kilometers on the bus, we passed a huge cement manufacturing facility. The heavy production of cement in areas that are barren of natural materials is so prevalent throughout the world. The buildings

15

here are made out of cement bricks or blocks, and then covered with stucco.

It's a city that is like so many in the world. It's there because of necessity, and without beauty. It's the gateway for the shipment of minerals and exportation of goods from the interior to this progressive seaport.

By noon, I get off the bus, and start to check out my next destination, which is La Paz. My quest is to continually go further north and preferably to another country. I find that there are no buses leaving for La Paz in Bolivia or as far as Pintados in Peru. I have a choice of either continuing north, hoping that I can find a route that's acceptable, or spend the day here and try to find some information at this point.

I know that the areas I will be going to now will have rougher roads and weather conditions will dictate whether the scheduled transportation is acceptable or has been abandoned due to bad weather. A lot of times with heavy rain the roads become impassable and the bus service is cancelled. In many cases, the bus runs only two or three times a week, but that's all part of the adventure.

My decision is to try to find a bus going further north. There's a small town on Chile's northern border called Arica. To my good fortune, a bus will be leaving for that city within another hour and a half. So, why not, and let it be said, let it be done. The ticket is purchased and in the short time that I have, I look around a bit at this metropolis and try to make a few purchases to replenish my food supply.

Soon it is back on the bus. Yes, onward and forward. Heading north, the mountain ranges become more dominant, but the conditions are consistent, very desert-like and even along the coastlines. This is a fairly harsh coastline when it comes to boating and not inducive to small coves or jetties. I do see some people camping as we motor along through the rugged terrain.

We are now entering the Norte Grande region, which contains the desolate Atacama Desert, and the Andeana Altiplano peaks. This is one of the driest deserts in the world, and the

SOUTH AMERICA
ENCHANTMENT

whole region is a reminder, with ghost towns from a by gone era of mining, for nitrates and the open pit mines at Chuqicamata, the world's largest copper mines and of mining for nitrates.

During the war of the Pacific, Chile annexed a lot of the copper and nitrate-rich lands from Peru and Bolivia. After the Chileans had won the war, they made one concession to Bolivia, which is now land locked, that they would provide an access to the ocean by means of a railroad a concession that is still honored. However political leaders have not given up the quest to try to win back that land that was Bolivia's to the ocean.

These mountains are so barren and foreboding; they have a majestic beauty all of their own. I have tried to capture some pictures of them with the changing light. No, it's not photography at its best, as we are on the move. The sandy ash terrain gives way to the ever-changing colors of sunsets and sunrises with gold's, greens, pinks and even purples. It brings to mind some of the sunsets I witnessed in the great Sahara. Whether it is day or night, the skies are clear and at night the stars blanket the sky to infinity.

On route to my final destination is a small town called Iquique. It's a collage of shanty buildings that were hastily thrown together during the mining booms of the period, along with some larger mansions. If I'd had the time, I would've taken a day to wander this rather unique place. It's quite small and easy to get around. There appears to be a lot of history here, from little wooden houses which you don't see too much of in this area, to sailors' bars dating back to the nineteenth century, to say nothing of the British leaving their stamp with a Victorian clock tower. During an ambitious period when mining was more in vogue, the Chileans built pipelines from the Andes to supply water to this region. Today, it has a duty-free zone and fishing, and a bit of trade and commerce seem to sustain this region.

When traveling, you can never be at leisure if you don't take the necessary initiative to always be organized and to question yourself as much as anybody else. Surprises, good and bad, happen, but mostly bad. I was sitting on the bus, waiting for it to park as I had been throughout the duration of my trip, only to have this good attendant advise me that I had a bus change! I must admit it wasn't an upgrade. Now this bus is very, very cramped, and I'm sure if they could get one more seat it would have to be put on the top of the bus. To my misfortune, I have the seat over the hub of the back wheel. I cannot stretch my legs out and for the next hours I am cramped into a fetal position. This causes my knee to develop a charley horse and an uncomfortable pain by not being able to stretch it out. To add to this discomfort, my stomach is bothering me a considerable amount and I have now been on the road for in excess of twenty-four hours, which is tiring enough on its own account.

I arrive at Arica and at a decent hour, about eleven o'clock; thirty-three hours of road travel and I've had enough. I'm travel-worn and going to stay here tonight, regardless of what one travel writer described as bleak, comfortless, miserable, a sandy waste. I'm too tired to really know or care. After getting off the bus, I've made a fast assessment of my strength and try to get some information on moving on to either Peru or Bolivia.

Yippee yay aye! Lady luck is riding strong with me and I've not only managed to secure transport to La Paz, Bolivia, tomorrow at two o'clock, but I've been able to get a *residencia* room in a home within walking distance of the terminal. So the tide has turned and I wearily make my way towards this home and a very nice clean room. Without any further thoughts on the subject, I take some aspirins for my splitting headache and another pill for my diarrhea and what else could one want besides a bed.

Good night, one and all. Good night, Marietta, and Wendy and Cole.

SOUTH AMERICA ENCHANTMENT

January 12, Saturday

Arica, Chile

Ah! Nothing better than a goodnight's sleep and medication to making you feel considerably better. I'm still not top of the mound, but I am feeling so much better. After a cold shower, a clean shave and a packed bag, I make my way to the bus terminal, leave my big bag at the terminal, and go and seek a breakfast. It's about 9:00 a.m. Again another beautiful day and my first impression is not that shared with the earlier travel-writer!

It's a charming town, with a laissez-faire feeling. It's clean, it's large enough for me, and the gentle breezes that rob the air of all its moisture still control the heat. I'm enjoying breakfast, which is a bun and some scrambled eggs, two cups of coffee and the local flavor.

This is an excellent place to make contact with either Peru or Bolivia. You can take taxis for a reasonable amount across the Peruvian border and they'll help you through immigration. It's not on my agenda, so I'm not enticed by it. It's also an excellent place to do some money changing which is a good idea.

The city does not have much more than two or three storied buildings and most of them are just one level building. To my surprise, there is a large shopping center and many stores, small by North American standards and probably family operations. I am always amazed in South America by the amount of auto parts and repair shops that blanket the downtown cores of the cities and this one is no exception to the rule.

The houses are unique - even the one that I stayed at last night; when you enter from the street, it looks quite foreboding with no front lawn and high walls, probably close to ten feet, with gates that are equal in height. The walls are concrete and most gates are metal or wrought iron. Behind this security are the nice little yards in front. Their homes are usually one level and not as large as the conventional North American home, but nicely laid out. In this particular region where water is scarce, they utilize small water tanks that are lit for immediate hot water by propane.

Arica is not blessed with large parks. However, I did find one to sit in the mist for a few moments with beautiful trees that produce a red, breath-taking flower. I don't have an obsession with death, but I do seem to always end up in cemeteries. The South American countries have a great respect for the dead, and the final resting places are works of art in their own right. Many families have crypts and they come in all shapes and sizes, and this cemetery is no exception to the rule. It is well maintained and the centerpiece is a statue of the Virgin Mary with the Christ Child. Up on the hillside, there is another huge statue of Christ, and within a short distance the flag of Chile flying.

I have taken pictures of some of the more interesting parts of this town on my way back to bus station. This is a very modern station and well laid out. I am able to send some internet messages as well as catch up on reading some of the news from the days that I have not had a newspaper and again exchange money. Most people converse fairly well in English, are friendly, well mannered and just pleasant to be around.

The bus leaves on time and almost immediately we start the high ascent into the Andes Mountains. On my way to La Paz, Bolivia, we soon leave the coastal region and the climb up into these mountains is breathtaking. At the present time, the mountains are barren and the sky is dotted with fluffy clouds. As they pass over the landscape, dark blackened shadows move across the mountains.

We do see some rather disturbing birds: 'vultures' is the right terminology, certainly not the great condor of the Peruvian areas. There are other smaller birds but at this point, this is the only life form that I see on these barren ridges and in the huge valleys. As we continually climb in altitude and

SOUTH AMERICA
ENCHANTMENT

the road winds itself back and forth, I get a glimpse of the miracle of what water can do in the desert. In the few valleys below, there are small creeks running from the higher altitudes, which turn these valleys into lush green oases. I saw this same wonder of nature in the Atlas mountain ranges in Morocco, surrounded by the great sea sands of the Sahara. However, each has its own beauty and should not be substituted or mistaken for other areas of the world.

The bus eventually reaches the summit and starts to level off, well above sea level. Amongst these rolling hills, I can easily see the small tufts of grass and each spot of sparse vegetation. The cacti stand alone, like proud soldiers defending a ridge on these barren hills above the flat lands below. They have a beauty all of their own and I have always admired the determination of these brave plants to cling not only to the arid landscape but existence itself.

As the heat of the day persists, the view from the window is always interesting, with so many different colors and formations on these majestic mountains. We are very close sometimes as we're passing through areas where the road has carved its way. There has been great erosion and in a long ago period of history of Earth there must have been great lakes in this area.

We finally reach the Chilean border. It's rather ironic that only a couple of days ago I was sweltering in the heat in Santiago, and now I see the military police here dressed in heavy parkas and toques. Being a Canadian, I find that it's crisp but not *that* cold to warrant such heavy garb. Immigration is easy and straightforward, "thanks for coming and hope you come back". Back on the bus, we travel a very short distance and are in Bolivia.

This crossing is equally as straightforward "thanks for coming", and there are a few moneychangers (all women I notice), so if you haven't done it in Chile, you can do it here. I really thought that the luggage would be taken off the bus and scrutinized, but this is not the case. Customs did impose some questions on one individual, but other than that, the delays were minimal.

Now in Bolivia I see snowcaps on some of the mountains. The wind is not harsh, but a chilling wind nonetheless. I notice that most of the Chileans and Bolivians are either sensitive to cold or much more aware of it. They have sweaters, heavy jackets on and almost everyone wears a hat or toque. The traditional Bolivian *Aymara* women's dress is quite notable and I have quickly fallen in love with these little women. Many Bolivian people appear to have an Indian heritage and are small in stature, both men and women, with very distinct and attractive features. The women are dressed in layers of more than one garment, looking like china figurines that you would put on a mantelpiece, and below all these layers are small little shoes that only emphasize their short stature. Underneath the remarkable bowler hat, their long hair is braided and joined further down by huge tufts of black wool (*pocaha*). They wear quite a few petticoats under their skirts, or *chola* dresses. The men, unfortunately, were not much for traditional costume, and their attire could be well placed in any community in the Western hemisphere.

SOUTH AMERICA
ENCHANTMENT

As we're heading to La Paz, the terrain flattens out with more shrubbery visible, and in the distance on both sides are the endless ranges of majestic mountains. For the first time I'm starting to see small herds of *llamas* and even a few cattle. At this altitude, their coats are very thick. Knitting with the *llama* and sheep wool is a popular past time amongst the women, and I hope later on to see some of their works in the market places.

It's the first time that I get to see some of the small, adobe-type dwellings. These people are very poor and it's sad to think that they are sitting 'literally' on a gold mine. Some of the expressions I have read about Bolivia are, "it's like a donkey carrying gold, it serves the animal no purpose and one Western person said it's like a beggar sitting on a pot of gold." Bolivia is exceptionally rich in natural resources. This has led to countries annexing Bolivia, like Chile and Brazil, both for the mineral wealth in the ground and in Brazil's case, the plantations of the rubber trees around the Amazon basin.

However, the largest single problem of Bolivia is that it's very difficult to get to these rich ore beds and the export trail is limited for getting to market. Agriculture has difficulties due to the altitude of the majority of the growing regions. This makes it a country that has a difficult time just feeding itself. It's very sad because as I am looking at this beautiful range of mountains, I can't help but drift back in time and think of the Incas and the ancestors of the local native Indians. No wonder they felt so close to the gods in all this vast beauty, and tranquility of the landscape. However, as I experience the sand blowing in the air, I can imagine the living conditions are and always have been harsh and demanding for all vegetation and animals, including the human race.

The bus has now reached the time zone when it's dark and way off in the distance I experience the first lights of La Paz. I've read where La Paz has reached those qualifications of cities like Hong Kong, Cape Town, or San Francisco that each has their own distinct characteristics. As we get closer to the designated spot, we do enter a zone that's heavily populated and extremely poor;similar to places I've seen in Mexico where poverty has equalized the population of the area. These people do not appear to have the standard of living I witnessed in other areas of South America. As we start to approach the vast amount of lights ahead, I take out my camera and hope maybe I'll get a shot that turns out. It is a wondrous sight, and looks like countless thousands of candle lights embracing the mountainsides and the valleys below. I am so very grateful that I am coming in at night, and although anxious to see the city in daylight, they always say first impressions are lasting impressions. I will always remember the mountains of candle lights. It is a sight to remember for the rest of my life.

We wander down the road endlessly, twisting and turning into the valley below, and eventually we arrive without incident. I get my luggage and am soon off to the Hotel Viena, as recommended in my Lonely Planet book. They suggest that it would be of particular interest to check out Suite 113, I not only checked it out, I am actually staying in it. The ceilings are at least 16-foot high; the suite is of the older baroque style, not in the most pristine condition, but for me, a unique place to spend the night, especially for US$20.00.

I have had my first Peruvian beer and some French fries. I have to confess, I am still not feeling up to the mound. Now, it could be a combination of a slight case of the flu as well as a bit of altitude discomfort, since I am also experiencing headaches.

Another e-mail off to my beautiful wife and off to bed I go. Goodnight, one and all, and that concludes today!

SOUTH AMERICA ENCHANTMENT

January 13, Sunday

La Paz, Bolivia

I went ahead with my usual toiletries and then made my way down to the lobby. I asked Alex, the attendant at the hotel, if there were any tours available and he informed me that yes there will probably be a city tour as well as one to the ruins. After a short discussion and a few phone calls, I am officially on my way to the ruins of Tiwanaku. This is probably one of the more important archaeology ruins in Bolivia. These ruins date back far before the Inca period of civilization, possibly to 1580 B.C.

The taxi meanders through the narrow cobble-stoned street before dropping me off. Now a small mini bus is going to take us to the ruins. Once in the bus, we start an arduous climb out of the valley that houses La Paz, which itself is the highest capital city in the world at 3636 meters. As we're moving up in altitude, we can't help but feel that the bus is laboring under the burden and maybe it too suffers from altitude sickness, but ever onward it continually climbs up the winding trail that probably dates back to the beginning of time.

I thought that La Paz was spellbinding as I entered it in the evening with the dancing lights of the buildings that cover the mountainside. But it's equally as enchanting and mystical as you see it in the daytime and you keep gaining altitude higher and higher, reaching the summit above this magical valley. There is good reason that this valley has been chosen by civilizations long before the residents of the present period. The harsh winds and the severe climate in this region of Bolivia taught the ancestors long ago that this valley would provide shelter and a safe haven for its inhabitants from the severe climates that prevail in the high Andes.

There is a hustle and bustle and congestion as we continually ascend out of the valley. As it is Sunday, I assume that there are markets to be set up for tomorrow, and people are

Robert F. Edwards

bringing their goods in and out of the local region. Once we hit the summit, the plains flatten off to rolling hills preceding the mountains themselves. Through the misty clouds you see the towering peaks covered in snow.

We continually level off for some distance, and there are small farms dotted with adobe huts. I see more cows, sheep, and even donkeys, and their coats are heavy and thick compared to animals in lower elevations. The people seem to be a gentle, easy-going group even amongst themselves. It's like stepping out of a storybook, seeing these women in their traditional garb herding their flocks of sheep. They look like they waddle rather than walk, with their traditional dress of many layers.

Our first stop is a small village along the way and it is so typical. The church dominates in the center *piazza* and people are gathered round lazily as their dogs wander about or lay sleeping, and older women have their wares out. They display their goods on the blankets they used to carry them to market, and all sit in rows talking, resting, just waiting for somebody to pass by and optimistically hoping that somebody will purchase something.

SOUTH AMERICA
ENCHANTMENT

I've met a few people from the bus and two young ladies from Uruguay. I recognize the *matei* that they are drinking and enter into a conversation. We discuss parts of their country, and how beautiful the beaches are, and how much I enjoyed it. Curiously, I asked the guide about some of the wares being sold in the marketplace. The peanuts and the vegetables I'm quite conversant with, but there are large mounds of an item that I am just not sure of. She explains to me that they are tripe (the intestines of domestic animals, which are cooked and then salted, or with sugar on them and they becomes quite chewy and edible.

As we continue our way to the ruins, which is about 70 kilometers from La Paz itself, the guide tells us more about the region and the Indian people and their religions and customs. Mother Earth is revered, and man is the Condor, the bird, among their mystical beliefs. So as we travel, I have more of an understanding of their strong commitment to Mother Earth. Much of this is only conjecture and hypothesis because little is known about the race that actually inhabited the ruins.

Tiwanaku (also called Tiahuanaco) has a nice museum and the different periods of this earlier civilization are well displayed. There isn't a great deal of knowledge of what happened to these people, but it is thought that they were farmers and had implemented irrigation. This particular site lent itself, and was constructed for the purpose of reserving water during the rainy periods. Then in the dry periods, canals enabled the valleys to receive the requirements needed for agriculture.

One of the interesting sights of this ruin is the sun gate. These people were unquestionably sun worshippers because it rains up here quite often. Even today, it's like having the four seasons in a short space of time as we've experienced a little bit of snow with the freezing rain, we've had very strong winds and then only moments later it's blazing hot. So, I imagine things haven't changed that much climate-wise. We met the four seasons in one hour and it must have been challenging in the days of this pre-Inca civilization.

Much of the construction was done with rocks and huge slabs carried from the mountains from a great distance. There are distinctly three types, sandstone, red granite, and the third is a black type of stone, which is the hardest and shows the least amount of deterioration.

The excavation site was discovered by an American archaeologist and many theories abound about its creation. The traditional belief that this ceremonial site was created by a race of giants can be believed upon seeing the huge stone slabs. One of the theories that our guide explained was that the ancestors of the Bolivian Indian ancestors came from Asia or possibly from Japan. This could be possible, as they do have an Asian appearance eye-wise and the color of hair, but there

is also a strong similarity to the Indians of North America that may have crossed over the Bering Strait, but anyway that's the theory.

As we continue seeing the ruins, an interesting point of history was brought to our attention. When the Spaniards arrived, they were accompanied by the Jesuits, who belonged to the strongest Order of the day. Not only did these priests have the zeal and fire of preserving the Roman Catholic faith but also of enforcing it through education and other means as well.

Many of the pagan statues' noses and other parts of them have been defaced, as the Spaniards wanted to destroy these pagan gods. They tried an exorcism of the ancient beliefs by

SOUTH AMERICA
ENCHANTMENT

carving the Christian cross and the Holy Trinity symbols on parts of the statues.

It seems man has always been forceful with his own beliefs, rather than respecting others that have gone before. The Spaniards took the stone slabs from many of the temples and used them to build their own churches and buildings. Throughout the world's history, conquering people have usually changed the structural phase of their predecessors and recycling has been going on for a lot longer than what we consider is in vogue today.

We have a short lunch break, and I order *llama*, my first taste of it. It's a pleasant meat, similar to beef, and was accompanied with rice and some vegetables. I have a soup which is very popular, with beets. After an enjoyable meal, we're back on the bus, and return to La Paz. The guide and I spend some time discussing other activities that I might be interested in doing. After a considerable length of time with her and a Peruvian man, I have the fundamentals of what lies ahead for my adventure. Now I realize that I'm probably going to have to cut out some of the aggressive parts of Ecuador and Columbia in order to see more of Bolivia and Peru. Both these countries are richly laden with history and culture of past civilizations, and of course I have to see Lake Titicaca.

Tonight I make arrangements to go a restaurant that provides local folk dancing. After discussing the evening's entertainment with my travel guide, I realize that little has changed in Bolivia. Their culture has remained virtually untouched regardless of intervention from the outside world, and their religion and ancient beliefs are no exception. I happen to mention wanting a talisman and my guide suggests a marketplace called "The Witches' Market", *Mercado de Hechicería*. She suspects that I am not just the average person passing through, and that I have some knowledge of different spiritual beliefs other than the Christian and traditional religions. She has agreed to contact one of her shamans to create a talisman for me. She stressed very firmly that first I must believe in it; and second, I must not show it to anyone. With this agreed, I may be able to receive this talisman possibly tomorrow. With that, I say my goodbyes and start heading back to the hotel.

The city is like a maze with its cobblestone streets. You really do have to climb and in some cases, you're huffing and puffing by going a few blocks. I have been in many cities, too numerous to count, but driving here is unique unto it. You drive through red lights; the horn is much more essential than the brakes; and if you can get through, you've won; if you don't, you have to wait your turn. The cab driver that's taking me back to the hotel is no exception. I'm sure that certain streets are one-way, (but only the locals would know for sure) and they are very narrow. The wider streets have no advantage to them because the two-way traffic doesn't seem to have any continuity. It's every man for himself, but the best vehicle gets through.

It looks like army personnel with their submachine guns, standing on the corner just looking blissfully by. Once in a while, you'll hear a whistle blowing to indicate that they're directing traffic, but I don't know what else they do other than that to collect their pay, because traffic seems to act on its own recognizance. But it just adds all the more flavor and sheer delight to this unique city where each street has a thousand stories.

So back at the hotel and I e-mailed my wife before getting ready for the evening. It is about seven o'clock before I head back down to the restaurant for the folk festival entertainment. The food is first class cuisine. I have garlic soup and *llama* in red wine. There's a salad bar with some of the hottest peppers that I've ever tasted in my life. I also have Inca beer, which is not a bad substitute for my favorite Guinness stout, a little sweeter but still a dark brew.

The performance started with men playing string and wind instruments, like flutes. As the evening progresses, the women folk dancers enter and invite the men in the audience to get up and dance. The only sad part about the evening is that there's just myself, a couple from Australia and two Frenchmen. The whole festival was an evening well spent and I thoroughly enjoyed both the food and the performance. After the performance, the Australian couple and I converse on many subjects and thoroughly enjoyed each other's company.

Eventually, I took a cab back to my humble abode and off to bed I went. Goodnight, my dearest wife. Goodnight, my beautiful daughter and goodnight to you, my little grandson.

Robert F. Edwards

January 14, Monday

La Paz, Bolivia

I got up rather late today and had a very restless night last night. Unfortunately, some poor person in the room next to me was suffering from Montezuma's revenge and using the toilet to relieve both ends of his or her agony, whichever the case was. I did my laundry and some of the mundane things that had to be done, before I checked the e-mail. To my delight, I had one waiting for me from my wife and an update on the events that had taken place in my absence.

As I strolled around town, I noticed some event taking place. It was a farmers' demonstration or protest march and I took some pictures of the people on parade. To this day, I'll never know whether it was actual shots being fired in the air or some kind of explosions, but I would think the first was more correct.

I had my first ice-cream in Bolivia; not the best ice-cream I've had in the world, but still real ice-cream. The vendor asked me if I wanted to try some white particles, to which I said, "Of course," and they were coconut. A delightful way to have an ice-cream cone, wrapped in coconut shavings.

I ventured into the Witches' Market and just spent the entire day perusing different alleyways and narrow cobblestone streets. I am fascinated by the display of wares both in the tiny shops, as well as the continuous row of vendors on the streets.

At two o'clock, right on schedule, the women had my laundry done and I continued searching out more 'off the beaten track' areas. I stumbled across a true Bolivian market, and their blue carts are filled with shoes, clothing and a collage of goods that the locals use on a daily basis. I believe many of these people live and commute everyday from the plateaus that we passed through before we entered La Paz. This is where poverty ranks at its highest level, and the women and men all look a little weather-beaten, as life has given them challenges. They have small builds, and the women are well-rounded off; partly due to their attire, but I would say generally that they spread out quite well after childbirth.

Robert F. Edwards

The thing that I've noticed, though, is their hands. Even though their faces are weather-beaten and show the lines of endurance, their hands are still very soft and delicate. These are not the hands of hard labor from agriculture that I witnessed in other parts of the world where rheumatism had gnarled and bent them beyond recognition. Most of the women are quite elderly and have poor dental hygiene. A lot of the older people are either without teeth or at least missing quite a few. Those fortunate enough to afford dental work have fillings of either gold or silver, no porcelain here yet.

I poked around endlessly in the shops, looking here and there before I found an antique carving blade. It is very similar in design to the ones used by the North American Eskimos, a fan-shaped blade used for scraping hides. I also admired the exquisite leatherwork, to say nothing of the woven goods, which in Bolivia are bargains at anytime.

The one thing that I've also noticed is that silver jewelry dominates the shops, whether they're antique stores or bargain stalls, the silver is ever present. I guess the Spaniards

didn't get it all. I did witness a local woman, probably from one of the villages, bringing in her hard earned goods from many hours of labors, to be bartered by a local merchant. A lot of goods, though, are manufactured products and one should be aware of this if you want to buy authentic products. It's worth learning a little more about what is actually hand-woven in the ways of ponchos or little mats or whatever.

For lunch, I had an absolutely delicious soup. I guess it would be the equivalent to Bolivian vegetable stew, with broccoli, onions and so much more - quite filling. As the afternoon moved onward, it became one of those days when I just became a mad hatter, going here and there, and dithering about, but thoroughly enjoying the spontaneous moments. I came across a little kiosk that was selling what looked similar to a fried doughnut or small fat pancake. I purchased one and it was absolutely delicious. It was pastry, deep-fried, but inside was cheese and some bits of vegetables and just a real delight.

I'm starting to step out more boldly to try the different cuisine around me. Later on, I tried what looked like a Cornish pasty and with all due respect to my English ancestors, their well renowned pasty is nothing to a Bolivian one. These *empanadas* are made on the same concept, with meat, onions, potatoes, and even olives and equally as delicious as their Chilean counterpart. The food here is good, and for bargain hunters, you need not go any further.

I continued on, up hills and down streets. Some of the architectural design is authentic baroque; others are a mismatch of today, tomorrow, and yesterday, all blending itself together. For a city that has an ancient background, it looked relatively clean. Yes, there are some open sewage areas, and I need not elaborate on the odor that prevails. Generally speaking, it's a city where the inhabitants do care, and mingle well with each other. Bolivian people are a gentle race and a congenial group of people. It has been my good fortune to experience these moments and these people.

I return to the travel agent and there's quite a fluster going on; they want me to return to the restaurant of last night (which isn't opened until eight o'clock, and it is now only

Robert F. Edwards

6:30.) It seems the proprietor has made a gross mistake. Instead of charging me one hundred and twenty-eight *bolivianos*, he had only charged 1.28 on my Visa slip. We quickly rectified it and he was more than just grateful, after having, I imagine, a worrisome night. He didn't want to have to feed people for nothing, especially rich foreigners.

My travel guide later introduced me to a shaman and I bought a talisman or an amulet. All over the world and throughout the ages, people have indulged in beliefs and rituals that oppose other religious attitudes. To me, God is everywhere and no one belief should have the exclusive domain. This shaman is rather an interesting individual and I noticed a bulge in his mouth, which I'm sure, was a ball of cocoa leaves.

The cocoa leaf (or cocaine) was used in ritual ceremonies by the affluent in ancient times. When the Spaniards came and realized that this wonder plant produced a much higher productivity amongst the Indians doing the mining for them, they cultivated the plant. Now this region has become one of the drug havens of cocaine in the global community.

There is no doubt in my mind that cocaine is a very addictive drug or intoxicant, giving an illusion of well-being. Sigmund Freud promoted it as the wonder drug of his period, only to become addicted himself and he never really managed to kick the habit. So, it's not something that is just today's problem. Sir Conan Doyle with his famous Sherlock Holmes went into stupors between cases with this drug of desire. Today, people in Bolivia use the cocoa leaf for an uplifting effect. In fact, the couple last night told me that they went into a place that is actually serving the leaf to the locals. It's quite different actually from the finished product of cocaine. For a comparison, I imagine one is like having beer and the other one is like having moonshine.

After my visit with the shaman, I purchased a poncho, and talked to the guide that will be with me for the next couple of days down in the Lake Titicaca area. Returning to the hotel, I settled up my bill and bumped into the young lady from Hong

SOUTH AMERICA
ENCHANTMENT

Kong I had met earlier. We started conversing and comparing notes on our travels. She is a very independent young woman obviously, to be traveling alone. Yum took the lead and asked me if I'd like to sit down and "how about if I buy you a soda?" So, we spent the better part of an hour just sharing conversation and philosophical views on many subjects. She was heading back to Hong Kong and I gave her my card with my e-mail on it, hoping she keeps in touch.

In the short period of time that I've been on the road, I've met some very pleasant people. At the travel agency today, I met a couple of young Irish women. They had spent the better part of six months traveling through Cambodia, Vietnam, Australia, New Zealand, Peru, and Bolivia and now are returning home to carry on with the day-to-day occupation of employment. A young Belgian couple that I met had warned me to be very aware of mosquitoes, saying they bite right through clothes and that strong insect repellants have no effect on them. These interesting travelers have enhanced today's adventure.

I'm ready for tomorrow now, so say goodnight to one and all. Goodnight, my wonderful wife, and thank you once again for all the things that you do for me. Thank you my daughter, for being you, and thank you, Cole, for calling me "Grandpee." Goodnight one and all.

Robert F. Edwards

January 15, Tuesday

La Paz, Bolivia

Well, it's early and I'm up at six o'clock. I haven't slept very well and can blame anything from dripping taps to just being restless, waiting for this moment to get ready for an exceptionally long day. I've had some cold showers in my day, but the water here feels like it has come right off those snow-capped mountains, and I just didn't have the intestinal fortitude to jump into the shower. So I had a sponge bath, which is refreshing in its own way.

While waiting for the bus, I talked to Alex, the attendant at this hotel. He's attending University also, studying hotel administration work. I sincerely believe that he will do well, as he has the right personality to deal with the general public in this profession.

The tour bus arrives at 7:30 and will be taking me to Lake Titicaca and some of the islands. As with any tour group, rounding up the rest of the people that were being transported, from La Paz to Copacabana, is a major undertaking. My guide and a Chilean father with his son are some of the people that are accompanying me on this tour. There is a wide variety in this group. A couple of nuns from Santiago, Chile, are on their way to one of the missions.

So, after loading all the people on the bus, and fuelling up, with all the necessary labors finally completed, we're on the road. They say, "All roads lead to Rome," but I think all roads lead in and out of La Paz. As the bus leaves town, I watch the people that have already started their day. Two women and their young children are sitting in a square, preparing breakfast. I guessed it to be some kind of porridge in a pot, and bread. The two children (one about three and the other maybe five) are very quietly eating and then the little one gets up and runs towards the pigeons, trying to chase them off. It's a very simple life here but they seem to weather any kind of condi-

SOUTH AMERICA
ENCHANTMENT

tions and just take life in their stride. They work to survive and survive to work, I guess. However, they have peace and contentment on their faces and when you talk to them, they are pleasant and happy and extremely polite - a race of people that the world could sure take lessons from.

We have now reached the top of the ridge and drive through one of the poorer districts surrounding La Paz. It doesn't matter what their age is, the women seem to sit endlessly on street corners and just watch life pass by. Men seem to be scurrying about, getting ready for another day. The food and produce that they bring in their blankets are now getting displayed.

As we motor along, passing small adobe homes, the people have started their day's work in the fields. We don't really have a great distance to go to get to Copacabana, but the drive is challenging. Up to this point the roads that I've been on have been in excellent condition. We arrive in good order at the entrance to the lake. From here the bus is driven on to a barge to make this crossing before we will able to proceed on to Copacabana (this is not to be confused with the more renowned Copacabana of Brazil).

It's cold but clear, so things are not too bad. I've got my jacket on and I've given my gloves to our guide to borrow. He

Robert F. Edwards

is in his thirties, married, with one little girl, and I enjoyed his company. Being a guide needs a lot of patience. Besides me, he has the Chilean man and his son in his group. I don't speak Spanish, and the other two speak absolutely no English, so our guide is like a ping-pong ball going back and forth. He never tired and was always assisting people that were not quite sure what to do.

We've arrived at the beachhead point of entry, purchase our tickets to get on small boats, and make our way across this end of the lake. Lake Titicaca is over 170 kms. long and 97 kms. wide. It is also the world's highest navigable lake, at an elevation of 3,820 meters. It's a very clear lake and dotted about in these huge 8000 sq.kms. are thirty-six islands. We make the crossing, obviously not at the 97 km. width, but at one of its narrowest points.

There is a very small settlement on the other side, and our guide asked if I'd like to have some breakfast, and believe me, would I! Just even a cup of coffee would give me a bit of stamina for this day. It's now about eleven o'clock and with that, I have a bun and coffee and cheese – it's delicious. The cheese is white, with quite a strong flavor like *feta*, but when I ask, he assures me that it's cow cheese.

After this much appreciated break, and without any further delay, we once again get back on the bus and now we're hugging the coastline of the lake. We soon get to Copacabana, a delightful little town, and every step a tourist city. I read that in the 16th century there were miracles happening when a statue of the Virgin of Canderlaria was presented to Copacabana, and even today a lot of pilgrims come here to pay homage to the Virgin, now the patron saint of Bolivia.

Once we get into Copacabana, we walk, not a very steep but challenging roadway, to a hotel and we are going to have lunch here. I've asked to be excused from lunch because I'm still full from my breakfast and I'm going to seek out a place to get an e-mail off to Marietta and hopefully, have one from her. To my great pleasure, my dear wife has given me an up-

SOUTH AMERICA
ENCHANTMENT

date on what's happening in her life in Canada and I quickly get one off to her.

Also, the connection that I'm supposed to meet up with has improved. I learn that my new guide is now in Copacabana organizing some other tourists. I concern myself more with future travel plans so as to have some order and consistency, as the travel agents here are not at the cutting edge of technology, and people living in these regions have a more laissez-faire attitude. For example, the Chilean father and his son didn't have tickets to accompany this particular leg of the tour. The guide just phoned and assured the people with the bus and facilities that "Yes, he's paid for it, and sooner or later they'll get the vouchers that are required." Just a bit more relaxed, but I have to admit still efficient. They might not have all the documents, papers and seals on their agendas, but they produce what they promise. In many cases, their word is much better than a lot of written documents that developed countries produce, only to be invalid.

Copacabana is the border town between Bolivia and Peru. Further back in history, when the Incas first came into this region, it was the entry point to their sacred islands, Isla del Sol and Isla de la Luna. These are the legendary sites of the Incas' creation. The Isla del Sol has been credited as the birthplace of the sun itself and the white god *Viracocha*, and the first Incas, and *Manco Kapac* and his sister-wife *Mama Huaca*, also had mystical beginnings here.

Their origins have some comparisons to Egypt's gods, *Isis* and her brother-husband. So, it's always interesting to learn that no matter how old the civilizations are and what unique situations they where created in, there are similarities elsewhere in the world.

This distance to reach the Isla del Sol is about half an hour ride by boat. So, you can imagine in the days of the Incas, when they rowed or used primitive sail on a reed raft that it must have been quite a labor of religious commitment to get to the sacred islands. Today, we use powerboats and the religious ceremonies are null and void, but the quest for the ex-

41

Robert F. Edwards

perience prevails and I'm no exception in my quest. This town exists more as a stop-off point for either going to Peru or the islands, and the locals have upgraded the accommodations and facilities to meet the developed countries' demands. There are many quaint-looking hotels, but it is highly commercialized and most of the shops have the usual trinkets that tourists purchase to drag back home.

Once back up at the hotel, I'm still full, so instead of having the meal I have tea called *matei*. I've had *matei* before in Argentina and Uruguay. It's a popular drink, an assortment of herbs that is steeped in a well-seasoned mug with sugar, and the spoon has a straw-like system to it. Boiling water is continuously added, and it's quite a refreshing, invigorating drink. However, here it comes in a tea bag and I asked the guide about this. He informs me that this one has three different types of herbs, and one of them is the famous cocoa leaf, which gives you a hit of rejuvenation. It's a pleasant drink, but I didn't notice any extra energy and, if I had the choice of the two, I probably would take the Argentine style.

After lunch, we head back down to catch the boat for the Isla del Sol. I've made a mistake in not communicating well

SOUTH AMERICA
ENCHANTMENT

enough with my guide. It would have been far preferable if I had left my heavy backpack at the hotel and just taken the small one for my trip to the island. However, now I have to bear the weight of my main backpack. I arduously get on the boat and I ask when we get off, "Where's the hostel", and he tells me about 500 meters up and God knows how many kilometers. I tell him there's no way that I can carry this for any great distance, and he suggests hiring a boy when we get there.

As we're getting closer to the island, one of the other tourists points out the challenge that lies ahead. It goes straight up. I'm now looking at the first Inca climb in my life and, believe me I have the utmost respect for these people's ancestors. We secure a boy, it's hard to say how old as these people's stature is quite small. I keep asking if he's okay and he assures me he is, putting my backpack on, and we all set off climbing up. I have only gone a very short distance and I'm huffing and puffing, but the rest of the tourists aren't doing any better.

It is quite amazing to see these locals running up and down this as if it was just a small flight of stairs. It seems an endless climb, and is all of 500 meters higher before we hit the top. This is where the facilities are located, both the hostels and the little buildings that the locals live in.

There is an infinite amount of small terracing and the guide tells me that this dates back over a thousand years. Long before the Incas ever arrived, the natives of the island were constructing the terraces on the hillsides to grow crops (anything from potatoes to lima beans to peas and other vegeta-

Robert F. Edwards

bles). Also, I've noticed some *llamas* and pigs and a donkey, but no larger livestock.

After taking numerous rest periods and watching this boy change backpacks with the other boys to try and redistribute the weight, I realize what a mistake I've made in bringing the camping gear, and all the cassette tapes and films. It's just made my backpack an unbearable weight to carry around.

The hostel's very nice - I have a private room and at this height, some breath-taking views. I've taken some pictures of the snow-capped mountains far off in the distance, and the beautiful little inlets below with small sailboats laying their nets for fishing. There are three or four different types of fish here, all white in flesh content. One that's the most popular is trout and when I asked (I don't know whether this is a fisherman's measurement or not) they show from the hand to the elbow, which would be an exceptionally large trout in Canadian standards. There is also one similar to a catfish and the other two are small, closer to the size of a sardine. One of the two has a blown-up belly, quite a unique look. The guide tells me that both these fishes are quite bony and I can believe it.

It's a nice day, although overcast, but the weather seems to be cooperating somewhat, bringing us some blue skies and then followed by clouds. I have taken a few pictures and recovered from the strenuous climb up to the summit, so the guide asked if I want to walk to the ruins. Together with a German couple and the Chilean man, off we go.

I'm really glad I made the effort to see at first-hand these little terracing crops and boy, they don't waste any land. Every little bit of dirt on these rocky ridges is cultivated (with an axe a pick). They diligently care for the soil, and the growing season is only one crop. For the rest of the year they let the animals graze about, so that the manure becomes the fertilizer.

Here are some of the most challenging agricultural developments on these ridges and in one of the harshest, most demanding climates, yet they are still producing an abundance of vegetation after a thousand years. In our developed countries, we're having trouble with crops due to the amount of pesticides and chemical fertilizing. We hardly have two hundred years behind us and they already have a thousand - who's going to win?

This terracing is a practice that I've witnessed in other areas of the world, in the Himalayas in the fall and in India. It's interesting how people, without knowledge of the other's existence, have adopted similar practices to meet the challenges of survival. As we walk along these trails, and up and down, the views are astounding. The distances are incredible, and give us an idea of how vast this lake is. It's supposedly one of the last of the great inland bodies of waters left behind when the oceans receded.

It's rewarding to see what the Incas must have felt when they chose it as a sacred place. When we get to the ruins, we find the guide very knowledgeable about why these ruins are built the way they are and he explains the sizes of the doors. They're very small doors that you have to crouch down to get through, but they're also very wide, probably close to a meter. The buildings are all stone, even the roofs, and are gradually integrated closer and closer together until they close over the top. The reason for the openings being so was to keep the heat in and since there were no doors in those days, just openings; it makes a lot of sense. People in ancient times were practical and knew what they had to do to bring comfort to their lifestyle. This is the first Inca ruin I've seen, and it's not quite what I had expected. The stones are well laid, with an earth-based mortar as the adhesive. This was the main temple the Incas used for their sacred ceremonies. You had to be a special person in Inca times to stay here and most of them were male priests.

The other smaller island, Isla de la Luna (Island of the Moon), was said to be reserved for women, and virgins at that. An anthropologist had told our guide that the high priest, in order to know whether a woman was a virgin or not, would escort them down to a pool of water and make them urinate. If they urinated in a very thin small stream, they were virgins.

Robert F. Edwards

If it gushed out, they were not virgins. When he asked us what we thought about this, my reply was "I guess you'd be pissed off if you're a virgin and you didn't qualify." The German did not have anything to say, other than laughing at my comment.

We continued being the typical tourists and took lots of pictures before we hiked back out. This was quite strenuous, as in addition to the climbing, I was experiencing some altitude fatigue as well. The guide is in excellent shape and keeps the pace quite aggressively. This was much different from when I've had guides before. On Kilimanjaro, they wanted the reverse; for you to slow down so that you don't experience the effects of altitude.

Back at the hostel, I find it's about 6:30 and I have to admit I am famished. A piece of bread and cheese is not exactly complete nourishment for the invigorating day that I have had. The amount of walking has now added up to four hours or better. I'm told that we will have supper at 7:30 and I'm not going to argue about that one. I'm just hoping that there's more than my share available.

SOUTH AMERICA
ENCHANTMENT

I stroll around a bit, and the evening is cool but not chilly. I am more than ready when supper is being served. I have a very nice soup, some buns, and I ordered some Sprite. The fish of the evening is a small trout served with rice and vegetables and for dessert a variety of fruit. Interestingly, the meal is good, but the rice is very dry and coarse and I would have done anything for some Soya sauce to give it a bit more flavor as well as some moisture. I noticed the young Chilean lad put ketchup on

his rice and stir it up. I haven't reached that stage but I'm sure before my trip is finished I may be putting ketchup on rice.

The German fellow didn't come to dinner, as he was suffering from altitude sickness and his companion/wife was eating alone. She was a quiet lady. I don't know whether it was her nature or whether she was not too conversant with English. The guide keeps the conversation bilingual and relays some amusing anecdotes of events, such as using the wrong words and the wrong language, which I did earlier. Instead of saying 'Puno', the city that I'm going to in Peru, I pronounced it as the Spanish word for 'Bitch'. We had a good laugh about that, especially if I had made the mistake with a woman at Customs and said, "I like *pinto or puto*" or whatever, and she'd respond, "I like you, you bitch." Communication can be hazardous at the best of times.

I find there's nothing to do and no television, not even a selection of books, and the chairs are meant for sitting in during meals, not really for lounging and relaxing. The guide mentions it's too bad we didn't have a deck of cards, and I agree with him. Being the only English-speaking person becomes tedious, listening to the conversation and as I've had little sleep the night before, I excuse myself and head off to bed.

It's cool, which is much to my liking, and without hesitation I go to sleep. At 12:30, I hear a pounding on the outside door, and it's also pouring rain. The noise wakes me up and the pounding continues for quite a while. I didn't know what was going on, so I take some necessary precautions by putting my pants on, and having my torch ready in case they kick the door down. There is a woman talking and some fairly loud conversation going on before the noise ceases. I guess whoever showed up at this ungodly hour needed a bed.

Good night, Marietta, Wendy, and Cole.

SOUTH AMERICA
ENCHANTMENT

January 16, Wednesday

Isla del Sola, Bolivia

In the morning, I got up at 6:30 and it was still very overcast and foreboding-looking. I managed by 7:30 to get a cup of coffee and started catching up on my notes, only to experience a hailstorm. The windowsills were covered with hail; and this is not a good start to the day. I'm glad that I had a great day yesterday.

There is no conceivable way I can get a shower here. The shower consists of a spout in the wall, and no showerhead on it. The water that you use to flush the toilet is in a barrel with a scoop. Besides that, I don't think I have the fortitude to endure the cold water.

I'm well packed and ready for the adventure today. My fellow travelers are awake also, including the guide. Shortly thereafter, we have a modest breakfast of bread and some eggs and coffee. It's six *Bolivianos*, which are quite expensive, but then there's little or no competition in this isolated area.

We all start making our way down to where the boat will be waiting to take us to Copacabana. We look like a bunch of trekkers that have just circumnavigated every high peak in the world, with our ponchos and rain gear over these huge humps on our backs (better known as backpacks). We're just starting to proceed down, only for the weather to give us a break. The sun god has blessed us by returning, and the crying god of the rain has receded. So, we are able to remove our heavy rain gear, and it is much easier walking down than going up.

As we proceeded on, the guide asked Camello, the young Chilean boy, what he would do if a *puma* (or mountain lion) came at him, and he shrugged his shoulders. He asked me, "What would you do?", and I said I would freeze. He wasn't overly impressed with that response, so I elaborated, and explained that any large cat has only a limited amount of pa-

tience when it comes to playing with its game. If you can remain stationary long enough, it abandons its prey. But the
boy wasn't convinced. He then asked, "Okay, if you're walking
down the trail and you came face to face with the *puma*", what
would you do?" I instantly responded with a huge growl and
raised my hands and attacked him. He was really startled
and laughed and said, "Yes, you would have scared the *puma*,
you have definitely scared me!"

With this bit of humor, we were in good spirits as we continued down the numerous amounts of steps to the bottom.
The boat was waiting and soon took us back to Copacabana.
I have about an hour or two in the process of waiting until we
catch the bus to Puno, so I take advantage of the time allotted
while others are going to have lunch.

I used the time to see the *Catedral*, famous in this part for
miracles that make Bolivia special. The church is an excellent
example of the commitment that the Spaniards had when
converting the natives and preserving their Faith in the New
World. They were not above desecrating other religions when
it came to using the materials at hand. They recycled a large
amount of the stones from Inca temples to build this Moorish

style cathedral and a large monastery behind it. The order that I've seen at the present time is the Franciscan Fathers. However, the life-sized statues represent both the Jesuits and the Franciscans. Unfortunately, the main altar of the cathedral is under restoration and they have a big tarp over it, so even with sneaking around and taking a peak to see, it's not quite the same as if you entered into the full blazing glory of it.

One of the first things that impressed the Spanish conquistadors was the massive amount of gold and silver that the Incas had used to pay homage to their belief, and the Spaniards shared this idea. The cathedral has more than its share of gold and it's comforting to know that not all was sent back to Spain. Being a Roman Catholic myself, I took a moment to kneel down and pray. The Franciscans do a blessing with a flower dipped in the holy water and sprinkle a generous amount on your forehead. I was emotionally moved and felt a spiritual uplift. The corridor leading into the cathedral from the *piazza* is lined with beggars and peddlers, and outside the church are many vendors selling candles and other religious paraphernalia. It is a beautiful church, but the commercialism takes a bit away from the spiritual moment.

I still had some time left to walk through the markets. These areas always excite me. They are just so colorful, and I admire the way that they display their produce and other foodstuffs. It never ceases to amaze me that in North American countries we have all our meat wrapped, weighed and inspected and we still have issues with safety. Here, it stands exposed, hanging on a hook as the butcher slices off pieces.

I joined up with a few of my fellow travelers on the way back to the bus station. I spent some time talking to our travel agent, and in the short time we've been together I've discovered we have similar thoughts and philosophies, such as the Arabic "my heart, my mouth and my mind".

Our bus journey takes us along roads hugging the shoreline of Lake Titicaca as we approach the Peruvian border. While awaiting the formalities of Customs, I take advantage of the break to get off the bus and stretch my legs. I silently say a fond "*adiós*" to the Bolivian people and receive a very welcome smile from the Peruvians.

It's getting late in the evening and darkness covers our first vision of Puno. Michael, the Chilean man, has prearranged our accommodations, and good to his word, has a young lady waiting for us. Rosina takes us to a *hacienda*, which is a much better upgrade than I have been used to, and for the same price as I had been paying previously. Once all of us have checked in, we receive instructions on how to get around the general area of this city and on what we'll be doing the following day. There is a group of us now, Michael and his son, myself, and Christina, the lady sitting next to me on the bus journey here. We all decide to find a place to eat. Michael and his son, Camello, and Christina are much in favor of pizza, and as Puna does not have franchised outlets, we get freshly baked pizza in a true stone oven. With a Peruvian beer, it was an enjoyable meal.

As we walking through the *piazza*, it started to rain. I have been in many countries that have monsoons or torrential rains and this one qualifies as such. Within a matter of minutes, there were rivers running down the streets and people were huddling against the buildings, just trying their very best to protect themselves against this onslaught of water. My humor always seems to surface when I am in the company of young people. The down spouts from the buildings were pouring out and I encouraged Camello to join me for an outdoor shower, and of course he's quite delighted to play along.

Christina had a real quest to try and get a cash advance using her MasterCard credit card, and after checking two or three banks, she did manage to get some money. I wanted to exchange the Chilean and Bolivian currency I had accumulated, and even though we were so close to the borders, this was not possible, to my dismay. I thought this was really a poor neighbor's attitude.

As we wandered through the *piazza*, there was a woman selling some of her knitted products that caught my eye. I knew she had been watching us through the window, as we've been eating the evening meal, probably hopeful that we would be customers. She had an assortment of knitted finger puppets in shapes of *llamas*, and other figures. As I was making my purchase, we soon had a crowd of children surround us, selling their puppets also. Camello bought quite a few from a young mother with baby strapped to her. The baby looked so comfortable and contented. He was wide awake, looking around at the world and just peaceful, so it must be a very nice way to be carried around when you're at that age.

The weather was still quite unsettled and, as the evening was drawing to a close, the four of us made our way back to the *hacienda* and said goodnight to one another.

Goodnight to my wife and dear family.

Robert F. Edwards

January 17, Thursday

Puno, Peru

Once I get up, I look forward to a shower. It's not exactly a hot shower but certainly better than freezing cold and after the number of days that I haven't been able to shower; this one is going to be my day. I pack, make sure that the luggage is secured, and with my documents I leave at the hotel. Christina's up but the Chilean connection is still in bed.

Boy! I know now what people mean when they say, "I need a cup of coffee" in the morning. I really want a cup of coffee to get some of the cobwebs out of my head, as well as the taste out of my mouth. So I asked Christina if she would like to join me, and off we go in the early hours of the morning looking for a restaurant. This proves to be challenging as we search up and down different streets. It's always interesting to see a city wake up, no matter where it is in the world. There seem to be two types of personalities: the ones that are finding their way back into their holes, and the ones that are going to start the day and win success. We managed to find a small café, gulped down a couple of cups of coffee and hurriedly ran back.

Everybody was waiting for us on the minibus that would take us to the boat. The day's excursion starts with a visit to the Floating Islands. This part of the lake is shallow, only three to four meters. There are quite a variety of nationalities on board, and I'm probably the lone English-speaking person in the group. I notice several people drinking the *matei* that I was first introduced to in Argentina. Yes, they are all from Argentina and before long we're talking like old friends and sharing their *matei*.

We continue motoring out further, past a peninsula, until we break into the open waters where we see the first island. These floating islands are world-renowned and home to the *Uros* Indians. They have intermarried with *Aymara*-speaking

SOUTH AMERICA
ENCHANTMENT

Indians, but their existence still remains totally unique. Everything about their lives is dependant on the *totora* reed, which grows abundantly in the shallow part of the lake. The

islands themselves are built entirely of reeds, layer upon layer, renewed on the top as the bottom rots away. Their homes and canoes are also built from reeds, tightly bundled together.

The islands are quite small and the total number of inhabitants is around three hundred, scattered about. We've landed on one of the larger islands; there are sixteen in all. I guess if one sinks or you want to get away from your neighbor, you just build an island. As the guide escorts us off the boat, you feel as though you're walking on a mattress – very soft and spongy. It looks like woven straw and my first desire was to take my shoes off. Most of the natives are all sitting around doing their crafts and obviously hoping that we're going to relieve them of some of their work and replace it with cash. They're a friendly people and have warm smiles. Even though this group of foreigners are stomping around on their homemade island and invading their space, they take it all in stride.

The guide explains about the reed and shows us how to peel back the exterior and it. He offers some to the group, and I

Robert F. Edwards

take my reed, peel it back, and start eating it. Before long, I notice some of the other people are experiencing it also. He asked me how I liked it and I said, "Yes, this is really delicious, I like it very much, and if these people don't behave, I'll go over and eat their house." So everybody had a little chuckle and we continue looking around.

The *Uros* Islanders are quite familiar with visitors and have become well set up in the tourist trade. I bought myself a few mementos, one being a replica of the reed canoe the natives use to paddle between islands. They fish from their boats which are large enough to take a whole family in. The catch of that day was the Lake Titicaca trout. By this time, most of us had taken as many pictures as we had film and felt the islanders could tolerate.

Back on the boat, it takes a couple of hours to get to the big island that we will be visiting for a few hours, Taquile Island. It is very similar to the island that I was on, Isla del Sol, near Copacabana. The farms on which they grow the crops look identical. Even climbing up to the summit or the peak of the island is similar; not quite as steep a climb, but equally as challenging. Once we got close to midway, the skies started to

SOUTH AMERICA
ENCHANTMENT

clear and we could see the snow-capped peaks in the far distance.

We continued on the trail and finally reached the village. The locals are all very industrious, the men knit and the women tend the fields. It seems every spare moment they have, their hands are busy. I was interested, watching some women spinning wool on their traditional spools. The saying that 'idle hands are the devil's workshop' must have really struck home in this area because nobody's hands were idle.

The museum was adequate and the village similar to so many, with the *piazza* in the main core and a few restaurants and souvenir shops. The islanders wear traditional costume; the men all dressed in puffy white shirts and a black vest. I was able to grab a bowl of soup for lunch, which was very good. The hours drifted by on the island as we made conversation amongst ourselves. A couple from Vienna spoke very good English and a

few Germans played chess on a small magnetic board and I spent some time talking to them about it. Generally, we're a pretty jolly bunch of people.

On the boat trip back we ran into rough waters, and some large waves crashed over the sides. This startled not only the captain but also everybody else on board. There were a few pale faces and one of the Spaniards that had been lying down literally fell off the bench onto the floor. It seems that the wind had come up very suddenly and we were all relieved when it changed to rain. Some of the things that you consistently see the vendors selling are ponchos and umbrellas.

57

Robert F. Edwards

Once we got back to the hotel, we had less than an hour to have dinner. There was still torrential rain pouring down, and the streets became little rivers. It's fairly sad to see these vendors trying to do trade and commerce under such trying conditions with tarps protecting themselves and their goods the best they can.

We just barely got our things together preparing for the trip when the taxi showed up to take us to the main bus depot. We will be departing at about eight o'clock in the evening. This is a very modern-looking bus station and probably the best thing I've seen in Puno. While the station was impressive, unfortunately the bus was not. We'd done it to ourselves, as we demanded a discount and it's surprising they gave us anything. The only thing that the bus had in common with the photographs and feature brochures is the company's name. The one in the brochure is a beautiful, sleek-looking bus with leather seats that recline, and a washroom. The bus that we're on has only the similarity that it has wheels and goes on the road the same way. This is a tired vehicle that had seen its best years long ago. The weather is grim. In fact, it's so bad that the seams on the roof of the bus are leaking into the passenger's area and one of the attendants is trying his best, mopping up the water with a towel as it keeps pouring in to the baggage shelf above. However, to keep us distracted they put on a movie as promised and it's a newer version of "The King and I."

In the wee hours of the morning, we arrive in Cuzco. When arriving in Puno, I did not have positive feelings but Cuzco is just the reverse. It's such a clean-looking city and it looks so Spanish compared to the adobe shelters of Puno. It was one of the capital cities of the Inca Empire and the oldest continuously inhabited city on the continent.

At 2:30 in the morning, we're still trying to find which bus Christina got on, and finally gave up trying. In addition to this mix-up, and due to our guide's lack of planning, the hotel that he takes us to is full and so are all the hostels. His best solution was, "Well, fellows, why don't you just stay in the

SOUTH AMERICA
ENCHANTMENT

lobby till five o'clock when people start getting up and go."
This does not go over very well. We're very exhausted and
have had a full day and are not prepared to accept this idea.
After three or four attempts, cruising around the streets in the
early morn, we do secure a room in a hotel.

On a positive note, we do get to see the city by cruising
around. It is a beautiful city, with a strong Spanish flavor.
The churches and the market dominate as the focal point of
the city. Our guide is heading off to La Paz, but he has assured us that his brother Mario, and wife, will show up to give
us a much-needed briefing for the next day.

*At four o'clock in the morning, I'm going to conclude this day
and go to bed. Goodnight, good day, whatever it is.*

Robert F. Edwards

January 18, Friday

Cuzco, Peru

A pleasant surprise at seven o'clock in the morning, I am wide-awake and full of energy. I get up and start my toiletries to have one of the greatest enjoyments I've had on this trip – an abundance of hot water. Yes, hot water! It sounds like such a mundane thing in many parts of the world but after two weeks of not having sufficient hot water, I have one of the best showers I have had, and savor it as if it was some great gift from beyond. Now I'm completely rejuvenated. I have breakfast of papaya and coffee served in a large espresso cup, before I set out to explore the city.

The population is about 300,000 and it's still an important hub for the travel industry in South America. Evidence of the Inca Empire can still be observed in many of the walls that serve as foundations to ancient and modern buildings as well. Cuzco's layout and design is attributed to Pachacutec, a famous Inca developer in the 1400's. The main streets are easy to distinguish. There are some very narrow lanes with doorways, which enter into another streets, all linked into a maze of networks from one area to another. Though it's an easy city to get around in, I did get lost a few times. I found the police very accommodating. No, they don't speak English, but with the map and a request, they're patient, polite, and efficient in trying to get you to where you ought to be.

The shoeshine boys in La Paz, Bolivia looked like terrorists or "banditos" in their occupation, wearing toques and full-face hats and their entire outfit was usually black. However, here in Cuzco, it has reverted to the more conventional attire, and I imagine the young boys are fending for themselves as well as giving extra support for their families as they run around with their shoeshine kits. This occupation is very prevalent here compared to some other developed countries where we wear running shoes which don't polish very well.

SOUTH AMERICA
ENCHANTMENT

I have taken pictures of the *piazza* itself and the large market square and I hope that they turn out. The balconies are

works of art from a bygone era which I enjoyed after seeing a lot of helter skelter design and necessity in construction. This well organized city requires two or three hours of walking round just for me to be familiar with the central core. As always, there is much vendoring and small kiosks do a thriving business; lots of little shops on wheels.

It is now late, so I return to the lobby, and spend some time reading my bible, "The Lonely Planet." While I was enjoying some *matei*, the rest of my group showed up. The three of us unite as if we'd been friends for years and the conversation gets more involved as we go over the program. A few more people come by and both the young ladies I met are going to join our group with Michael on Saturday, the 19th. So, we're all delighted on how well this is working out. I spend a little more time with Michael and his wife, and their only child, a little girl. Again, I am impressed with how children here are well behaved, not just quiet but also observing what life is all about.

Robert F. Edwards

After many good-byes and thank you's, I start on a quest trying to find an Argentine *matei* cup. This is harder than I would have thought possible I covered most of the main core of shopping in this region. People know what a *matei* cup is, people are more than happy in trying to help you find it but I'm still unsuccessful. Finally after many shops, I did found one place that usually carries it. Yes, but they're out of it, maybe next week they'll have some more. However, I purchased some wool socks and a wool hat, chocolate bars, and biscuits for the expedition since I was there.

By now I felt I deserved a glass of cold beer. A Brazilian couple allowed me to join them at their table. The young man was feeling the effects of altitude sickness but both spoke exceptional English and I enjoyed the conversation over dinner. My being familiar with their city, Rio de Janeiro, enhances our conversation and the young lady has been to Toronto once, so it was soon like old friends talking about what's happened lately.

After dinner, I send another e-mail off to my beautiful wife and to my delight I received one from her, just an update. For me, e-mail is certainly one of the most wonderful things that technology has given us over the last century. It's like never being away from home. I returned to my hotel and, as I lay down, I could hear a bit of music coming through the windows.

And that concludes another day of adventure in the life of Robert F. Edwards. Goodnight one and all! Goodnight my beautiful wife. Goodnight my wonderful daughter.

SOUTH AMERICA
ENCHANTMENT

January 19, Saturday

Cuzco, Peru

Let the adventure continue and let the Inca trail begin! I'm
going to enjoy one last hot shower for the next four days. I've
packed some chocolate bars, cheese, crackers, to say nothing
of an extra set of clothes, and will be ready to leave between
6:30 and 7:00. Camello and Michael and I have just enough
time to catch a quick breakfast of coffee and biscuits. This is
without too much conversation because Camello and Michael
speak little or no English and I speak little or no Spanish, but
the feeling of comradeship is evident.

We return to the main lobby at 7:15, and the group is assembling, all ready to take part in the Inca trail. With our
gear on board and seat reservation made for us, we're now
part of the adventure. The bus continually weaves in and out

of these fascinating streets, and we are aware of the Inca
presence, more than just a memory. A lot of the walls and
many of the cobblestone streets still have small polished

Robert F. Edwards

stones embedded in concrete. It interests me that these structures of four or five hundred years old are in full service still, while in North America we're lucky if we get five to eight years before we have to repair our asphalt roads.

The bus winds and turns as it climbs the hilly streets. We stop periodically and more bodies arrive, and more gear stowed away. By now the bus is quite full. With the help of Camello, we now realize that there's going to be sixteen people in our group that's going to take part in this adventure. Victoria and Jimena have now joined us, a bonus for me as these two young ladies from Argentina speak English. There's a warm welcome from the three males, and now our mini group is intact.

The bus stops in the main square, and the hiking gear, food, tents and other equipment that will be accompanying us on the trek are all loaded on top. By now, it's well past 8:30, and most of us were naïve in thinking that the bus would just drop us at the city limits. The Inca trail starts at 88 kilometers outside the city, so, we travel on in high spirits as we anticipate getting started on this first day.

The scenery is very majestic. The rolling hills are dotted with small farms and adobe buildings. The farmers are just starting to make their way into the fields and I can easily spot the odd woman as they are wear very colorful reds and oranges. On the fields there are crops of corn in different stages of development. I'm looking forward to trying this corn on the cob. These corns are gigantic and I watched the local people eat them in quite a different way from what we do in Canada. We pick it up and gnaw on it back and forth. They use their fingers to pick these large kernels off and eat them daintily. The kernels themselves are the size of a fingernail, some as large as my thumbnail.

It's a beautiful day, just what you would hope for to start the trekking. We have the better part of a couple of hours behind us and I'm getting hungry. Everybody's wishing that their bag contained a Big Mac or at least some potato chips. We're told that we'll be stopping for lunch shortly and, sure enough, we

SOUTH AMERICA
ENCHANTMENT

stop at a little village. We have a forty-minute layover, and both the young ladies and I decide that we're going to buy some walking sticks. We asked Julio, our guide, what was a fair price and he tells us about three *nuevos soles* of Peruvian currency. At first the woman asks five SN, but as the bus fills up, ready to leave, the price drops. Now, the three musketeers have three distinctive walking sticks.

The bus spent another hour making its way winding through the foothills toward the mountains. Theses ranges change just as you blink your eyes; some are tall and majestic, others are softly covered with foliage, and patchworks of small farms endure at this high altitude and diverse climate. My eye catches a sign on the road "68," so I am thinking we have another 20 kilometers to go before we actually reach the trek. About 10 kilometers up, the road is washed out and we're told that we're going to have to walk.

So, we all load up our gear and start walking. My canter hasn't changed much over the years and before very long I'm taking the lead. There's one fellow outpacing me, but I'm not out for a race. Julio comes strolling up to me and he says, "You really like to walk, don't you?" And I say, "Oh yes, I enjoy a good walk." We'd been walking now for the better part of an hour when a bus that was able to reroute itself stopped and picked me up along with another couple of girls from my group. The girls motioned shortly after that they wanted to get off the bus, and as they got off I was prepared to go with them. Luckily, one of the porters was also on this bus and he motioning to me, "No, no, no, stay." Like every person, you want to try to stay with your group because you have no idea what's going to happen if you get separated. With my limited vocabulary, I'm quite concerned. However, they assure me that this is perfectly fine, this is the right bus.

I start talking to a young lady, about 25 or 26. She's studying law and has two to three years left. Her English is just perfect and she's Argentinean. She is absolutely gorgeous. Her eyes are dark chocolate brown and her skin is ivory, and I wonder that such a beautiful woman is so determined to take on such a brutal profession. We talked the rest of the way and it makes the short journey endurable. We get off the bus at about two o'clock in the afternoon and I'm starving. More importantly, I'm concerned where the rest of my group is. Then, another bus rumbles in with the remaining part of my group. We're handed out bananas and I'm starving, and the rest of them, I notice, consume this small token of food very quickly also.

We're told that we have to walk about a kilometer to where the inns and the national park registry are. Our merry group is soon joined by others as we all head towards the entrance of the park and the beginning of the trail. It has become very congested, but we are highly motivated to get started. When we reach the entrance, our trekking documents are presented and stamped, and they require your name and your age. I feel that 60 is a wonderful year, but I'm Horatio at the bridge on this one, as I stand alone. Most of these people are in their mid to late twenties.

We start our trek by crossing over a bridge and the river below is a torrent of brown water, frothing and rising due to the rainy season. The upward grade starts here; it's not difficult,

SOUTH AMERICA
ENCHANTMENT

just a continuation of upward and onward. As I wind, weave and twist with the trail, it continually builds grade. This is not going to be a walk in the park. I remember my guide's advice when climbing Mount Kilimanjaro, "slow, slow, slow." So, taking it slowly, without the long rest breaks that a lot of my fellow backpackers are taking, it's pleasant.

We alternate between putting the ponchos on and taking them off, depending on what the weather wants to do. When it rains it's forceful and I am anxious to try to keep my backpack dry, as well as myself. We stop for a lunch break of *sopa*, or soup. It's a very thick, nourishing, broth, with rice and little beans and a scoop of tuna on top. I smiled to myself about this, as tuna must be the most popular fish in the world. Even in the great Sahara sea sands, I was eating tuna, and here on the Inca trail, again eating tuna. They serve quite a variety of teas. One tea is even a cold type, in tea bags.

So after lunch, we have about another four to five hours of walking, depending on the pace of the individual. It's all upward, but the views are becoming breathtaking and we can see the river that we crossed; the bridge appears as a small line below. To my understanding, we've covered approximately 12 kilometers, the total trip being around 45 kilometers.

By eight o'clock, we arrive at the camp. After carrying my small pack plus my sleeping bag, my body belt with my camera gear, I feel more like a pack mule than a trekker. We stop for a drink and Julio, our guide asks me how I'm doing. He's developed a very sore throat. So I said, "Well I'm actually doing quite a bit better than you," and offered to buy him a pop. We try to talk for a bit, but he sounds like he's getting laryngitis, which doesn't enhance his English by any means.

The shirt I am wearing is supposedly water resistant, but it is soaking wet, not from the rain but from my perspiration. Even the padding on my backpack straps is soaking wet. We start to set up camp where they've permitted us to pitch the tents and our porters have it all well organized. They've got us all in the same general area and I am pleased to find that I have my own private tent here up in the Andes. Dinner is somewhat a repeat of lunch, a thick broth, almost porridge.

It's dark enough now, and I say goodnight to my comrades and head off to my tent. Before crawling in, I take one last look at the clear sky with the infinite number of stars twinkling above. When I slept out on the great sea sands of the Sahara Desert, my Arab guide had commented that, "In my country, we have a Million Star Hotel."

So, with that, I conclude tonight. I'd like to say goodnight to my beautiful wife that I miss very much and to my daughter that I love very much and my little Coleman, I'm looking forward to playing with him and his trains.

SOUTH AMERICA
ENCHANTMENT

January 20, Sunday

Inca Trail, Peru

According to the schedule, we're supposed to be up by 6:00 and hopefully on the road at 7:00 am. As usual, I'm one of the first awake, and it's a beautiful morning. The view is breathtaking. The clouds are at different levels on the mountainsides and I quickly grab my camera and become a real shutterbug. So, I'm up and dressed; no, I didn't shave but I did brush my teeth.

Gradually, heads appear from the other tents and the day starts to get underway. My friend Michael has blisters on his feet, which he is trying to repair with bandages. I offer him an extra pair of socks and he says, "No, no, I've got that too." Soon his son is up and breakfast is served. This morning we have porridge, not the traditional oatmeal (I really don't know what the main ingredient is), but one that's very unique. It has got cloves in it and I enjoyed the flavor of it.

The Incas considered Machu Picchu a very sacred city and it was a pilgrimage site in their religion. The more that I learn about the Incas, the more I realize that history has revealed little of their culture. Although they had a language, it was not written down and recorded, so a lot of theories about them are highly speculative. This Lost City of the Incas was stumbled upon almost by accident by the American historian Hiram Bingham in 1911. The overgrown vegetation was cleared in subsequent years to reveal the most spectacular archaeological site in South America.

This hike is said to be one of the most popular hikes on the continent and this pilgrim is thoroughly enjoying his pilgrimage. The girls and I are somewhat concerned about the altitude that we'll be experiencing today. Now we're at 3,500 meters and we're going up another 1,000 meters today. Julio has stressed the fact that it will be very cold and he has a very warm toque on and a heavy woolen jacket and more gear on top of that. Who knows how many other layers are underneath, so I'm not questioning him by any stretch of the imagination. I've put on my Gore-Tex pants, which I know will add extra warmth for my legs. I've got my wool Peruvian hat, mitts, and the mud-gaiters around my ankles. They provide no warmth, but are just something to protect my clothes from the trail's grime. The two girls and I have decided to hire a

porter to carry our packs. So, we'll be aristocrats and just walk up the mountain with our walking sticks. Now with twenty *nuevos soles* less in our pockets, off we go.

Here again are the Inca's stairs that were so predominant on the Isla del Sol. These are not as high but they're still good-sized steps. I marvel at the size of these, as the Peruvians themselves are short people, most of them being just a shade over five feet. It's interesting to realize that the Incas of similar stature would be able to climb up these ladders to the sky. However, let there be no mistake. That's exactly what these Peruvian guides do, as well as the porters with back-packers' heavy loads, and all at a good pace. One of my fellow trekkers, an Austrian commented, "You never see any Peruvians in the Olympic Games and they would probably do exceptionally well." Looking at the calf muscles on these men's legs, I would agree with him.

The day is turning out to be quite a strenuous one, especially with the continual gaining in altitude. This is when I try out my cocoa leaf. Yes, it is one of the main ingredients of cocaine, the drug of choice for the new generation of addicts in North America. With the leaf, which you fold up two or

SOUTH AMERICA
ENCHANTMENT

three times (whichever your choice is), you tuck it in your cheek, very similar to chewing tobacco, and chomp down. I'm not sure whether it works or not. Julio says that it's part of their mystical belief in aphrodisiacs. If nothing else, this particular leaf keeps your mouth moist, and I do feel I've got an extra surge of energy after swallowing some of the juices. I am more impressed that after climbing for hours, my mouth hasn't become parched. Julio instructed us to drink a fair amount of water at the beginning, take very short rest periods, and to go slowly but keep moving. As we get into higher altitudes, our breathing will become labored, and we may have signs of altitude sickness, some more severe than others. When I was at a lower altitude, my mouth had become parched and I grabbed the water canteen to relieve the dryness, but without success. Now with this particular leaf, I have no problem.

The views are breath-taking, but as we take a turn, we face upwards towards the summit. I see another arduous trail that seems to demand that we hike forever. Then out of nowhere, I see people near the summit. As I hike closer to the top, they all stand up and cheer me on, clapping and shouting "hurrah"

71

Robert F. Edwards

for me. I was taken by surprise; it's not even my group. There are five or six different groups and obviously some of them have left earlier than us. As I reach this plateau, many of them come over, and welcome me. It's a United Nations. There are some Spaniards, Germans, and Australians, but the Argentineans dominate. While I am resting, the rest of my group starts to appear and there's an exuberance that is felt by all as we make a bit of conversation. We are all grateful there are toilet facilities here. It is quite cold now, and I met a British chap, from London with whom I exchange some biscuits and camaraderie. It is nice to be able to talk to someone without all the gesturing; to know what they are talking about, and vice versa.

There are probably close to a hundred young people working their way up this challenging trek. It is fairly evenly divided between men and women. I'm (without any stretch of the imagination) at least twice everybody's age here, and then some. Many of them have come up to me and expressed a sincere admiration for my efforts. I'm very proud and amazed that these people have respect for an older person. From the Peruvian group a young man approaches me and asks how old I am? I tell him I'm sixty and the whole group raises their hands and bows back and forth to me. Then he says to me, "You're a very strong man." I said, "Oh, I don't know; I just try to do my best." He says, "No, you're very strong and in good shape. I'm impressed." I didn't realize until later that he was the guide of that particular group. Not knowing who he was, just thinking he's another poor mortal making this pilgrimage, I was even more honored and deeply touched by their encouragement and respect once I found out he was their guide.

After this short break, I start climbing again, higher and higher towards the summit. I go down a very short distance, only to start heading back up. They say 'All roads lead to Rome'. This road, I hope leads to Machu Picchu and not the world beyond. I can't believe how high we are and still these beautiful mountains command more of the sky. It changes,

SOUTH AMERICA
ENCHANTMENT

almost by the minute, a heavy mist clouding in and covering us. It becomes very cold and the winds are quite strong, but with our exuberant attitude and as we concentrate on the trail, we don't notice it so much. Just when we get dressed for an Arctic adventure, the sun appears and together with the energy that we are putting into this walk causes perspiration to form, which soon is running down our faces. I'm not referring just to myself; even the porters were sweating, mind you they're going faster than I am, but under the same conditions.

This is not a walk in the park by any stretch of the imagination. If you're going up, it takes all your concentration and your strength; and if you're going down, it's equally as demanding because you're putting so much weight on your knees and stretching to go down these stairwells.

The moment we had at the summit is more than rewarding. I am so grateful to just be present and accounted for. I feel blessed to be able to re-live the experiences of the Incas on this remarkable trail. As we start downward, we find it is a very steep decline. I have no idea why the Incas chose these high plateaus to cross over rather than keep to the riverbed through these passes. However, the scenery alone warrants full admiration for their accomplishment.

I am thankful to be well seasoned for walking the mountain paths in my own country. This is supposed to be the hardest day and until we got to the top and started our way down, I was still in full fighting form. Actually, I still had a considerable amount of energy to burn on the way down to our camp. I arrived before most of the others. I wouldn't say I was first, but I was in the top five to get there. We're shown the tents that each one is designated to, and soon the porter carrying my bags and the girls arrive. We rejoice at our accomplishment and the adrenaline is running high.

We're informed that in two or three hours they will be serving tea and then the evening meal shortly afterwards. Victoria says she's not highly motivated to have a *siesta*, but Jimena said that she's prepared to have one. There's really little to do here, other than go for a walk. The only place to walk is the trail itself and I don't think anybody today, tomorrow, or any other day arrives and then says, "Well, I think I'll take a little hike up the trail." So, after everybody expresses their feelings of excitement at their accomplishments of today and compliments all around, the *siestas* begin.

We all end up crawling into our private little tents for our afternoon *siestas*. To my surprise, I sleep until five o'clock, when the rustling of my tent indicates that it's time to get up and enjoy some of the beverages and cookies presented. I have great admiration for how hard the porters and cooks work. There's a lot of effort needed for these trekking expeditions to be successful, even small things like taking a stick and making a small groove around our tents so that when it rains the water runs away from the tent towards the ravine. These men know what they're doing and it's a hard, demanding life. Anybody that's in the service industry and looking after people knows this is one of the most difficult job assignments. I commend what these men can accomplish working at these altitudes and preparing the amount of food, the tents, and everything else.

SOUTH AMERICA
ENCHANTMENT

We are served a variety of teas, one of which is cocoa tea. The more I chew this leaf, the more I think it does have medicinal effects. My digestive tract seems to be in full form and I feel good. As we are enjoying our tea, there's a sad moment. Michael and Camello arrive. Michael is supporting Camello, almost carrying him in. The brave young lad is extremely sick, and his father is understandably distraught. He's more than prepared to have his son even air-lifted out. This is the sad part of this trip. There is no communication; no radios, no telephones, and above all there's no medication or medics. I had learnt a bit of Michael's personal life and could understand the stress he was experiencing. Many years ago; he had lost one of his sons to meningitis. He was now very adamant that safety was a priority rather than adventure.

We're all feeling the deep concern Michael has for his son. This is the first time that the two of them have shared an adventure and Michael had often told people how much this meant to him. Also, it was evident how much Camello enjoyed being with his father on a one-to-one basis. This is the time in life when a boy of thirteen becomes a man and he was sharing his manhood with the man that he had always respected and loved ......his father, and Camello was having this experience with his father. My heart and my emotions are going out to the distress that this wonderful man is enduring as he's trying to find people that can help him. We can only hope now that with rest, Camello will improve through the night.

After supper, I bring out my chocolates and now more and more people are enjoying my little treats, which I'm happy to share. The Australians really help me out but, despite all my preparations and diligence to do things right, the batteries in my small flashlight have died. One of the Australians has an extra set and generously gives it to me, so I'm not roaming in the dark or falling off a cliff. We spend some time talking about tomorrow and know that we've accomplished the hardest part of our adventure today, and that in record-breaking time, so tomorrow should be most enjoyable.

Robert F. Edwards

Our guide outlines the plans for tomorrow and, though we'll start about the same time, it's going to be a much longer day as we'll be visiting ruins along the way and should cover around fourteen kilometers.

The night is clear once more and I gaze at the stars and somebody points out what we think is a satellite, but no, Julio says it's just an airplane. All I know is that it looks like a bright light moving faster than the rest of the bright lights far beyond. In the darkness I can still see the proud majestic mountains commanding attention from the skies above.

And with that, I'd like to conclude this day in my life, a remarkable event. Goodnight, my beautiful wife, I love you dearly and I miss you a lot.

SOUTH AMERICA
ENCHANTMENT

January 21, Monday

Inca Trail, Peru

We're up and at it. The most that I can do is brush my teeth and pack my gear, so this is the third day of growth on my face and I have no idea how scruffy I look. It's a nice day and I take some pictures and feel full of vigor and determination. The rest of the group is in good spirits, also. So, we start off again and guess what? We're going up. Yes, and up and up and up. We're getting used to the conditions of this trail, but I have to admit to myself that it's still very difficult on this seemingly endless rugged trail. Climbing the heights and then going down again is not only difficult, but somewhat repetitious. So, this process is a continuation, hour after hour. I marveled at the Spaniards' commitment to work these trails for greed and obsession for gold, but then I was told that they took the riverbed, and were determined to get there faster than those of us that are trying to re-live the moments of this civilization.

We get to the first ruins, probably built as a defense or a lookout post to the paths below. It commands full attention of the valley and we can even see the river below. I'm sure that the man that guarded this area had a tremendous advantage over anybody trying to make their way up to it. This site being an outpost is limited in size, but the facilities are well built and obviously in their time offered comfort. I believe this out-of-the-way station offered people a place to spend the night resting, and that to me makes a lot of sense. I've been told that marathon runners could do the entire trail in four or five hours. Marathon runners were remarkable people but I would still think that the average person even in the Inca period would appreciate this resting place.

The scenery is endlessly fascinating. The more I'm up here and gaze at these beautiful mountains, their different shapes and natural designs; I can't help but wonder in my mind, "Is

77

Robert F. Edwards

Machu Picchu going to be a disappointment?" Can anything man-made compare to the beauty that I'm experiencing with this endless trail? As with people no two mountains are alike. However, I'm amazed that each one is distinct.

Most of the group is complaining of the cold, and it was bitterly cold last night, few slept well. Leave it to the Canucks though, at least this Canadian slept like a stone. I was chuckling to myself that here, sleeping in a tent on a wafer thin mattress in a sleeping bag, I still have a better night's sleep than when at home in my own bed. My wife's observation of me is quite correct when she says, "I think you were a peasant in another life." It doesn't take much to satisfy my needs.

The time seems to have stopped on my watch, even though my feet keep moving and the hours seem to take days to move their little hands to the next point. When we do stop and talk a little bit, there's always the same encouragement, "Yes, we aren't getting tired." We meet up with a couple of Spaniards, young men, and they comment again on how awesome everybody thinks I am, trekking through these mountains. I can't help but start to blush, I'm sure. I thank them very much -

SOUTH AMERICA
ENCHANTMENT

the camaraderie and the people that I have met along the trail have been a great part of this experience. Even if there had only been a few people, it would not have taken away from these moments of beauty and excitement, but meeting so many young people from different countries has added to this exceptional moment in my life and I'm thoroughly savoring every conversation.

We get to the next ruins, which are much larger and they even have baths. I've taken pictures of the ceremonial rock that was used to perform rituals. Julio has stressed the fact that humans were not used in their sacrifice. One of the animals that was sacrificed was the *llama*, in a blood ritual. The black *llama* was considered more pure on the inside.

These ruins are not as intact as some left by the Roman Empire or those in Crete and Egypt that command so much attention. However, these are informative. The Inca society wasn't as advanced in technology as some of the other civilizations, but is still interesting. Incas used a twine of tree bark to make ropes. Wood is scarce up here so it wasn't a commodity to be used other than for their roofs. Julio explains that an Inca door is a stone slab placed across the entrance as the wood has long since disappeared, so if there's any wood present in the reconstruction, this isn't true Inca. The dwellings have stones jutting out from the wall at higher levels for hanging things on or to support the roofs. A wood or thatched roof was the order of the day. Of course, these have long disappeared and you can only see the framework.

Some of the ruins are more crudely put together, probably originally made for more common use, and small chips of stones are used to stabilize the structure of the walls. In the more important places however, the stones are ground to fit into each other, needing no mortar. This reminds me of the pyramids, but the Egyptians had it easier as they used the softer sandstone of the desert, rather than mountainous granite. I know very little of what tools they used, but the Incas still must have been totally committed in order to construct these building, now ruins.

Robert F. Edwards

We still have about seven or eight more kilometers to go. It's well past mid-day. I've taken out some chocolate and eaten that along the way. This hiking is strenuous work and we are starting to feel the effects of altitude and fatigue. All seem to limp more than walk. The saddest situation is my little friend Camello. When he got up this morning, he could barely stand. He was wrapped up in a blanket and strapped to one of the porters, who literally piggybacked him up the mountain. However, along the way, I was able to catch up to them, and he was sitting down, resting with his walking stick. I encouraged him, and suggested he put his arm around the waist or the shoulder of the porter to help him take some of his body weight. I understand his strong sense of pride and my heart is going out to him.

This is supposed to be a night of celebration and the campsite where we are heading to will have a large number of tents. There are a lot of people that are doing two-day hikes instead of the four-day trekking and will all congregate there before we all approach Machu Picchu at the same time. My heart is not in the celebration; my thoughts are with Camello and his father, just praying that once we get to this site they will be able to get the medical attention they need.

The trail seems to drag on endlessly and all of us seem to be waiting for that magic moment when we can see the facilities that lie ahead. Supposedly, we will be able to secure a bed and a hot shower and there's a restaurant. The previous day, I probably would have gone the extra mile just to get a Diet Pepsi. I crave a bottle of pop as much as one of the girls was craving a smoke. We'd be teasing each other, saying that we'd keep count on how many cigarettes she was going to have because then I would to have equally as many bottles of pop. I hate to admit it, but I think I'm a popaholic as I just love that beverage.

The hours seem to drag and even though the scenery is breath-taking, my enthusiasm is waning. I'm tired and I can't believe how long the day is. We finally get in around four o'clock. It looks like a military campaign and a congregation of armies coming together, with each regiment finding its own designated spot. Tents are everywhere on this terraced terrain. Because of the rains that we've had, everything is slippery. I eased my backpack off gently as I didn't want to fall face down into the mud, although I notice my sleeping bag's outer case is already suffering the effects of mud.

Whether it's my age or not I don't know, but there's an air of consideration bestowed upon me by the group and I'm very honored by their commitment to look after me. When I find my tent, I realize that I wouldn't want to jump out of it first thing in the morning. The first step would be devastating, a drop of four or five meters. It's already dark and it's only 6:30. There is a beehive of activity with people everywhere and, surprisingly, I know most of them. Jimena and I relax, sitting on the ledge, and yes she has her first cigarette and I enjoy two bottles of pop. We watch as more and more people gather in the facilities below. There are no two ways about it, there's going to be a party tonight. By now there must be in excess of a hundred people, probably closer to a hundred and fifty, and I'm still the oldest person in this entire group. The majority is under thirty, so these people have a lot of vigor left in them.

Once we settle in, we are informed that the evening meal is about to commence and each group is designated their own spot. It's been the first time in three days that I've actually sat on a chair. Most people are enjoying a *cerveza* while I'm salivating on more pop. I'm somewhat disappointed over the last meal, but it's understandable as each group has brought its own supplies, which are now running low. The soup is almost water with a touch of cinnamon for flavor and the rice is spartan, to say the least. However, the party mood prevails and nobody is too distraught with it.

The highlight of the evening comes. Camello arrives to take his place and there's a standing ovation for him. He's the Hero of the Moment and my heart jumps out of my chest to see him there well enough to join us. I'd said to the girls that I thought Camello was suffering from altitude sickness. The attendants basically confirmed that Dr. Edwards' diagnosis was correct, not that it helped his condition at all, but I can't help but be grateful to God: "Thank you very much for looking after my young friend."

Now there's a renewed air of exuberance at our table as we are grateful and relieved. Michael is a shy man, yet he gets up to face the group and gives a speech on how much he and his son love me and appreciate my support during the last few days. Victoria's doing the translation for me, but even she is starting to choke up and I can tell by the way he's expressing himself that he's pouring his heart out. I walk over to their end of the table and Camello stands up and cheers in Spanish, "My hero!" It's a very emotional moment. We are all hugging each other and the entire one hundred and fifty people are clapping, crying and sharing the moment of three men.

We take up a collection for the porters and for some reason the group has decided that I've got to be the one that presents this remuneration to them. One of the Australian fellows has made our gift bag into the shape of a little bird and I added a cocoa leaf for the beak. I asked Victoria if she would do the translation for me and explained to her roughly what I'm going to say; that these porters have made each and every one of our dreams come true, we appreciate their sharing our dreams with all their labors and endurance on the trek and we appreciate their commitment to making our dreams a reality, and with that we present this little bird that will grow into the condor to share their dreams.

Everybody claps and there is more hugging and cheering and the evening is a celebration for all. I'm quite overwhelmed by the enthusiasm of the young people wanting to involve me in their party spirit. Women are coming up and asking, "You dance later?" and I reply, "Oh, I'll see". The only negative aspect of the evening is that we have to get up at four o'clock in the morning to start our final approach into Machu Picchu. At this moment, six o'clock would be early and four o'clock seems completely out of the question.

SOUTH AMERICA
ENCHANTMENT

The meal is cleared away and the party is now in full swing. The Brazilians have taken the lead and have a musical rhythm going with a whistle and some beating of pans on their table. As I walk by to get another pop, they look a bit embarrassed that they may be making too much noise compared to the rest of the group. However, I encourage them to keep going, putting gasoline on the fire. I laugh and have some fun with them before I return to my table, only for them to ask, "Please come over to our table." It's a good thing we weren't on a boat, as before long we had all the people gathered at one end of the large hall and had cleared the floor for dancing. Everybody is happy and exuberant and probably like myself, somewhat relieved that this arduous trek will be coming to an end.

Tomorrow we'll see Machu Picchu. I am concentrating on that four o'clock wake up call and make my way back to the tent. The second set of batteries in my flashlight is starting to show fatigue. Batteries have been a plague to me.

It's too late to worry about that now, so goodnight, one and all.

Robert F. Edwards

January 22, Tuesday

Inca Trail, Peru

Yes, we really do get up at four o'clock in the morning. The battery in my flashlight is hovering from weak to dead, and I pack and get dressed in the dark. I put the light on only when I absolutely need to find something. I feel as though I haven't really slept and have to confess I had a restless night, worrying about having to get up at this early hour.

As I open up the tent, the stars are still winking at me. There is movement in the tents around me and other people are starting to awake. I try to make my way up this muddy trail with little or no power from my flashlight. Luckily, one of the porters has a proper flashlight to give me guidance up to the first part of the walkway. I manage to get to the top, staggering with the weight of my gear and my walking stick, using the faint flickering glow from my flashlight.

People are congregating, but we don't look like the same group that was singing and bouncing around the night before. This is a bunch of tired, misplaced refugees with bewildered looking faces. It's a spartan breakfast with just a few pieces of bread and some coffee. Nobody seems to be in too much of a mood to talk.

Victoria, Jimena and I are ready to go. I have explained to Victoria that my battery is no good and she runs off to buy batteries for it and soon the three musketeers head out into the darkness. I take the lead because compared to both girls, I'm the fastest walker. As we're heading up the trail, I call back to them when we're approaching stairs, etc. The girls continually compliment me and say I'm the best guide in the world. I have such appreciation of these young people, very few of whom speak any English, and the ones that do are limited. Yet they make the effort to express to this old man their admiration and respect for his accomplishments. If there's ever any doubt that the world was going to be in good hands

SOUTH AMERICA
ENCHANTMENT

in the future, I feel assured that these people have the right ingredients to advance civilization. I'm so proud to be with them, they will always be in my heart forever.

We've been on the trail for three-quarters of an hour when dawn begins to break - it's always the coldest moment of the night. My eyes grow accustomed to the darkness and I've turned off the flashlight. It's a different experience, watching the mountain ranges develop their formations out of the darkness of the night. As we are descending, the surrounding terrain becomes more visible. For the first time we're starting to see flowers, butterflies and birds.

Earlier, at a previous site, I had visited a museum and was amazed to learn the number of species in this general area: locusts, a tremendous number of butterflies, some with beautiful fluorescent wings, bats, birds, and lots of hummingbirds. One hummingbird is no more than three inches, just a little puff of blackness. Of course, there are snakes, both poisonous and otherwise, and many small animals that were presented in the museum.

We're now in the full force of the sun and I see some freshly made mud tracks on the trail. When I tell the girls that there are some people ahead of us and explained why, they said: "You're absolutely remarkable. You know everything." And I'm thinking, "Oh God, if only I did, how happy I would be", but I suppose there's benefit in that experience does come with age. Along the way, we take a few moments to share the sheer beauty of this trail's majestic landscape. Now, the river does again appears and it looks like a brown pencil-line far below in the valleys that meet it. All of us are in awe and we marvel at the view.

We have nicknamed ourselves 'the three musketeers' and use our walking sticks to pledge our allegiance to each other as in days of old when knights used their swords to pledge their bond. Then we always laugh and say, "One for all and all for one." Onward and forward down the trail which now has lush tropical foliage and is much warmer. I can't get used to the climatic conditions changing almost hourly on this trail.

Robert F. Edwards

Since the very beginning we have experienced torrential rains, mist, burning sun, and then bitter cold when the clouds cover the skies.

As we take a turn on the trail, we see another outpost station of the Incas. These ruins are interesting in that they have areas set aside for the baths used before ceremonies. This

particular temple has such facilities. There's a huge rock slab which we take advantage of for some posing of pictures. It seems, since last night, everybody's aware of our presence and we're almost celebrities.

There's a group of maybe eight to twelve people ahead of us on the trail, and they ask us to stop. One of the girls says "No, Señor ..." and something I didn't understand. I thought maybe I'd taken the wrong trail. What actually happened was a few in their group had to go to the bathroom and decided that they would alternate. We haven't had this problem yet, and it is difficult as there's a sheer drop on one side of the trail and an impregnable wall on the other side. There are no facilities along the way, so you just have to use a spot on the trail to relieve yourselves.

SOUTH AMERICA
ENCHANTMENT

Once this issue is resolved, the three musketeers are once again in full stride, back on their quest to see Machu Picchu. We all feel the air of excitement, knowing that we're getting closer to completing this remarkable trek. I am anxious to see if my imagination has any continuity with the reality of Machu Picchu. The trail continues on gently now, going up and down, ever closer. We come to another ruin and there are a few people sitting there resting. As we climb more stairs,

again I think of the Incas. As we follow in their footsteps, climbing up and down these very narrow, steep stairs, I think the Incas must have been some of the most sure-footed people in the world at that time. We get to the top of these ruins and it takes my breath away. There in the valley below is Machu Picchu.

I will never know whether it's the ruins that hold me fast and won't release my fixation on them, or the beautiful majestic surroundings of this 'Lost City of the Incas'. My eyes are overwhelmed. I wonder which beautiful presence to gaze upon longer than the other, the range of mountains and valleys, and peaks, and the river far below, or the wonder of building a city so remote from the world. But it's the place; it's the setting that is as magnificent as the city itself. I try to imagine what it would have been like for an Inca to have made a pilgrimage to this sacred city, and first gaze upon it at this very spot.

From this viewpoint the ruins take shape and you know Machu Picchu was a city; not just a mere construction of a few buildings of a bygone civilization. This is a city planned in some of the most majestic settings of the world. We rest and make some conversation with our fellow travelers, marveling just at the sheer beauty that we're witnessing, and of course, more pictures. The three of us, again, break trail. We're now beyond exuberant. I haven't got a word for the enthusiasm and the renewed energy levels that we're experiencing. To get to this ancient city without any further delay, we're trekking down with a new zeal, wanting to achieve the entrance and explore the wonders below.

As we go down, we've been instructed to turn near the electrical pylons of the hydro plants below us. Shortly thereafter, we're rewarded by seeing them and know that we're almost there. By now we're able to see the railroad tracks for the first time and some of the buildings that are available for the *turistas* and the entrance to the actual ruins themselves.

The trail is progressively going downwards now and the steps are numerous in our quest to get to the city. Once we get to the entrance itself, we pass through a security check that we have the right documents and our passes. There are also instructions that we're not allowed to use our walking sticks or allowed to carry our backpacks or other supplies in.

SOUTH AMERICA
ENCHANTMENT

However the men on duty are more than pleasant and ac-commodating. Once we check our gear in we feel that we should be rewarded by having something to eat. As I men-tioned earlier, Jimena and I have had an outstanding joke that whatever number of cigarettes she wishes to have, I'm allowed to have as many bottles of pop; so with that, I jokingly ask how many, and she says, "You can have at least three, maybe four."

Once we enter the restaurant, we find surprisingly that the mood has changed. My fellow trekkers on the trail were a rug-ged group, survivors in their own right and adventurers by full definition. Now we're mingling with the people that have come up by train or bus. These tourists are a different breed. They have walking sticks that are contractible and state of the art. Their guides are first class, or at least have a better pro-nunciation of English or whatever other language is being spoken. The age group has shifted from the mid-twenties into the mid-fifties and beyond. As I look at these older people, I reflect that this is my age group. Oh thank God, thank you very much for allowing me to be with these wonderful young

people that have adopted this old man to be a part of their adventure!

Looking at the others in my group waving and yelling "Bob, Bob!" letting me know that they've arrived, I'm so very grateful to be a part of the trekkers. I mention this to both Victoria and Jimena and they laugh and say "you're one of us, don't forget it, you're one of us". It only renews my great love for all of them and the respect and honor that they've bestowed upon me is still something I have a hard time

89

Robert F. Edwards

comprehending in my own mind and feelings. Together, the three musketeers have fulfilled a dream that I've had for a lifetime.

We break the tradition of our spartan lifestyle and quickly go back into the convenience of modern civilization. I have a ham sandwich on a Kaiser bun and a light cola. My comrades, as they enter the open-air restaurant are looking exhausted much different from those people that have arrived from their five-star hotels. We are a ragged bunch, worn out and dirty, but a very happy group.

Our group starts to congregate and we're just waiting now for Julio to show up. He's going to take us into Machu Picchu and explain the different parts of the city that waits below. I want to compliment the guides, whether they're the ones that have trekked these endless kilometers on the trail or the ones that have lived a more comfortable life with the tourists. They've chosen different sectors of Machu Picchu to start their guided tours, so that we don't all look like a huge glob of flesh standing on top of each other. It is well planned and they've dispersed each group, almost like a private school within the great walls.

From Julio I learnt about the demise of the Inca civilization, after which the surrounding forest and the lush vegetation quickly engulfed Machu Picchu, leaving only the legend to persist as with ancient cities like Troy and other well-known archaeology sites that have now been unearthed. Machu Picchu was very similar. The legend persisted, but nobody really knew where this lost city of the Incas was. An American, Hiram Bingham, on July 24th 1911, more or less stumbled upon this site. This man wasn't a true archaeologist but more of a historian, studying the occupation of that period under the Spaniards. However, after finding this remarkable place, he quickly returned to the States and in 1912 and 1915 accompanied an expedition and started uncovering the remains of Machu Picchu.

In all the ruins that I visited, I could tell the original Inca structures from the improvised ones they've reassembled.

The original ones are intact, and the replacement ones have numbers on them, so it's easy to distinguish. The ruins are very much a city; there is no two ways about it. Some of the more significant buildings are the Hut of the Caretaker of the Funerary Rock and up a small hill is Intihuatana, the major shrine here. There's the carved rock on one of the summits where the sundial is. The Incas were sun worshippers and they had devised calendars that were very accurate according to the seasons. Their calendar was actually divided into ten-day weeks.

The Incas had three major gods that were evident in their ceremonies. One was the *puma* and this represented Mother Earth. It plays a very significant part in their religious cultures including Lake Titicaca, which is supposed to have the appearance of a *puma*. Throughout our journey, we've been shown different rocks and told of ceremonies that were related to the *puma*. The next is the condor, representing the gods of the sky. Another important god was the snake, or the serpent, and this symbol is often seen in the ceremonial temples in the stone carving of a cup or chalice. If the blood of the sacrifice went one way with the snake, it would mean prosperity in the crops and a good growing season. If it went in the opposite direction, there would be crop failures and famine.

Robert F. Edwards

Incas had their own beliefs and attitudes towards events of the coming year. They did not have the farmer's almanac but their own unique methods of forecasting.

The stone available in this mountain range is very hard granite. I was curious, and asked Julio the guide how the Incas managed to use this difficult material in their buildings. Thinking back to Egypt, most of the pyramids and temples were made with sandstone. Egyptians were able to achieve a tight formation by putting sand between stones and using it as a grinder. The Incas must have had some process to produce the smooth continuity of stones linked together. I understand they used a chisel type instrument, obviously very  strong, and would break into the huge slabs of rock by inserting wood and letting it expand to eventually crack the slabs.

There were two stones that caught my attention in a temple or a sacred place. They were elevated about six to seven inches and countersunk about an inch. Since we've had some rain, this small depression is full of water. The imagination of archaeologists has given three interpretations to these two stones. One is that these represent the life-giving milk of a woman's breasts and the beginning of life. Another idea is that one represents the moon and the other the sun. I am inclined to go that route, as one does seem to be a little bigger than the other. The other theory was that during the ceremonies that these pools of water provided reflection. Today I think that probably no one really knows what the interpretation is. The real feat of accomplishment was in

SOUTH AMERICA
ENCHANTMENT

working with the stones of all shapes and sizes, with no mortar. The site is well over 400 years old with little deterioration.

The city of Machu Picchu did not have many flat areas other than the terraces built for agricultural purposes. The Inca civilization at its peak covered vast amounts of South America. This linked Peru, parts of Chile and Bolivia in their central requirements. The people on the coastline turned to fishing, while those in the jungles were hunting, although some historians have said that the Incas were vegetarian.

My good guide said to me, "You look tired," as I was sitting on one of the stones. For the first time on this trek I did feel a bit of a fatigue and blamed it on the early hour that we started. The three musketeers and our faithful friends, Michael and Camello, have now become our own private walking unit. We decide to descend the steep trail to the Temple of the Moon, about a two or three hour hike round-trip.

On the way down, we are able to walk on some of the large terraces that the Incas had built on the mountainside for their crops. *Llamas* take advantage of the grazing here and we take advantage of the picture opportunities that they present. Camello was having great fun with his father's camera and, as

Robert F. Edwards

each day passed, I could see this young boy growing from a timid child to a competent young man. I've had experiences on this journey that will last me a lifetime and I will always cherish the moments, good and bad. For him, the experience was passing from adolescence into manhood, and his over-coming of the suffering and fears have given this fine young boy the confidence in himself to overcome situations that he's not experienced before. His air of confidence is evident, as he grows ever bolder, getting closer to these *llamas*. We're all in high spirits, as we sit on the grassy terraces, just enjoying each other's company. Two Chileans, two Argentineans and one Canadian seem to speak a common language. Michael's opinion was jaundiced towards Argentineans until he went on this trip and he has now felt their kindness. I wish I could speak Spanish and converse with Michael on a one-to-one ba-sis, but I know we have a respect for each other and the im-portant things are felt.

It's well after 2:00 p.m. by the time we return to the main area and grab a sandwich. We then decide that it's time to take the bus down to the train station, so without any further delay we get our packs and our walking sticks and get on the *turista* buses which cost three or four *nuevos soles*.

Jimena was telling us about a little boy who runs down the mountain and yells: "Good-bye! *Buenos dias!*" and we hadn't gone a great distance before this little boy appeared in true Inca attire, yelling at the top of his lungs these farewell greet-ings. As the bus twists and turns down to the next level, there he is waving again, "Good-bye!" This continues all the way down and although the boy was taking short cuts, it was still about three kilometers for him. The bus benevolently stops, let's him on, and the cheers contributed to his worthy cause in good jest.

We ended up at the marketplace. I was expecting the prices here to be exorbitant, but after checking, no, they're quite reasonable, after some bartering. With that, we go to a res-taurant and Camello gives the "high" sign for his choice of pizza, but his dad squashes that idea. Julio shows up with the train tickets and here iss an example of where problems arise in tours. To my dismay, I have some woman's train ticket, not mine. When I mention this to Julio, he says that he will be down at the train station to explain the situation. Michael is still distraught about the experience with his son's problems and the lack of facilities. Also, the two girls are jaundiced by the tour group that we've chosen for they know they can get a cheaper tour if they negotiated. The main reason they picked this tour group was they wanted to be with me and they were disappointed that we didn't get the quality for the premium price.

We wander around a bit. Some of the other fellow trekkers are still suffering the effects of the hike, with chills and general fatigue. We don't have very much longer to wait before the bus takes us to the Cuzco train station. I go through three separate security checks before I'm on the train, passing through all of them as a woman. Michael and I are making hand gestures of me being a woman and the three others are getting big chuckles out of it.

We start off in daylight on the train and it's a very enjoyable ride. I comment to Victoria, sitting beside me, how much I really enjoy trains and she completely agrees with me. The people across from us are from Switzerland and I learn that they paid as much as $200.00 for their trip on the Inca trail. The young lady tells me that there was a bottle of wine on their table each night and they were woken up every morning with juice, an upgrade from our experience. She spoke highly of the professionalism of their expedition that had about five members.

The train stops at different stations, bringing back memories of when I traveled through the Ukraine and Russia. The local women and men would be selling beverages and freshly prepared food that you could purchase through the windows. Sometimes if the train stopped long enough, you could get out and check the variety offered. Here it's no different; the women are going up and down very quickly with huge corns and they're steaming hot. Besides the food, they are also selling little dolls, souvenirs and blankets, you name it. You can't say these people aren't industrious. It's funny though; the person I see that buys a doll is not one of us tourists, but a Peruvian for his little girl. It goes to show that you never know who the next customer is.

The train continually passes through one city after another and I wake up my poor friend Victoria thinking that we are nearing Cuzco, only to find out we have another two and a half hours on the train. However, when we do start to reach Cuzco, it's a remarkable sight, and I'm very grateful that I did get to see it at night and at this altitude. It's much larger than I anticipated and looks a much greater city in the dark. You can distinguish the two cathedrals and the great *piazza*, which signifies the city's uniqueness.

Now that we're entering the city's parameters, we're all excited, only to be disappointed as the conductor walks by. He informs us that we have at least another twenty, thirty minutes before arrival, which is bewildering to my mind. Then I learn the reason for this is that they have to shunt the train down these tracks to different elevations so it stops. They throw a switch and it goes all the way down to come to a screeching halt, throw another switch and it proceeds forward, going down again and so forth until it reaches the level of the train station.

With that we arrive and are exhausted. Mario's brother and wife are present and we are concerned about the behavior and attitude of these two people. The biggest issue that we have right now is the unethical behavior, but we've chosen a game plan. Michael is going to "cross swords" about the danger his son was in and the lying that this agency has done. He's more than just distressed and upset. He is angry and livid because he had stressed so adamantly that medical facilities would be available or he would not have taken his son on this adventure.

Anyway, our priority now was to get to the same hotel we stayed at the previous nights. I ask the agent if the girls can collect their luggage that he was storing for them. We found out that these people live in a very poor area and roads are so bad that the taxi can't even get into it. The young man gingerly wades through all this mud and brings the two backpacks to the girls. I don't know which one of us musketeers was the most relieved. These people might be a little bit shady, but they weren't criminals by any stretch of the imagination.

When he returns us to the hotel, I ask the agent for a meeting the next morning, under the pretense that I would like to discuss further journeys. Michael, being a little more Latin American than I am, continues to express his dissatisfaction. I'm just barely back in my room, flopping on to the bed, when I get a phone call asking if I would come down to the lobby. By now it's around ten o'clock at night, and I'm exhausted, but five against two, whether it's in a street fight or a debate, is better odds.

Michael was adamant that he has been charged twice as much as anybody else for the same facilities. He also expressed his views more than adequately of his discontentment about the quality of the trek. Michael is livid and Victoria is sitting beside me translating, so I am aware of his total frustration and resentment about what has transpired. The fact that there were no facilities, no help, and no way of rescuing his son, had provoked his anger to almost rage.

As for myself, I personally felt that I got dollar value for dollar spent, but I was distraught that there were no medical facilities. There were no provisions to take anybody out of a life and death situation. What really provoked me was the knowledge that Michael had already lost one of his children and so was more than just sensitive; he was deeply concerned for the welfare of his son. He wouldn't have jeopardized his son, no matter how enticing the adventure had been if the medical facilities hadn't been intact. In fact the agent had blatantly lied.

With the help of Victoria translating, I became as much of a Latin American as any of them, and asked the agent what he was going to do about it? He said that he could reimburse a

Robert F. Edwards

little bit, about sixteen dollars per person. I retaliated by saying that this was a terrible insult to my friend's son's welfare and life; and became quite vocal and started banging my fingers on the small table. Somehow these gestures seemed to express my feelings clearly, and today, tomorrow, and forever, I will always feel that that was the focal point. It was not the money, it was not nit-picking on whether our food was as good as the others, or our guide was bilingual. Yes, I was promised a porter to carry my belongings. Yes, I did get a porter but I still had to pay eighty *nuevos soles* more, so I was pretty close to the two hundred mark. These things happen, and even as I expressed to the girls, we had made a business deal and sometimes you make good business deals and sometimes you don't. Maybe we were taken advantage of because of our lack of knowledge. But I'll never forgive the agent for promising something that is as precious as life itself, medical facilities and the availability of medicine that Michael had requested so strongly before he ventured out.

We made arrangements to all meet at ten o'clock the following morning and we left on rather a sour note after one of the most remarkable days that I've experienced.

At about eleven-thirty at night, I'm going to say goodbye to a long day. Goodnight my beautiful wife, I love you dearly and I miss you very much and I think some of these new friends along the way realize that you're always present in my heart. Goodnight one and all!

SOUTH AMERICA ENCHANTMENT

January 23, Wednesday

Cuzco, Peru

I'm going to refer to this day as "the lost day" because I'm very sick. I start by getting up in the morning feeling exhausted. However, it's about eight o'clock and I want to get a few things done before our meeting transpires with the travel agent in two hours. As I look at myself in the mirror with four days' growth on my face, I have a slight hesitation whether to continue the beard or to revert back to my normal facial attire. This impulse is soon taken care of with a razor. I'm then clean shaven and I have a hot shower, get dressed, and join my comrades for a Continental breakfast, which I eat very little of.

We have some discussion about the demands Michael is going to make, as well as Victoria and Jimena, with the agent. I leave them to it, as I would like to check my e-mails and at

least get one off to my wife. The very odors of the food that are coming from the shops give me the first indication that this is not going to be a day when I'm going to be at the top of the mound. I get to the Internet store and log in and I'm most grateful to receive an e-mail from my beautiful wife. With that reward, I quickly send another one off to her telling her that I have arrived back in Cuzco and will give her a progress report as soon as I know my next destination and departure time.

By now, I'm feeling quite exhausted, perhaps a hangover of fatigue from the endurance of the trek. Once we have had this meeting with the agent, I'll be happy to have a little *siesta.* I return to the hotel only to find that I'm about ten minutes late and neither the agent nor my traveling companions are there. However, I discover a fellow Canadian, and a further pleasure, he's from Invermere, B.C. He is in his mid-40's and has experience climbing mountains in the ranges in B.C. We enjoy each other's camaraderie and discussions of our native land. I relay some of our experiences on the trek and tell him about the lack of medical facilities or emergency evacuation for people on the Inca trail. He is quite dismayed by it and he does inform me that his travel agent has assured him that they do have radio-transmitting devices in case of emergencies.

I feel it's not so much the agent, but more the government of the day that hasn't provided any rescue in the event of an emergency. He tells me about a situation in his own case just last year. When he was climbing mountains in the Rockies, he started to take a severe drop and so jumped. He was saved from the fall and received only a broken ankle.

He commented that this would be a great country to use the motorcycle in, and he enjoys that type of recreation. A California man overheard our conversation and interjected that he had just completed an adventure of that nature in Colombia where he had been arrested and detained for the better part of three weeks with his motorcycle. We asked him, "Did you get your motorcycle back?" and he just laughed and said, "No, but I've got another one that I'm gonna continue my adventure with. It's just outside."

I say farewell to both of them and venture back upstairs. By now, the cramps, nausea and fatigue are a dominant factor. I lie on my bed to rest and along with all the other discomforts that I experience is a twisted knee. Now I'm limping

SOUTH AMERICA
ENCHANTMENT

and my left knee cap is extremely sore, so even when I'm lying in bed it's distracting as I compare the pains that I'm experiencing in my stomach and in my leg. I don't want to take any aspirins because my stomach is still feeling the stress and discomfort of something that I've eaten the night before.

After we had the meeting with the agent last night, we all went out for something to eat. Camello and I shared a pizza, and the other three had chicken and French fries. There was also a salad assortment available, which I nibbled on. There were chopped onions along with some hot peppers that I enjoyed at the time. However, as I reflect, I remember that when I drank a little water, it hit my stomach like a bomb that had found its target.

I use the utmost precaution when it comes to water. I always buy bottled water and I check to make sure that the cap has not been tampered with. In other words I take many precautions to prevent what I'm experiencing today. However, the cramps intensify and the mad dash to the toilet starts and diarrhea becomes the order of the day. By midday, I'm ailing even worse, and I take some medication to relieve the dysentery.

I'm hoping to try and find some of my fellow travelers, just to tell them that I am sick and will not be able to do anything other than try to put myself back together piece by piece. I go to the Tourist Bureau of Information to find more about the itinerary that I wish to start working on; to see the Nazca Lines, and then on to Lima and Iquitos. After that I try to make the best of it and place mind over matter, but matter seems to have the upper hand today. I visit a few more travel agents to confirm that the information that I'm getting is accurate. It seems to be consistent. "Do it yourself, mate, unless you're going to fly from Cuzco to Lima and then Lima to Iquitos". If I were to fly to Lima, then I would have to take a bus back down to Nazca, which is in the southern part of Peru. It seems inefficient to me to spend the extra money and time on airfare, and then still have to take the bus to where I want to go in the first place.

Robert F. Edwards

Unfortunately, my pills have not taken effect yet, as I am still experiencing excruciating cramps. I return to my room to try and secure a little more rest for the day, but this was not meant to be. I started throwing up and having further diarrhea. I'm also experiencing chills and heat waves, so I guess along with all the other discomforts my body is experiencing I must have a full red alert. I'm fighting with all the natural resources that I have. Not a very pleasant day, to say the least.

At about six o'clock, I venture back out to try to get some yogurt and bananas to fight whatever I have with natural ingredients as well as medical science. To my delight, Victoria and Jimena have just entered the hotel lobby - talk about a uniting of friends! We discussed our day and my being sick while they had spent the better part of the day at the police station filling out complaint forms. It's either feast or famine; no sooner had they told me about their situation, than Michael and Camello came into the lobby. We're all back together, and it's heart-warming to me to have friends that, while they may have been short in time, are long in compassion and concern. I assure them that I'll be okay, I'm just going to get some yogurt and bananas, and that tomorrow will not only be another day, but it will assuredly be a better day for myself.

I returned to my little food store that I had first purchased cheese, crackers and chocolates for the adventure on the Inca Trail. They remember me and with a lot of gestures I try to express my needs. Again, I am impressed with the patience that people have when somebody is really trying to communicate in a foreign language, these wonderful women have the patience of Job when it comes to this. I can see the yogurt, which is no problem, but all of it has artificial flavoring and fruit supplements in it. I just want what we call "plain yogurt." In Spanish, it's "natural yoga," and with a big container of it in my possession and a lot of good will on behalf of the store clerks, I return to the hotel with at least half the supplies.

SOUTH AMERICA
ENCHANTMENT

It's disappointing, as the last time I was in Cuzco I saw many vendors on the street with bananas. This would be a safe purchase as there's little or no risk due to the fact that

you have got to peel bananas anyway. However, no luck today, and with only half of the supplies needed to make my recovery, I return with my liter of yogurt to sulk in bed. I have to say that, "Yes, this has been a very lost day. Sickness wise, I'm feeling ill." After eating some of the yogurt to suppress the excruciating cramps I'm experiencing, I return to the bed turning and tossing.

At eleven o'clock that night Victoria phones and tells me that Michael has been served by the police to appear the following day at eight o'clock at the police station, and he's asked for my presence and requested that I bring my ticket with the woman's name on it. The two girls, during the day, had gone down to the police and filled out a large comprehensive report on the connivance and the exorbitant price that was charged by this agency and its failure to provide the quality services promised. Michael was summoned because of problems with the travel agent, and his not paying other amounts of money still owing to her. I was concerned for him and was somewhat apprehensive about myself. I knew that none of us had done anything wrong and that we had all had justification to be upset, especially Michael.

However on the other hand, when in Rome, be Roman. I'm not in any way implying that the Peruvian police are not as honorable and respectable as any police force anywhere in the world. But some of the reports that I have heard indicated that bribery and connivance do exist in Peru. I was concerned as this lady is a citizen of Peru, whereas we are foreigners, and each from a different country. Maybe the law would show more tolerance or more understanding to one of their own rather than to foreigners.

After talking to the girls for a few minutes, I agreed to help in any way I could the next day. After seeing Michael and his son, and Victoria and Jimena I felt wonderful, that I was amongst my friends and they cared about me and were concerned. I checked one last time for e-mails, just hoping that maybe my beautiful wife would have got my last one and sent me an update, but it wasn't meant to be.

With apprehensive thoughts in my mind, I retired once more, and the rumbling and pains persisted well into the night. As the hours slowly passed from one to another, I would get up periodically and gulp down some of my delicious "natural yogurt."

With those thoughts in mind, I would like to say goodnight to my wonderful wife. I wish we were together tonight. I miss you very much and I hope that you, Wendy and Cole, are doing well - I miss you too. Love and prayers to you and everyone and goodnight.

SOUTH AMERICA
ENCHANTMENT

January 24, Thursday

Cuzco, Peru

I've spent a very restless night. However, I've stopped vomiting and the diarrhea is less intense. My stomach has still got the thunder and rolling and gurgling in it, but it seems that these pills and yogurt have counter-balanced the discomfort. Along with that, my knee is still exceptionally sore, but not as bad. In general, I guess you'd have to say I'm in much better shape.

I get up and do my toiletries and I would have preferred to have arisen later, but we have to be at the police station at eight o'clock in the morning. With that in mind, it conjures up all the problems that have gone before us in our relationship with this agency. There are always two sides to every story and I'm hoping that fairness and justice will prevail in this case.

As I meet my other four comrades, I find they're already eating buns and drinking their coffee and obviously discussing the events that took place last night. It's a great strain on all of us and especially Michael as he is the one that's charged. With my liquid breakfast of coffee and the remaining yogurt, off we go to the police station. I'm sure that a lot of people have visited Peru, but few ever want to visit a police station. As bold and self-confident as I am, this is not a place I would recommend any tourist to check out on their "things to do" list. The first things I see are holding containment areas. Maybe they are nothing more than drunk tanks and the men inside look as though they are the worse for wear. Out front is a parade square, where a military-type commander is giving instructions to his subordinates. The building is a three floor terrace style, quite dilapidated compared to some of the magnificent buildings in Cuzco, but it has a power that few of the other present.

Robert F. Edwards

When we enter, we're escorted into a waiting area. The lady from the agency and her little child are already there. I can honestly say with everything that's decent in me, I just wish that this had never happened. I wish that Camello had never became sick, of course, and I wish that Michael had never been put through the agony and torment in his parental responsibilities. This young woman is representing her family while her husband is in La Paz, and is not even escorted by his brother, and she seems to stand alone as a victim of us, the tourists or foreigners. Michael is taken into an interrogation room along with the woman, and Michael's son, Camello, is very tense. The three of us try to calm him down and assure him that we're not leaving this place unless all of us go together. Jimena takes Camello out to get some candy to keep him distracted, and also because she has such a sore throat that she can hardly talk.

I could tell that Michael was feeling the strain. His eyes seem to be red, probably from fatigue and a restless night. He said to us before he went in, "If I have to pay, I will pay, but I want to get out of this terrible country. I'm going to leave tonight regardless," and with that in mind the hour that we spend in the police station seems much longer than it is. I had fully anticipated that police would want to question each and every one of us, especially when one of the clerks came out and got the statements that the two girls had submitted the day before. I was sure that this was going to be a day that we would spend in an area of Peru we wish we had never known about, let alone visited.

However, within about an hour Michael appears and he's very jubilant. Just as his young son had predicted, his father doesn't lose very often. Translating, my two musketeers inform me that in essence Michael had said he did owe the money; yes, he refused to pay it, in order to force the issue against the agency. From his side, he wanted to be heard about the deplorable attitude and irresponsibility of the agent and the poor conditions of the trip. The police listened to both sides and Michael got a reduction in the price including the

SOUTH AMERICA
ENCHANTMENT

original sixteen dollars that he had offered before and a further reduction for Camello to cover the expenses incurred for the porters needed to help him when he was so sick and unable to walk. The bottom line was that of the US$180.00 debt that Michael owed the agency, he had to pay $45.00. He did so and all was completed.

Reflecting back on the situation, I realized it was more a matter of honor than a monetary issue. I thought to myself 'We're all from countries more affluent than this one and all five of us are richer than the people that we've demanded compensation and justice from'. On a more upbeat note, I must commend the police of Peru, not because Michael won but because of their handling of the situation in a very professional manner. They were able to resolve the conflict between Michael and the agency in an expedient and efficient way. I give my full compliments to the police force of Cuzco, and have a new respect for the authority and the administration of Peru.

Once this is behind us, we are all in a state of euphoria and, knowing this is the end of the matter, we feel much better. On the other hand, I felt sorry for the lady and asked if I had any indebtedness towards her agency, and she said no, so that's fine. Michael had been granted a reduction of $16.00 from our fees also, but between the girls and myself, we basically had enough and felt justice had been served.

There was a bit more discussion and I couldn't help but interject and said: "Look, I would far rather be in a more congenial and pleasant setting than this." There was a general consensus among us as we left the police station and proceeded into the general street area.

Now that we were free, we discussed plans on what we wanted to do for the day. Michael and Camello were thinking of going horseback riding and the girls were receptive to this as well as doing a city tour and seeing the ruins. Without much discussion, we all agreed on going horseback riding and seeing the ruins. The girls kept questioning if I was well enough to do this. Even though the rumbling stomach pains were prevalent, and I must admit I didn't feel that exuberant, I felt I could do this.

We all rushed over to our new travel agent's office because the horseback riding was supposed to start at eight o'clock in the morning. It was now closer to nine-thirty, but the travel agent was elated on having five more people to go on this particular tour. She quickly made a few phone calls and before I had a chance to go back to the hotel to get my camera (or anything else as far as that goes) we were off and on our way to a rural area where the horses were waiting before taking us to explore the ruins.

It took us awhile to get saddled up and, although all of us had ridden before, Jimena had the most experience. There were also two other Argentinean girls waiting to join our group. We set off, finding these trails were not exactly the Inca trails, but still quite steep, and the horses took their time. These horses are well trained in the sense that the only bridle that they use is a rope; the stirrups are welded iron and the saddle not much better. My horse either got up on the wrong side of the bed or just had a really mean disposition. Most of the time his ears were laid back and for the first half-hour of the ride he tried to buck me off two or three times. He also couldn't bear to have any horse beside him and would try to nip the neck of any such horse. Not withstanding Jimena had the meanest horse of the group.

One thing that all the horses had in common was a real dislike for water. As we went across creeks, they tried to bolt and bucked against doing this, and poor Jimena's horse actually fell over in the first creek. Thank God she wasn't hurt as her horse rolled around. Between her horse and mine we had the most obstinate and unpredictable horses. To my surprise however I actually enjoyed riding. After I gained some confidence and the horse realized that I knew what I wanted and would not let his wishes prevail, we seemed to develop a bonding. As long as I kept him in the front lead without other horses interfering, he even perked up his ears a few times.

SOUTH AMERICA ENCHANTMENT

There are primarily four ruins around Cuzco. The first one is *Tambo Machay* and it is a small ruin with a ceremonial bath situated about 300 hundred meters from the main road. From here we can see *Puca Pucara*, and this particular ruin, which translates as "the red fort", is quite distinctive, as the name implies. Along the way, the locals are dressed in colorful costumes and have numerous amounts of things that tourists buy. One item that Camello bought was a water jug and I probably would have bought one for Marietta if I had had a way to carry the darn thing. They were large and my journey was still fairly extensive.

It's just amazing how these people have such a pleasant, passive way about them; but yes, in the *piazzas* in Cuzco, children do get pretty aggressive and whether shoe-shining or selling post cards, men and women canvas hard. However the bartering or pressure that these people put on tourists is small compared to that in other parts of the world. The people are also very pleasant. As soon as you show an interest in their wares, they are anything but indifferent. They'll be more than happy to barter and of course as in any bartering society the price is only as high as the individual is willing to pay.

Each time we go into a different ruin, we have our tourist pass cards punched. Unfortunately for myself, Michael and Camello, we won't be able to see all of the exhibits permissible and the pass is good for almost two weeks. I'm probably enjoying the scenery and riding back into the hills and off the main roads as much as I am seeing the ruins. In fact I am just about 'ruined' out. At each of the ruins, there's always a volunteer guide, whether it's a middle-aged woman or a young boy that offers to explain the whole Inca civilization. The only comforting thing that I can say about these guides is that their heritage makes you feel that at least the story has some truth in it.

Many of the explanations center on animals; the *puma*, the condor and the snake being more mystical. As they point out different rock formations that have some type of animal configuration, your imagination has to be at its highest level.

109

Robert F. Edwards

However, I did see one formation at this temple that appeared to be of the *llama* and, once they pointed it out, I could see the shape was distinctly a *llama* configuration. Also, they showed us where the Incas performed both rituals and surgical operations. One that is most notable for archaeology is the cranial operations. Not brain surgery exactly, but if somebody's skull had been broken, Incas knew how to remove the broken pieces of cranial bone and I assume that the patients survived.

As we get back to our horses and the trail, this Canadian is in the lead, mainly because of his mean little horse. It's extremely hot. I don't realize until after mid-day that even my hands are sun burnt and my face has a beet complexion. The scenery is very majestic and even as we're gaining altitude there are still little farms and some of the *llama*s and other animals are present and accounted for. At the second temple we were at, it was unfortunate that I didn't have my camera, as there were lots of young *llama*s. There was a white baby *llama* that I pointed out to the girls; it still had some of the umbilical cord attached. As we watched it tried to stand up and was a little unsure about walking, but managed very well. Both the girls said that they would send copies of their pictures on to me via the internet and I had no doubt that this would be done.

We took our time wandering through the temples, but for me the most enjoyable time was riding the horses. Poor Jimena's horse just kept bucking her and one time she did fall off and received a very nasty scrape on her mid-section and a cut on her finger. She's a remarkable young lady, very good-natured and a determined person. It just hurt me to hear her talk because her throat was so sore, and I'm hoping that she isn't getting really sick as she also has a bit of a fever. It seems to be a mutual "worry" society – she's worried about me and I'm worried about her. For what it's worth, my cramps seem to be subsiding, but boy - am I ever still in quite a bit of discomfort!

The day wears on, and by now it's past two o'clock. I seem to be rallying around the clock and Jimena is starting to deteriorate. We're all getting quite familiar with our horses so there are a lot of *gauchos* or cowboys in the making. We stop at a small midway center to rest the horses, more than anything else. Camello and I go into the little shop and find a bunch of *sombreros* or Peruvian-style cowboy hats. I put one on his head and before long, I've got one on too and we're doing our own remake of the 'Stand off at the OK Corral'. We're both whooping it up pretty loudly and I think sometimes his father must be glad that this Canadian isn't around all the time, because "my son is really enjoying himself, but picking up some bad habits." In all sincerity, Michael is pleased that Camello is having such fun and he has told the girls how much I mean to Camello and how much Camello loves me. So he realizes that all my bad antics and bad habits are done in good humor and faith.

The next ruin we come across is *Qenko*, which means zig-zag, and this particular ruin is exactly what the name relays. It's primarily a limestone carving of canals and the ceremony that it was used for involved *chicha*, an alcoholic beverage. There are tunnels and carvings below in the mystical caves and when the sun is shining above the shadow of an altar forms a rectangle directly onto the temple itself. We spend some time listening to a self-appointed guide. These guides are entrepreneurs as much as anybody and, after they go through the motions of explaining everything from the creation of the Inca to what we're witnessing, they naturally expect some monetary remuneration.

Robert F. Edwards

The next and the largest of all the ruins is *Sacsayhuamán.* The name means "satisfied falcon" and it relates back to a brutal battle between the Spanish and a rebellious Inca force. The Inca leader, *Manco* narrowly lost the battle and retreated to Vilcabamba, but his forces were killed brutally by the Spaniards. As the men lay dead, large flocks of the great Andean condor swarmed in to pick at the carcasses.

Today, you see only about 20% of the original Inca structure left intact. When the Spaniards conquered this area, they tore down most of the structures and reused the materials for cathedrals in Cuzco. However not even the most ambitious conquistadors would have the strength or the manpower to move some of the structures, being 300 tons or more.

There's a legend here of the water giving eternal youth to men or fertility to women. I asked the guide as I wanted to make sure that I was on the correct side, and found that right is for the men, promoting eternal youth or becoming younger, and the left side is the women's, which gives fertility. Believe me, at my age, I would prefer to have eternal youth.

Both Michael and I had some fun, horsing around, and putting on quite a performance for the rest of them. We all had a pretty good time, laughing about the whole thing. Even the new companions to our merry band are enjoying themselves. My two musketeers had brought some *matei* and a thermos of hot water to add to it. At first, both Victoria and Jimena weren't sure whether I should have any because of my stomach problem. This herbal drink is primarily served in Uruguay and Argentine. I did drink a little *matei* however, and to my surprise, whatever parasite or bacteria had shown stubborn resistance to the medication I had, now gave way to this magical herb.

Back on the horses, we make our way down, towards the last ruin. We leave the horses very close to the station. Our mode of transportation is now walking, so we walk to the next ruin which is less than a kilometer away. At this point, both Michael and Camello said, "Look, we would like to leave by bus. We'll take a taxi back to the hotel, get our things and head to the bus station and get out of town."

There were a lot of emotional goodbyes from each and every one of us and a little bit of fun and camaraderie between Michael and myself. I'd given him a coin and he had paid me back with a coin. We had been playing a game with this coin, back and forth for a while, originally over some small amount of remuneration that we were supposed to give to our guide. It was only half a *peso*. As he was hugging me and wishing me well, he slipped the coin into my pocket, laughing. When he was in the taxi leaving, he said to Victoria, "Tell Bob that I've given him the coin back. It is in his pocket." And sure enough, when I looked in my shirt pocket, I found the coin. But, the game wasn't over yet.

When the three of us were ready to continue to the last ruin, Jimena realized that she still had Michael's documents and cell phone in her backpack. We were now anxious to get these returned to Michael before he left the country.

The other two Argentinean girls were tired and agreed to return with us, so we bargained with one taxi driver, but he was uncooperative; however the next one accommodated us by meeting us halfway on the fare. We dropped the two girls off at their hotel and preceded to the one that Michael and Camello had been staying at. I gave Victoria a plan of action that she would jump out and go into the hotel to see if Michael was still there while I stayed with the taxi driver; if they'd already checked out, then we would precede to the bus station. I told the girls that I'd picked up the tab both ways, since I had my bus ticket already to go to Nazca.

Victoria came running out and yes, they'd already left the hotel. So, off to the bus station and we said to the taxi driver, "Look, if you wait while we check the bus, we'll take your taxi back to the hotel; if not, we'll settle up with you." He said, "Yes, that's fine." So he parked the vehicle and actually came in with us. I don't blame him. He has got ripped off more than once with somebody crashing out to the bus and leaving him behind unpaid. He had already been helpful and told me

Robert F. Edwards

about a luxurious bus line called *Ormeno*. Because I still wasn't feeling that good and some of the buses I've been on didn't have any toilets, I didn't want to find that out the hard way, on a long arduous bus ride to Nazca.

We were all running around, looking for Michael and Camello and start checking the buses. Jimena managed us to get permission to go into the restricted area where passengers were boarding but they were not anywhere to be found. Now we were more than just concerned; we didn't know what was going to transpire. Then suddenly up popped our two comrades, a total surprise! We had actually reached the bus terminal before them. Then with more hurried goodbyes, hugs, and best wishes again, they rushed to get on their bus.

As I was giving Michael one last hug, I slipped the coin back into his pocket and whispered into his ear, "You have the coin" and of course he did not understand. As he was going through the security gate, he asked Victoria what I had said and he started laughing and laughing. This just shows that men of all ages are little boys and boys like to have fun. Often grown-ups forget how to have fun, but these last days together, five people of different age groups, nationalities, and personalities, have had an enormous amount of fun with each other on a very adventurous trek. The three of us were quite emotional, knowing this was really our last goodbye to Camello and Michael.

Tomorrow I will be facing my next bus trip, a long journey of over thirty-six hours on an indirect route to Lima, passing through Nazca on the way. However, the roads are said to be much better than on the previous trip and this bus is supposedly quite luxurious. I pay a premium to get lunch, dinner, and breakfast, and I'm supposed to arrive in Nazca around eleven in the morning after traveling for a full day and night. My departure time is at nine tomorrow morning, so give or take a few hours it's going to be a long bus ride.

With those arrangements behind us, we head back to the hotel. We haven't had anything to eat at this point, and I've been promising the girls (or myself as much as the girls) that

SOUTH AMERICA
ENCHANTMENT

before we left each other I'd take them out for dinner. We'd have a grandiose meal in an upscale restaurant and we would really splurge - my treat. I had been feeling so sick the previous day, but had been gaining my strength back today, so we decided this would be the time.

Once settled into the restaurant of choice, I ordered a Peruvian steak (which looked almost as if it had been put in the blender). There were little chunks of meat, tomatoes and onions, and *papa fritas* sort of hashed together, and then to add to this mulligan stew, rice. Not quite what I had in mind, but then I haven't had a piece of meat in this part of the trip that would even come close to what I experienced in Argentina. The girls had different types of sandwiches and juices, and I had a beer and lemonade.

After our meal, we went to a travel agent as the girls needed to discuss arrangements for flying back to Argentina. I wanted to check my e-mail, so I found a different Internet place. Yes, I did pay a little more, but I was able to send another e-mail off to Marietta and read some of the ones that were there for me. I'm still feeling fatigue, and my face and hands are severely sun-burnt. I look like the red man of the Peruvian hills.

So when I returned to the hotel, I put some cream on my face and did my final preparations of packing and getting ready for the continuation of this adventure tomorrow. I want to get the girls something that would be a bit of memorabilia for them and Jimena has already told me that they've got me something. They've been more than just a pleasure and enjoyment as companions. They've touched my heart in so many different ways with their enthusiasm, admiration, support, and just by being two wonderful young ladies.

I was thinking of getting them either a Peruvian blanket with the design of the Inca trail on it or something else of that nature. The only thing that was available was T-shirts. I just have a bad attitude, I guess, when it comes to T-shirts and the fact that they look so tacky, and every *turista* has one spelling out places and events. I even tried jewelry stores, among other places, to find something that would be appro-

115

priate, but was unsuccessful. I eventually found a bookstore and purchased three books, two in Spanish and one in English, on the Inca Trail.

I also bought myself some postcards, which I paid a hell of a premium for, as I soon discovered. When leaving the shop, a little Peruvian kid came running up to me and said, "Postcards?" I said, "No, I've already got them." Not to be discouraged, he continued, "Two for a *sesentas* or one Peruvian *peso*." I said, "No, no, no." He says, "Okay, three for two." So I did end up buying from him, better postcards than the ones that I had paid up to two *sesentas* each for. You never know who's got the best prices in town.

I returned to the hotel at about 9:00 p.m. I had said to the girls, "Look, what I'll do is I'll just put a note in your slot when I'm back in and you can come and get me when you're ready." So I started going to bed, until at about 9:30 p.m., there was knock on the door. My two little musketeers are there, so I quickly throw some clothes on. They said, "Well, we got a present for you." It is a picture of the three of us at the beginning of the Inca trail. They'd got it blown-up and framed and they wrote a beautiful letter.

Bob,

We are very grateful because we have had the possibility of being part of your life, and because we could discover the real kind of person that you are. Perhaps, we don't know why, but it doesn't matter the ages, nationalities or languages, when three people are meant to meet each other, it happens .For all

SOUTH AMERICA
ENCHANTMENT

that we were seeing before, Inca Trail was much more than an adventure. This is how we want to remember you.
The Three Musketeers
With all our love, Jimena and Victoria

I gave them their presents, and had written in both of the books ' as they turn these pages that I hope that they'll remember the wonderful times and the enjoyment that I'd experienced with them, and that I will miss them very much and I'll always keep these thoughts with me'.

Both girls are very emotional, and if somebody asked me before which one was the more sentimental, I probably would have said Victoria. However Jimena proved herself at this point to be the more sentimental. She just started crying, she couldn't help herself, and we were hugging, all three of us. Earlier that day, we talked about the possibilities of all five of us organizing another adventure together, perhaps even including Marietta, Wendy and Cole, and Michael had thought of his older son also. Maybe all of us would go to Cancun or another area in Mexico for a month and rent a *hacienda*.

In these last moments, we reminded each other that we had a date for next year. Let destiny and God decide whether it would materialize, but I know these young ladies would enhance any adventure that I would ever have just by their presence. With that, 'youth' is going to go out dancing and 'maturity' is going to go back to bed and prepare for the long bus trip tomorrow.

Marietta, I love you very much, and also Wendy, and Cole, and I hope all is going well on the home base. Goodnight one and all.

Robert F. Edwards

January 25, Friday

Cuzco, Peru

I am up at five in the morning. I'm feeling quite chipper and try to catch up on some of my notes before I forget. I start my final preparations with a long hot shower before breakfast, which is a couple of buns and a cup of coffee. Now, also I say my goodbyes.

It's a remarkable thing that happens when I go on these sabbaticals. Not only do I remember the people that I've met, but also they always seem to remember me and there develops a warm sincere camaraderie in a very short time. The young man that serves me breakfast speaks no English of any consequence, but in the short time that I've been staying here, we've enjoyed each other's company. We shake hands and hug and I tell him that I'm leaving and he thanks me very much.

As I am checking out at the front desk, the manager comes out of his office, shakes my hand and wishes me a safe, wonderful trip and tells me how much he enjoyed meeting me. The boy at the front desk was going to charge me an extra night because I checked in so early in the morning on the 17th, but the manager said, "No, no, no." I said, "Four nights, twenty dollars, that's what it is." These are kind people, trying to make a living, and they are hard workers, but when business comes to friendship, friendship always succeeds over business. The longer I'm in this part of the world, the more distasteful I find the North American attitude of self-gratification and material success. In this region of the world, I find the quality of man at its best, with the true spirit of giving and kindness.

I head off to the bus station and I don't mind admitting that at this point I'm still apprehensive. The fact that the short route takes around ten to twelve hours versus this one I am booked on, which could end up as long as thirty-six hours,

118

SOUTH AMERICA
ENCHANTMENT

seems questionable. Again, I checked to make sure that I'm not going to Lima, but to Nazca, and yes, everything is prepared properly.

The only thing that I hadn't been informed about was the fact that I have a bus transfer at the border of Bolivia. This particular route is going to take me back along Lake Titicaca to Punta, and then to the Peruvian border where the other bus transfer takes place. At 9:00, right on schedule, I get on the bus and Wow! It's the most luxurious bus I've ever seen, let alone been on. There are leather seats, it's a double-decker, and "Yes, Britain, I hate to tell you this, but your London double-deckers couldn't hold a candlestick to this bus called The Royal Class". There's even a front observation deck and the bus is deodorized so that there's a nice fragrance throughout. I have probably ridden more buses in South America in the last two years, than most South Americans ever have, and I say this is *Uno*, it is first class.

A young lady shows me to my seat and across from me are two Brazilian people. They're a married couple and have spent two or three years in Japan doing research on pollution as well as in Britain. What I find unbelievable is that there are only three of us on this huge bus. I have no explanation, but it seems so ludicrous that this Rolls Royce of the bus kingdom has three passengers. The young lady is suffering from the same problems that I've been plagued with, diarrhea, and I give her some pills that assisted me in my discomfort. She's not only suffering from cramps and diarrhea, but she and her husband both also have problems with motion sickness.

I'm very grateful that I have the constitution of a warhorse. Some people are meant for travel, but for others travel is really an endurance of their tolerance. I'm very grateful for good health and should never take it as lightly as I do. We're served a delicious lunch; I've had many meals on buses, some of them better than others, but none of them were worth much comment. This one was better even than the meal I had in that expensive restaurant last night. There were nice chunks of meat, rice, and gravy and for dessert, fresh peaches in a sauce.

The airlines could take a lesson from these people. If only I could have a seat like this on a plane. You can stretch your legs out and when you put the seat back, it is almost like a dentist's chair; it reclines to a comfortable position, but you don't have to open up your mouth!

I am thoroughly enjoying the conversation with the Brazilian. I'm finding that when you really do know something about a person's country and they realize this fact, you can have a very close association with each other. People will open up to you about their personal views of their governments, and tell you about their way of life and their attitudes. This man was obviously expressing his concerns about pollution and nature, but also sharing his concerns about the changing of his cultural base. The fast-food restaurants and the super malls, and so forth, are now becoming a global phenomenon, rather than an American way of life.

He was telling me about how he enjoyed a certain type of chocolate and that when he was a boy Portuguese descendants owned most of the bakery shops. This is where the chocolates were made, with recipes handed down through the generations. Today, it's more convenient to go to the large supermarkets to do one-stop shopping in our fast pace of life. It is very nice to realize that some of the problems that people have all over the world are common problems. I'm sure when the first man rolled over another the first complaining began. But there seems to be a general consensus the governments of the day are not really working to understand the problems of the people. Throughout history, we find that usually when there's a general collapse of sincere dedication on the part of the government to the people that they're ruling, and taxation becomes the burden of the reward of serving the master, then it's a time in which realignment is taking place. And right now, throughout the world, people realize that the governments that are controlling them don't understand the problems that they are experiencing.

SOUTH AMERICA
ENCHANTMENT

This Brazilian man I was speaking to is well educated and knowledgeable about diversities in cultures. He expresses these same thoughts about his country, Brazil, and refers to it as the corruption of the government. The Argentinean young ladies were saying the same thing about their government's corruption. In my own province of British Columbia, the ruling political party of the NDP was just voted out, and lost the election due to what we felt was their corruption. Corruption seems to be the dominant factor in the global community when it comes to leadership and part of the problem is the unprecedented amount of debt that these countries or municipalities have built up. In a lot of South American countries, the average individual doesn't have much debt because he or she has very little or no income to achieve credits on a regular basis. But in the most powerful nation in the world, the United States, the average individual has less than two months of savings before the burden of debt becomes collectible. We live in a debtor society and, like the 'Merchant of Venice,' Shylock's interest has become unacceptable.

As this educated young man and I talked in great depth, I realized that in his country there's a hopeless feeling, even despair, about this burden of debt and failure to take the responsibility to rectify it. I assured him that it's much the same throughout the world. Although we discussed these problems for some length of time, we weren't able to come up with answers for ourselves, let alone make a contribution to the success of overcoming these problems.

As we motor along in this luxurious mode of transportation, we're now taking the route along the shoreline of Lake Titicaca. This wouldn't have been the trade route that I am taking since it's the longer arduous route, but the roads are much better than in the other route. However, I'm very grateful to see the lake from another perspective, especially the part where the reed islands are.

With all the explanations that the guide has offered and through my own observations as I travel along this shoreline, I now have a much deeper understanding how these people

Robert F. Edwards

work with the reeds and how the reeds dominate their unique way of living. This part of the lake is marshy and very shallow, and Mother Nature has provided vast supplies of this reed for an unusual way of living.

From the bus I can see the little boats going about and the people busily cutting reeds. Once they've accumulated bundles, they bring them ashore, and lay them out to dry. When they become dehydrated, the reeds are used for building boats, islands and homes. The reed takes three or four months to gain back the moisture that it has lost before it starts to decompose. I have a much deeper understanding now of how these people live their unique life on these floating islands, and the processes which they use with the reeds.

For quite a few hours we travel along the shoreline as we move closer to Puno. We pass by lots of small farms, with anything from cattle to sheep to vegetables, and they work by hand on these plots of ground. The adobe buildings are constructed in a "finish when you have time" or "when your neighbors and you are motivated fashion."

Now that I've traveled to many places in the world, I have become aware that the developed countries are really the only

SOUTH AMERICA
ENCHANTMENT

ones that have completed homes when you move in. They're also the ones that carry a debt burden with them. I remember being in India and other places as I crossed the Middle East and finding the inhabitants couldn't comprehend owing money for your home any more than most North Americans can comprehend having a debt-free home.

A lot of these homes are not finished. I'm now passing by an area where they are cutting the adobe bricks from the earth and stacking them. Of course, no matter how many mud bricks I could produce in my region of the world, the Vancouver area, the next good rainfall would just make one big mud pie. So, the arid conditions here are perfect for drying and warrant this type of construction.

We're now less than an hour from Puno. My Brazilian friends are getting off there and we've all enjoyed our discussions on everything from pollution to biotechnology to the adventures that we're taking part in. The three of us wish each other well and the bus lets them off, and believe it or not, only one Peruvian gets on. So now we're equal; there are as many staff as there are passengers on this bus.

We're heading towards the Peruvian border. At about four in the afternoon, we arrive at the designated place. I ask the girl, a very nice attendant but who speaks no English at all, what's happening? She tells me that this is where I have to transfer from this bus to the next bus, which should be in about twenty minutes. They call in to a filling station and the only thing I recognize is Shell. It's not a bus terminal or anything like one.

I'm not overly partial to borders at the best of times and being the only person waiting for the other bus makes me feel even more vulnerable. To add to my concern, the attendant makes a motion for me to get off the bus. The bus driver tries to explain to me also that I have to wait for the other bus. So, I attempt to explain to him about my huge packsack and he and the attendant try to reassure me that this is no problem that they'll look after it. I have a vision of them driving off and God knows where the larger part of my supplies would be then. However, they assure me, with a lot of talking that I don't understand, and with a lot of encouragement, to come with them.

Well, we walk less than a quarter of a kilometer, and once we arrive I understand this is the bus agency. On my behalf, the bus driver tries to explain my situation to the ticket clerk regarding the next leg of the journey. I show my ticket and the clerk and bus driver talk back and forth and I find it surprising how much more I understand of the general conversation these days. I wouldn't have been able to translate for myself, but I do have the ability now to understand what the gist of the conversation is. Now I understand that he's waiting for the other bus driver and bus to arrive before he can leave.

The three of us start towards the Peruvian border and I take a few pictures of it, but nothing will do it justice. It's wall-to-wall traffic, the larger portion of which is on foot. People are going both ways, and there are quite a few of these unique little "bicycle taxis". The locals build a huge box with two wheels on the front, something like a wheelbarrow in reverse, with the seat behind the bicycle apparatus, which the individual pedals. I'm hoping that I've caught one or two of these on film because they're such an inventive form of transportation, and there's no pollution with two legs for pistons. There are also huge transport trucks going through the border with supplies. Once they reach the Peruvian side, they have to stop and be sprayed with some pesticide, for control over agricultural changes between Bolivia and Peru.

The border itself, or the actual line, is on a bridge and both flags fly. While I'm waiting there, I watch the military procedure with all the rituals of two men lowering the Peruvian flag. They are authoritatively telling everybody to take their hats off out of respect for the lowering of the flag. Nobody seems to think anything of the procedure, including myself at the time.

The other interesting thing on this bridge was the local women with their wares of mostly produce and one of the most all-around pieces of necessity, the large blankets that both Peruvian and Bolivian people use. The women carry not

SOUTH AMERICA
ENCHANTMENT

only their children in them, but also their food, and probably all their utensils in these huge bundles being stowed on their backs. The blankets serve as the mat for sitting on, and another blanket inside is where they display their wares, anything from tomatoes to bananas, potatoes, onions, beans, and different herbs. The ones that are a little more entrepreneurs or little less agricultural, have consumer goods that are traded for a profit. They sit there patiently, and are quite eager to please if you show any interest.

The young lady from the bus is walking along beside me, trying to translate the Spanish for me. I find the people here kind and there's no other word for it. What a pleasant place to be. Yes, in a lot of developed countries' eyes, it's nothing but squalor, poverty and just deplorable living conditions. For me, I think these people are beautiful and I neither feel sorry for them, nor despair for them. I admire and respect them, and enjoy their presence. I'm eternally grateful for the opportunity to share their openness, and sincere wanting to communicate, and their patience, their patience at being alive.

Most of these women are old before their time, by the harsh climatic conditions and the spartan way of living. Others are young and starting this journey of hardship, but their faces don't reflect bitterness or resentment or hate, only patience. This fine young girl, as we keep using the words and exchanging them one for another, like the papaya is *papaya*; I learn many of the Spanish words are similar to English words, but then others are completely different. A potato is *frita*. I tell her that she's my baby-sitter and we're both laughing, as we're waiting for the bus. It's well past an hour when the bus is supposed to have arrived.

One thing I can't help but notice in developing or poor countries, young mothers with large families seem to be the norm. As an example, the two Argentine young ladies that I have enjoyed my trek with, were in their mid-twenties, and not married. When Argentine women usually do get married, one to two children are about the average. A young mother sitting at the border, I noticed has already three, but they're beautiful

125

little children. The oldest, a little boy of maybe five, is looking after the new addition. It's so funny, the little baby is in a wooden crate, which serves as the crib/playpen, and the young boy is babysitting while the mother is trying to sell her produce. He's doing a wonderful job, and when the baby wants to get out, he lets her toddle around. When she gets a bit out of hand, he plunks her back down into this wooden crate, with no crying or fuss. There's a bond of caring for each other, and it starts at an early age. They're rich in a quality that has been abandoned by developed countries. They're never alone.

We head back to the square and by now it's dark, but still a beehive of activity. The young lady again takes me around to different parts of the market square, where they are selling musical CD's. I'm getting a tremendous education. Instead of being distraught and disappointed over the length of time the bus is taking, I'm using the time to observe the culture. The mayhem that I see taking place is done in a very orderly and consistent fashion, with both nations mingling together, working hard. We sometimes think that these people aren't industrious since they are poor. It's late at night and there's a chill in the air, but they're still working their trade and commerce.

The locals showing their wares and produce are receptive to having you reach down and check the produce, and even sample the goods, if you wish. There isn't any resentment when you walk on by. There are a few stalls selling popcorn, or *palomitas*. I buy a bag, and as I was walking down the Avenue of Life eating popcorn, I am enjoying it as much as if I was walking down the Champ des Elysses in Paris. We strolled back towards the bridge to see if the *bús* (as pronounced in Spanish) has arrived. No, just the continual flow of interwoven traffic that moves back and forth on its own time schedule.

Again we walk over to the border, all that's holding it across is a rope and they let it down accordingly. My young companion stops for a drink, it's basically lemons with sugar in boiled water, and the locals just drink it out of a glass. God knows what they washed the glass with. Anyway, she takes a sip, and it's warm, not hot, just warm. She offers me some, and I'm thinking, "Oh no, please God, if I keep on saying no, I'm just like a typical *turista*; and if I do take a drink, I'll probably have to go to the pharmacy and ask for more pills for diarrhea." I choose the latter and take a sip of this drink. It's delicious. With that, I take a few large gulps out of her glass and we're happy.

I can't overemphasize the generosity, not just for the drink but of sharing, and the sheer enjoyment of watching another person enjoy something that you find pleasure in. She's finding real pleasure in being the teacher, and I want to have a picture of drinking this and the fellow that's serving it. The vendor who has the juice on wheels straightens up his hat and you'd think that he'd just had an interview from Hollywood. We asked a policeman to take our pictures. I can't

Robert F. Edwards

help stretching my luck, and ask the policeman if he'll have a picture with me. Without any hesitation, he stands beside me and the young lady takes our picture.

I'm reflecting on this trip, and many other adventures, but it has been very prevalent on this one, that people enjoy being with me and I thoroughly enjoy being with them. We have one ingredient that's common and that is that we're human beings and we enjoy having fun. When people realize that I'm enjoying myself in their presence and the gifts that they are bestowing upon me with their presence, we all seem to revert back to the simple pleasures of youth and innocence. I've found a new ingredient in my life that maybe I am a 'Peter Pan'. When I do meet people, like this policeman with a lot of authority and control, he also shares a moment of reflecting back to just being a child, of having fun.

The two of us wander back to another square and meet up with the bus driver. He is also starting to share our concern about the other bus arriving, which is now two hours late. We're now standing in the area where the moneychangers are, and with some quick calculations, I realize that the exchange rate here is better than any bank. Even though these fellows work on a little wooden table with just a drawer in it, they're more on the cutting edge of exchange rates than any bank teller in the financial community. They know exactly within a fraction what the exchange rate is on any given amount. It's fascinating to watch.

The bus driver enters into our spirit of merriment as we're having fun with an exchange of translations, and of being around people that are just in a good frame of mind. I get out my little translation book and he puts on his glasses, as he has also reached that age when the arms are too short. He starts looking up different words and he comes across "egg" and in Spanish it's *huevos*. He asked me how to say it in English, and the pronunciation just struck him funny and he started laughing. I added a little bit more to it, I said "We have egg in the morning" so you could say "*Buenos dias*, egg" and all three of us are roaring with laughter. You'd think it

SOUTH AMERICA
ENCHANTMENT

was the joke of the year. Soon everyone is calling each other 'eggs'. It may sound absurd, that on old man, a middle-aged man, and a young girl, in the midst of mayhem, are laughing over saying "Good morning, egg." These are the enjoyable moments that I have in my adventures throughout the world, just basic communication and happiness.

While waiting for the bus, I watch a young woman and her small baby as she has pulled her little cart into the area behind us to set up her wares. She has a big pot that she's prepared a rice pudding with different syrups and accompaniments. She's as efficient as any McDonald's restaurant in serving, with her little baby tucked comfortably on her back. No, he's not asleep; he's just looking at life from the warmth and protection of his mother's back. In the meantime, the mother is conducting business as briskly as any fast-food restaurant. She rolls back the cloth that's keeping the food warm, serves the rice, offers the different options of syrups and seasonings, does the money changing, and all in a very professional manner. It's a different world that I dropped into for a moment. I don't know if I could, even if I was conversant in the language, be as competitive and as congenial as these people are with each other. You don't hear any yelling or screaming from the taxi people, whether they're carrying three or four people in the front of their tricycles, or whether it's a huge weight of goods. Some have a little horn, others will just say, "Would you please get out of the way?" People are basically nice to each other. What a totally different perspective, unlike what I and other people experience in the Northern Hemisphere.

By now, it's really starting to get cold. The bus driver has got a couple of heavy sweaters on, the young lady has at least three different sweaters on, and I've got my Gore-tex jacket. Somewhere around nine o'clock, the bus finally arrives. It's been a situation that could have been frustrating, but turned into a memorable moment. The bus drivers hug each other, wish each other well, and the young lady gives me a big hug and gives me a kiss on the cheek as I make sure that I'm on the right bus, and my luggage is on the right bus, and I'm thinking, "I've never had that kind of service in my life anywhere in North America."

Finally, I start the long arduous journey into the night. This bus is equally as luxurious as the last one; and it's full of people. I'm no longer the sole controller, as being the *Uno* passenger. I try to settle down for the long night ahead. There is a Peruvian man sitting beside me and we make a few gestures, both in our limited amount of each other's language; in other words, "Good night, *señor*."

Goodnight, Marietta. Goodnight, Wendy. Goodnight, Cole. I hope all things are well in the land of Canada. Goodnight, everyone.

SOUTH AMERICA ENCHANTMENT

January 26, Saturday

Enroute, Peru

I can't say what time it is, somewhere around 6:00 a.m. Yes, I'm on the "*bús*" and we've traveled throughout the night as the bus makes its way heading north on the Pan American Highway. It's very deserty and in some areas, it looks like there are sand dunes. Sure enough there are even some sand dunes going across the highway.

I've had a relatively good sleep through the night, but not overly generous. The bus has, for whatever reason, got extremely hot before they did finally cool it down. Now that I've got my eyes open and looking out the window, I can see the ocean below as we're following the coastline. As we're passing through this mountain range that hugs the coastline, I couldn't help but think, "Gee, the Spaniards must have sailed great distances along this coastline looking for a safe cove or inlet." There's no possible way that you can anchor any type of vessel, in those days or today, along this rugged coast.

We are moving along at a progressive pace, and I am hoping that I can meet my own itinerary to see the Nazca Lines today. Just as I'm feeling optimistic about this, that I will only arrive two hours late, lo and behold there is our first indication that there might be some trouble ahead. People are on foot walking, and the bus slows down to ask questions. We have just arrived at the entrance of a tunnel. My first thought was an accident, and then my overly vivid imagination came up with a worse case scenario, that there were *banditos* ahead. I quickly dispelled that idea, thinking that they might attack one bus, but they surely wouldn't attack a colony.

Still wondering what had transpired on this particular delay, the passenger beside me told me that there had been a rockslide and that obviously cars and buses cannot get through. So, I gave up any hope for what kind of day it was going to be and joined the other passengers outside. The weather was accommodating, as I stood around listening, trying to get a bit of information on the whole situation. They said there have been two rockslides, one bigger than the other. A crew has been working on them, but they're waiting now for a large piece of equipment to remove the big debris. Some of the small passenger cars are now able to get through; it's just the large transport vehicles, trucks and buses that have to wait. It should be about 9:00 a.m. before the equipment arrives to remove any rocks too big for the labor crews to do.

I get back on the bus and they serve us breakfast. It's not anywhere near as "gourmetish" as the first meal I've had, but it suffices. I have a ham sandwich, a tart and a bun, with some coffee, as well. I overhear a conversation between two passengers. The lady is from Holland, near the Amsterdam area; and the gentleman is from Scotland, in the northern area around Edinburgh. As I have been to both places, we soon start sharing our travel experiences.

I can't believe it, right on time, at 9:00 a.m. a large piece of equipment with a big scoop makes its way through. By 9:30 a.m., we're starting our journey towards our destinations and traffic seems to be moving relatively well after the horrendous backlog that took place.

As I had said to the young lady from Holland, there was no conceivable way that I was going to be able to get to see the Nazca Lines today. Most of the planes fly over them in the morning, due to the high turbulences of weather that pick up in the afternoons, and this particular afternoon looks worse than normal. It's quite forbidding out there, overcast and hazy in most directions.

I see a signpost, and I'm only 128 kilometers from Nazca; so, at least I'll arrive before the twilight hours. This terrain stays the same; endless desert. We pass a few villages, the same adobe bricks and sparse living is the order of the day. The children I see playing look a bit dirty at times, (but that's what Tide commercials are made for) their clothes are not torn or worn out. They look well-dressed and other than the odd

SOUTH AMERICA
ENCHANTMENT

runny nose, they seem well cared for. The one thing that I've noticed was the rosy cheeks of Peruvians and Bolivians. It may be due to the high altitudes that they endure or allergies, or just the complexion that persists.

I arrive in Nazca about 4:30 p.m., and as I get off the bus, there are about six to eight 'touts' (as they call them in India,) eager for our business. It's people that are waiting at transportation areas to tell us that they've got the best hotel, or the best accommodations or the best deals, whatever happens to be the flavor of the day. This is the first time I've met with this kind of aggressiveness in South America. Usually it's just a person asking, "Do you need accommodations?" Now, these people are as close to their counterparts in India as I've ever come across in South America.

I tell them, "No, I don't want a taxi. I want to get to the bus station." My first priority is to get a bus ticket to Lima prepared so that I'm not finding that I have an extra day in Nazca. Even with the attendant, this pack of wolves pursues me to the ticket desk, and it's really annoying me. Even the desk clerk tells them to back off, "You know, we'll do this business first and then address the issue." I also turned to them and said, "Okay, fine, I'll take you all outside and listen to each and every one of you", which I did. I listen to them in the order that they first approached me, and heard all of the "I've got the best *hacienda*, I've got the best hostel, I've got this, I've got that, I've got the right group of people to make arrangements for the plane, and on and on". When finally "push comes to shove", they realize I'm going to listen to every one of them, and I finally choose a man that I can get a room for ten *nuevos soles*. The plane tickets are consistent at US$35.00, with transportation out to the airport, the flight and transportation back. Nobody's going to fight you on that price. So, the cartel is well and alive.

The man I decided on takes me to the hostel and it's clean I end up with a double room, a bathroom and hot water; exactly what he promised, and its two blocks from the *piazza*. I'm satisfied, so we make arrangements for the next day,

133

which is the mother lode of their business, booking the different tours.

One of the more popular tours is to *Cementerio de Chauchilla*, a mummified cemetery that's been exposed by grave robbers as much as anybody else. Now the government has stepped in and is taking their rewards from the deceased. A tour of a pottery factory is strongly encouraged, and the opportunity to buy ceramics is the final gratification for the touts because the commission must be quite exorbitant.

The plane tour to see the Lines is my only priority, and that ticket is booked, at the best price. For the other tour, he wants ten dollars, and I'm not overly motivated one way or the other. However, the fact that if I take part in that tour, the taxi driver would drive me to the designated hotel where the bus meets up. So, I do a quick calculation and think, 'Well, I'll play a little bit of poker here, or take a Berber attitude.' I said, "Yes, I'll take the plane tour but not the other one."

With the expertise of his salesmanship, he said, "I just need one more for the trip and if I give you a special discount, would you consider?" I said, "Well, what's the discount?" He says, "The whole package for $45.00 complete, including the bus or the transportation back." "And the taxes?" I ask. "Yeah, forget about that." There is another four or five dollars worth of taxes involved. So, the bottom line is the tour to the cemetery would probably be about US$5.00 or half price.

After this is agreed on, I checked into the hotel room which I find is almost as good as the pictures that the fellow had shown me, not only a pleasant surprise but amazing for ten *nuevos soles*. The more I stay in Peru I realize anybody that tries to struggle with what is the 'real' price is playing with illusions. I'm sure that if I had walked in on my own accord and spoke Spanish fluently, I would have gotten it for seven or eight *nuevos soles*, a far cry from the twenty that was first quoted. However, I've never begrudged in any country, but especially poor countries, paying premiums, provided that I don't feel that the person has lost respect for me or taken too great an advantage of me. The small premium I pay provides a little extra for essential needs for the families that they're trying to support. People who have an obsession that they've are paying too much or they're being ripped off, have attitudes that are as oppressing as when the Spaniards abused the native Indians.

By now, it's about 6:30 p.m., so I'm going to try and find an Internet as well as something to eat. I've lost some weight, if nothing else, just by the sheer lack of eating on a normal schedule, as these buses stop for no man. I stop in a small grocery store to pick up a bottle of pop. Either my Spanish is getting better, or my body language is reaching a new level of communication, as these people seem to comprehend what I'm asking for. I'm finding as I continue this journey that communication is becoming less challenging. My Spanish is improving slowly, and I seem to be able to understand a lot of the conversations, especially if the individual speaks distinctly and slowly.

As I'm walking along, I come across a travel agent. I thought I'd just pop in and see what he had to offer as far as the flights from Lima to Iquitos. I've already got the ticket from Nazca to Lima. The agent, Roberto, tells me that he can have somebody meet me at the bus terminal, take me to a decent hostel, and pick me up and take me to the airport. With taxes included, he can offer about US$30.00 and the flight should be another $69.00. From what I've read and gathered from other travel agents, these flights are often full and should be booked well in advance. Two days advance is not well in advance by any stretch of the imagination.

Without any hesitation, I ask him to pursue this quest for me and as he's making phone calls, I continue my conversation with him. These people are very free with their information until it comes to booking, and then of course their price has some very big premiums built in. My interest is peaked when he tells me about a trip from Iquitos to Manaus that he had a very good time on. It's a passenger ship that a lot of locals take down the Amazon River. They have facilities to stow your luggage in, you sleep in hammocks, and since he's done it twice himself, he claims it's an enjoyable experience.

I'm getting closer to that part of my adventure, so I'm feeling more confident that I won't have to build a raft and be Tom Sawyer hoping that Huckleberry Finn will join me on this voyage down the river. By all indications, many vessels are continually leaving, so it's just finding one that I like with the price that is acceptable.

For my flight reservation, I've been waitlisted on the first plane out which is 7:00 a.m., the next at 9:00 a.m., and then another one at 1:00 in the afternoon. It's a short flight, about an hour, and Roberto advises me that if I come back at 8:00 p.m., he should have a confirmation on one of the times.

While waiting, I decide to get something to eat, find an Internet, and check the e-mails. I was hoping for one from Marietta, but it wasn't meant to be. So, I send her a short one telling her that all is well and that I'm in Nazca. The restaurants don't open until about 7:00 p.m. This is pretty well the norm for all of South America. They eat late in the evenings and they spend a considerable time on the evening meal. They also practice the *siesta* which makes a lot of sense, especially in this hot climate.

SOUTH AMERICA
ENCHANTMENT

Once the restaurant opens, I order a large beer and what I thought was stroganoff. As in families, each recipe is a little different and in each country, the recipe has been altered so I didn't recognize this dish as anything I had eaten before. However, it's quite tasty, pasta with bits of chicken, and garnished with tomatoes and a few other vegetables and a salad. The rice, of course, is present and accounted for and I've been able to get some *pan* or bread. With the great distances that I am traveling and spending a large amount of time on the buses looking out the window, I haven't been able to eat three square meals a day. So, when I find a restaurant with a nice décor, I take advantage of the opportunity and hope for the best.

After having a pleasant meal, it is 8:00 p.m. by the time I get back on the streets. There is still much congestion and activity going on, but it's very orderly and reminds me of an organized anthill. Everybody's moving back and forth, but there's no bumping or collision with each other. Carts are pulled aside to let traffic move in, and there doesn't seem to be any irritation in the process.

When I get back at the travel agent, Roberto, he doesn't have the best news for me. He is able to secure the hotel, the ride in and out; however, the airline hasn't gotten back to him, even though he has phoned on numerous occasions. While I'm talking to him, he tries again. This time, "Yes", I can get passage on the flight, the later flight at 9:00 a.m., but the price from $69.00 has gone up to $84.90 plus the airport tax." I agree because when I first started this quest, I was quoted $99.00, so I am within the corridor that I'd thought of.

With that decided I pay him the money and am assured that everything will transpire. This is the tremendous difference between doing business in Peru than in Canada. Instead of having a ticket issued there, or even written out on a ticket voucher, I am given a little scrap of paper that he has neatly written the times on and the flight and the confirmation number. Normally in Canada, if that had transpired, then I would pay for the ticket at the ticket bureau. I know that of course,

137

Robert F. Edwards

he's going to get a commission and if he doesn't send the money in, then he doesn't get paid. I'm assuming, and I'll be very surprised if I'm not correct, that he has quoted me the price that the airline charges me, plus his commission. Just to reassure me that this piece of paper is not worthless, he phones the airline on my behalf, so I can talk to a woman that speaks some English. This is not the norm of business travel throughout the world, so I'm sure a lot of people would feel dubious and ill at ease. With myself, I've always felt that you have to trust people, and believe in their goodness, rather than looking for the devious and bad part of their character. I toddle off hoping that all is well.

On my way back to the hotel, I treat myself to a couple of chocolate bars and a bottle of pop. 'Sprite' this time, I'm changing brands, as 'Coca-cola' is very sweet and prepare myself for the day ahead. The two young ladies in the grocery store, again really help out. My pronunciation of *chocolato* was quite puzzling to them, but I eventually get my chocolate bars.

Back at my room, I've asked the attendant on call to wake me up at 5:00 a.m. We're supposed to be ready at 7:00 a.m. for the flight. I enjoy some of my chocolate bars, which were a nice finishing touch to my meal.

Goodnight, my beautiful little wife. I miss you very much. Goodnight, Wendy. I hope you're having a good holiday. And Cole, I hope you're enjoying yourself. Goodnight.

SOUTH AMERICA
ENCHANTMENT

January 27, Sunday

Nazca, Peru

I don't need the wake-up call, as I get up at my usual time. I sure can't say I'm sleeping in. By 5:30 a.m., I've got every-thing done that I need to get done, and I go downstairs to see what the day is like. Also, to see if I can get a cup of coffee and maybe a bun, and they tell me that it is also pronounced 'bun' in Spanish. So, I am improving in my Spanish, espe-cially if the words remain very much in English context.

Out on the street, there are a few people walking around, and it's a beautiful morning. I am up early enough to see the *pan* or bread being delivered. The houses in this part of the world all have huge iron gates across the front. Some of them are also enclosed with reinforced glass mesh and as I watch the bread being delivered, a little window opens up to take the delivery.

I sincerely believe that not everybody has to fear for their life; it's a form of insurance on the contents in their house, and fending off *banditos*. The two Argentine girls had talked about the amount of guns and concealed weapons that in cer-tain South American states are permitted for the residents. They told me that because of the high unsettlement now in Argentina, a lot of people would have guns in their homes. They have to protect themselves and their belongings more than we would in Canada and the United States due to having no recovery if the loses take place.

There are some men standing over in a corner, and as soon as I see the beer bottles, I realize these men have done the night shift. They are still celebrating that they've survived the breaking of the dawn and are in good spirits. They are en-couraging me to come over and join them, and I shake one of the fellows' hands and make a bit of greetings. This is far too early for me to have a drink of beer, and the type of thing that I avoid in my own country, let alone here.

Robert F. Edwards

Back to the hotel, the attendant is just putting himself together. It is déjà-vu of India, where attendants slept where they fell. Behind the reception desk is a small room for storing luggage of people like myself when not in their rooms, or have checked out and are awaiting transportation to the next destination. Sure enough, not a cot but a mattress on the floor is his bed. He is on guard duty not only of luggage but on the front desk also, for anybody pounding on the door that wants to rent a room at some ungodly hour. Their lifestyles are so different to ours.

After having some coffee, I feel much more energized and meet the two people that will be flying with me today over the Nazca Lines. Eli and Anita are two American young people, in their mid-twenties. Soon our guide shows up and off we go to the airport. We go from one airline to the other and the second encounter, yes, they have a plane for us and yes, there are three seats for the passengers, and yippee doo! I get the front seat with the pilot. The young people are in the back and I did not arrange this or make any preparations in advance, it just happened. I am finding down here (maybe it's my imagination, but I don't think so) that there is a respect for age and I've reached one of the golden milestones in years. It could just be that they were a couple and I am a single.

Without too much further ado, the captain takes us off the runway in this small aircraft, I am inclined to think is a Cessna-150, a very light plane. The Nazca Lines I've wanted to see all my life. My interest was captured as a young boy, from 'The National Geographic' magazine, and television programs that talked about the Nazca Lines; these unexplainable geometric designs drawn in the desert that are only visible in their entirety from the air. I am fascinated even today with space and all the unexplainable events recorded in Man's history. These huge outlines that can only be seen from a high elevation have been speculated as being readings for the gods of space, (better known as astronauts). A tremendous amount of theories abound as to why these people labored so long in the desert, building gigantic lines that cannot even be identi-

140

SOUTH AMERICA
ENCHANTMENT

fied from high elevation of any mountain ranges. In this area, it's a flat desert, with just small protruding mounds.

We flew over the outlines, seeing a 180-meter long lizard, and a 90-meter long monkey, and an elaborate condor, which has a 130-meter wingspan. The figures were achieved by removing the dark stones from the sands. The governments of today are very determined to keep people away from this area to prevent any damage to these remarkable geometric figures. I've taken a whole role of film, hoping that some of these straight lines will be identifiable from the air. They are as straight as any pencil line drawn with a ruler.

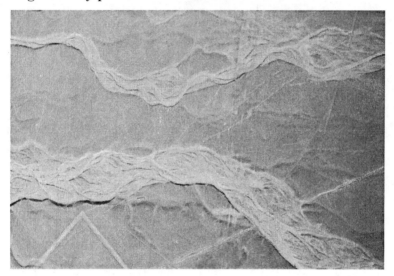

Scientific information today places the dating of these lines anywhere from 900 B.C. to 600 A.D. These people were the ancestors of many settlements throughout the northern parts of South America long before the Inca ever dominated the area. With a bit of math, this region had about 700 years of occupation. The Incas, better known as the dominant civilization before the arrival of the conquistadors, had a very short empire of around 400 years.

I said to the American couple once I got out of the plane: "You know, I would have done this just for the ride alone." It

Robert F. Edwards

cost $35.00, but between the banking, the elevating and acrobatic performances of getting us to be lined up properly so each passenger has an equal chance to see these lines, it was a far better value than any thrill ride at an exhibition. I was told, "Don't have breakfast before you go." Of course, I didn't listen. Now I understand, for anybody that suffers from mo-

tion sickness or fear of flying, this was certainly not the event to take place in. I couldn't help but think of my beautiful wife who is quite nervous in commercial airplanes; she would have been in a bad state if she had gone on this particular ride. The pilot did a great job of pointing out the symbols and the figures and letting us take enough pictures. Myself, I've got the better part of twenty-four pictures, so I'm sure something that I've shot will reflect this by-gone culture and its remarkable contribution to the world.

Once down on the ground, we are then taken back to the hotel. I have the better part of an hour before I go to the graves and my two entrepreneurial agents hope to take advantage of the extra time. The leader says to me, "Would you like to see some originals", which is the same as artifacts. Being polite, he assured me that "no pressure, you just have to see them, if you'd like." Of course, if you didn't like, I'm sure he'd persuade you a bit more before giving up. With 'liking' and an hour of nothing to do, I felt, "why not?"

We drive into a residential area; I think it's his sister's house or one of his relative's. It's quite an attractive home, with an iron gate across and a pretty garden filled with flowers; probably one of the nicer looking ones in this row of

houses. All the homes here are one-storey and made out of
adobe, then whitewashed or painted. This particular one is
painted a sandy color, with a nice wooden door, and small
from the outside appearances.

As we go in, my mouth drops open, what a transition! You
go from a mud hut appearance on the outside to very enjoyable living quarters on the inside. Also, by now, the heat of
the day is evident but it's cool in here. Just really pleasant,
and I've learned something. Boy! Does mud ever produce a
good insulation; soundproofing, too. The furniture would be
welcome in any living room, all nicely laid out, and exceptionally clean.

By now, two other men appeared. He's just a unique character, almost an artist's sketch of a man from another era.
He's wearing an old cowboy hat and a big Harley Davidson
belt buckle. At the very best, he stands 5'1", is slightly built,
and he's my age, but he's got jet-black hair and a meticu-
lously groomed black mustache. He's obviously the grandfather and we try to talk about our children, although he
doesn't speak any English, he's the *Uno* of this operation.

These people have a nice lifestyle. Yes, they're poor and by
our standards, they haven't accumulated worldly wealth, but
I'm sure that they have a better quality and enjoyment of life
behind these closed doors. This older gentleman and his son-
in-law start to display some of these 'artifacts' for me, mostly
different clothing and so forth. At this particular point, I haven't gone to the cemeteries and I haven't heard what the
guides have told me, but I'm still thinking not quite nega-
tively, but somewhat jaundiced that these are "originals".

I really don't have any strong interest one way or the other.
Some of the graphics and artwork on these very faded pieces
are quite remarkable and probably as good as any museum in
Lima would have to display. There are two things that have
caught my eye: One is, for a better word, a slingshot. You put
the stone in the middle, and have two long strings to swing it
for aiming at the target, and as you release the one string, the
stone becomes a projectile. Anybody that has read his or her

biblical history of David and Goliath will have the best imagery.

My first introduction to this weapon was a crazy man that guarded a temple in the Rajasthan province of India. He had pinned down two Swedish people and I by hurling rocks with this particular type of slingshot and I couldn't believe the accuracy. This can be a very lethal weapon in the hands of an expert.

After going through these artifacts, they showed me something that does appeal to me, which is a pouch. There were about eight pouches, different sizes and designs, and they were used by the Incas to put their cocoa leaves in. I don't think these are really Inca dated, more likely to be *Wari* artifacts. With some strong negotiations from my Berber, North Africa training, I'm drawing these men down to a new level of bargaining. They eventually agreed to accept my price on this one pouch that I've got my eye on. It's one of the larger ones, and unique in that it has tassels running down it. The designs are equally as good as any of the others even though they are extremely faded.

We return back to the hotel and I still have lots of time before I take the ride out to the cemetery. I see a slingshot in the display window at the hotel, and I'm actually prepared to purchase it. They want US$45.00, but I'd think somewhere around $20.00 to $25.00 would be the flavor of the day. I feel terrible, even thinking about this now, but it happened. I am testing the parts of the sling and, to my dismay both the ropes fall off from the main part of it. These guys are freaking out; it's like damaging a mummy. You can't really go out and buy another one. After a lot of effort, even trying to staple it together, this thing is crumbling before our eyes. We feel like three *banditos*. We gingerly put it back into the display case, and put the display case back up against the wall as if we were three kids being caught with our hands in the cookie jar. Once we're back out in the street, we all start laughing at the terrible deed that we've taken part in. The two locals tell me of another man they think has one.

SOUTH AMERICA
ENCHANTMENT

These entrepreneurs are not going to give up that easy. Just as we're driving over to one more place, our little grandfather shows up and hops in the car. We drive off and find another door to knock on. It's really surprising. These people know who is home and who isn't. I tell them, "Oh, nobody's home", but this small figure of a great *gaucho* kept pounding on the door and finally, a woman showed up, and opened the door to us. Her house is not quite as elaborate as the first one, but equally as clean and well furnished. I can't believe my good fortune in being able to enter these homes and seeing first hand their quality of life. This changed my attitude towards adobe construction.

More *authenticas* come out and of the three slingshots displayed, there's one there that I have fallen in love with. This time, gently testing it in front of the owners, this one is in much better condition and workable order. This one has an added feature, a very small loop at the end of one of the ropes, which you put on your little finger. When you have the right velocity and direction to release the stone, you let go of the entire rope. Of course, the rope remains in your possession due to the fact that it's looped to your little finger. This is an effective way of keeping an adversary at a great distance. When I was under siege in India, with this kind of weapon, the range was up to 300 meters and the Crazy Hill Man demonstrated his accuracy within centimeters.

With that complete, now it is really time to get back to the hotel, before my tour to the cemetery. This cemetery is called *Cementerio de Chauchilla,* and is about twenty to thirty kilometers outside the city.

In the tour group now is a young Japanese girl that's been on the road for about nine months and she's heading back to Tokyo. There are two young men from Hungary who don't speak much English and, of course, Hungarian isn't one of my native tongues either, but very nice people.

The first part of the cemetery is conventional, with the typical crosses that you see today on graves. Further down are the gravesites that have wooden canopies over them. Most of

Robert F. Edwards

the mummies and artifacts in this region are believed to date back to the Nazca period. There are over three thousand graves that had been exposed. Some of them were family graves like crypts in today's society. They were mummified; both children, and those that had reached full maturity in life. An interesting custom during that period; they didn't cut their hair in any way. It was against their faith and some of the mummies found in these tombs had hair up to three meters long.

The tombs are usually rectangular or square in shape, and a good two, sometimes three, meters deep into the ground. They use the same principle of adobe system as in our present-day society. The individual that was mummified was put in the fetal position because they strongly believed in reincarnation. They would cut the tendons of the back of the legs and the arms, so that they could place the deceased in the fetal position. Historians believe that the people realized that the fetal position was the one in which the baby or life began in the womb, and they also made the individual face East to see the beginning of their reincarnation. Like the Egyptians and other cultures, anything that the individual personally enjoyed in this world, was usually brought along for the next world, so they would have a head start.

SOUTH AMERICA
ENCHANTMENT

The guide tells us also, "Please don't pick up any bones or shells or pottery throughout this vast area." He said that now the police and the government put guards 24 hours a day in this general area, but they have no idea how large this vast cemetery is, and there is still grave robbing. Even in the large museums in Lima, the artifacts belong to private collections. He was saying that, "You know, the pottery and a lot of the accessories are being reproduced, but the one thing that can't be reproduced is the cloth." All of a sudden, I grasp the significance of what I've just purchased, and am going to treat this little piece with more respect.

We visit twelve open sites. They are all in different forms of both skulls and bones, some pottery to actual mummies.

Like any ghoul, I've taken my share of pictures to bring back. I was thinking cremation is a way in which the next generations won't be looking down on you. When they say, "Rest in peace," I'm beginning to wonder if that might be the only alternative to fulfilling that prophecy.

On a personal note, when I arrived at the gravesite, I bumped into the Austrian couple I had met earlier. Talk about a reunion! It's most rewarding, plus the fact that they

147

Robert F. Edwards

had information on the young German nurse from Berlin. We got misled and these people informed me that yes, she finally did get to Cuzco, and she was able to do the Inca trail. We exchanged e-mail addresses and I asked if they'd be good enough to forward mine on to the nurse, so that was just an added bonus to this remarkable day.

From here, we went to a pottery factory and were shown how they do the clay throwing process , the firing of pots and the painting. The paint pigments are ground from different stone alloys, and once decorated, the pottery is placed in a kiln to fire for three days. This work is not cheap, but then it shouldn't be. It's art, and one should never try and take advantage of an artist telling the history of Man, whether it's with canvas, pottery, writing or any form of art. I think of some of the authentic works that I have seen today, and don't have much respect for people that take artifacts and sell them for profit. However, since time immemorial, there wouldn't be museums to visit if money hadn't changed hands for the gifts of the past.

Soon it's time to go to the bus station and the girl from Japan and I am traveling together to Lima. We are dropped off at a beautiful hotel. I have no idea what the cost would be, but before my adventure is up, I'm going to spend at least one night in a hotel that has some kind of similar facilities. There's a big open square around the rooms, and just a breath-taking swimming pool in the center. Mind you, my clothes are dirty; I'm dirty and I've been on the road for a considerable length of time, so this looks very appealing.

I take advantage of their toilet facilities, probably the best I've used in all of Peru. I say to the Japanese young lady that I'm just going to get some pop and a few biscuits for the trip ahead when no sooner than that, the bus arrives and needless to say, "On the bus!"

Again, it's a small world. As I get on the bus, I run into some people who say, "We remember you. You were on the trail." They're from Switzerland and I enjoy some conversation with them. I know the reason that I keep meeting up

148

with these same people is that it is a small circuit that we travel in. Yes, I meet new people along the way, but one of the most gratifying things is that these people remember me. I'm honored and deeply touched by their welcoming of our reunion.

The bus continues to travel the highways and byways and coastal regions as we work our way up 600 kilometers to Lima. It's the same bus line and they're all a little different layout, but on the same concept. This one isn't quite as luxurious as the very first one I was on, but more than adequate. We stop along the way to have little breaks, and it's tedious. I'm glad I'm doing this, but the desert is endless in this part of Peru. I had no idea how isolated and barren some of the northern parts of Chile are; and now also the southern part of Peru, the only word that describes it is - bleak.

I haven't seen any of the giant condors like the large one I saw in Melbourne's zoo, which left an imprint of fear and awe for this great bird, but I have seen more condors than I can possibly remember flying in the air. They have a very graceful appearance, as they glide above. I can assure anyone that's never seen a live condor; their beauty is when they're in flight, not when they're on the ground. Even thinking back now, I get a cold shiver of that gross beak and long neck that is associated with the vulture. The word 'condor' has a much more pleasing connotation, but their purpose in life is exactly the same as the vulture. As they soar over these long corridors in the desert, I know that some poor creature is reaching its expiration and these birds of prey are searching for that last breath of life.

As we continually move endlessly towards Lima, I can't believe that I see the lights about six o'clock but as I talk to people from Switzerland, they don't share the same enthusiasm that we'll be there quickly. They said that the bus was leaving late and that we'll probably be arriving closer to eight. It turns out that they were right. We don't get into Lima until well into around nine o'clock.

Robert F. Edwards

I get off the bus and collect my luggage and as the agent promised, a gentleman was waiting for me, not with a big placard but a small scribbled piece of paper, but he recognized me and approached me (along with about twenty different taxi drivers). He didn't speak much English, but showed his credentials like his driver's license with his picture on it and assured me both with the identification and with just his sincerity, that he was the right person.

Both of us made our way through the crowd and Pablo is his name. We find his old Impala, one of the dinosaurs of the large period, waiting for me. With some help, he takes the small pack and I have my huge backpack on my back. I don't know whether I'm getting stronger, but there is no conceivable way my pack is getting lighter as I've been adding things to it rather than subtracting from it. My muscle tone must be improving, since I can handle it much better than when I first lifted it off my own bed at home.

 With all my gear thrown into his vintage car, we're soon rumbling down through the streets of Lima. As I look at the city, it doesn't take my breath away by any stretch of the imagination, but it's nowhere near as dismal or foreboding as some of the stories I've heard about Lima. It's a very large city, and it's spread out without many high-rises. In the downtown core are some high-rises, but it's a mixing of old with new. The Spanish period of occupation is present with the massive cathedrals, but the streets are relatively clean and the main arteries are exceptionally wide. Throughout South America, their inner cities' layouts are far superior to North American's in the width that they have provided with these massive boulevards and *piazzas*. Traffic flows much better here than

SOUTH AMERICA
ENCHANTMENT

in major cities like Vancouver or Toronto, or New York, as far as that goes. Down here, they're a little more visionary when it comes to expansion of population.

It is still relatively early, but there's sparse population on the streets. It's only about 9:00 p.m., and other than traffic, there aren't really a lot of pedestrians, or shops open. I see the odd street vendor, and a few corner stores open, but the rest are well bolted down with corrugated steel doors. There must have been a hell of a marketing program on them, as they all use the same. There's a little door on the inside of this metal door that they've cut through, which is reinforced with heavy gauged steel bars, bolted and then locked with huge padlocks. I'm sure that the only way to penetrate these doors would be with a tank. The proprietor, with his life savings and inventory behind these corrugated steel panels can sleep very well at night in his own *hacienda*.

It's not a pretty city from the little I can judge at night. Again, the general condition of such a large city reflects the economy of Peru. We are in the core of the city as we rumble over the old tired cobble roads and finally make our way to the hostel. It could have been a mansion from a different era, now it's run down. I remember my agent Roberto, saying that he was getting exceptional value and the best prices, but this is a downgrade even from the place I was staying at for ten *nuevos soles*, which is about US$3.50. I'm bearing in mind that yes, cities are always expensive, but I'm paying about US$20.00, pretty well at the top of the mound. I've been given a room that is little better than spartan. I have my own bathroom and that makes a huge difference in these hostels. If you want your own bathroom, you pay a premium. The room is adequate, with two small single beds in it. The staircase on the first floor is quite conventional, but the next two flights are a spiral staircase. If I ever wanted to see if I could manage a backpack on my back, the spiral staircase is the ultimate training program.

The most important issue now is that I'm quite hungry. I haven't eaten much all day and the few biscuits that I brought with me on the bus just appeased my appetite rather than sufficed it. With both my packs out of the way, I get down to the main floor and ask if they have a café, and to my pleasure, "Yes, it's right in the building." They even have a *restaurante*. The ceilings in these places always amaze me and this one's at least 6 or 7 meters high. There is grandeur of another time and this building must have been exceptionally elegant, but both age and neglect have severely taken its toll and now it has become more of a flophouse, not even a high-grade hostel.

In that negative attitude, I find an Internet and not much news, other than the regular stuff. I try to get an e-mail off, a short one, to Marietta, just to let her know that all is well when I'm interrupted by one of the women from the front desk. They've asked a French man, his name is Allan, to act as interpreter for me because he's the only one that speaks English. I had a message from Pablo that he wants to pick me up at 6:00 a.m. in the morning instead of 6:30 a.m. because something is wrong with the road on the highway going to the airport, which is more than fine for me.

Allan and I spend some time talking. He lives in one of the suburbs of Paris, was born in Algiers, and has taken a sabbatical like so many men of his age. I would gather he's in his mid-30's, but with a receding hairline, he could be younger than his appearance. After the better part of ten or fifteen minutes, I said to him that I would like to continue the conversation, but I also wanted to get some internet mail off, or at least read some of it.

By the time I finish with the Internet, I am more than hungry, so I go upstairs and to my delight, Allan is there drinking water. I offer him a beer, juice or whatever and he declines, but I have a beer and a ham-cheese sandwich and some *papa fritas*. The food is surprisingly fresh, and good for the surroundings that I'm in. As I talk to him, the hours are passing and before long, it's 11:00 p.m. The restaurant personnel are closing up, so they move us to some open-air seats on the fourth floor.

SOUTH AMERICA
ENCHANTMENT

Long before the Western world ever thought of the word sky-light, these parts of the world used the open-air roof so that the main square in their house was open to down drafts. This keeps the buildings cooler and it also gave them small court-yards in the larger cities. Even in dense row housing they still had open courtyards within them to enjoy a little bit of na-ture's gifts to man. Also, the terraces or balconies are on the inside facing the courtyard, to take advantage of the cooler night air.

Now that we're in the dark, I quickly finish the last bit of my beer and *papa fritas* and start to head back to my room, only to find out that I can't, I don't know where it is. I've got the key but it's a maze; it's absolutely a maze in this place, with no more than three to four meters on any one level. So, after trying a couple of doors that have a D on them, (I thought I was D-4), I'm having no success. Cautiously, I make my way back down to the front desk and the gentleman, a young man, is more than accommodating. He goes up with me, only to have the same problem of not being able to find the door. But, he discovers that on my key tag that it's not just D-4, the A has been removed. Talk about the left hand not knowing if the right hand is even attached, let alone where it is. The better part of ten minutes is behind us before he finally finds the room. We both have a bit of a chuckle about that one, and I'm now behind the door.

While I was searching, the rooms that I passed were dormi-tory-style, with six to eight beds to a room. The young people need to be into communal living, but it fits the price. During my wandering I met Ian, the man from Scotland. He dropped off his girl from Holland and now he has one from Scandina-via. Even this young blonde says: "Oh, he's really a ladies' man." She has just returned from the Amazon, and I would have liked to talk to her about that trip, but they were going to venture out into the streets of Lima. By now it's 12:00 mid-night and I knew that 5:30 a.m. is going to be my time to as-semble both my goods and myself to venture down the 'fire-

153

man's' spiral staircase to the main floor and then on to the airport.

With the bewitching hour shortly passed, I'm going to say goodnight to one and all. Goodnight, my beautiful little wife. Goodnight, my daughter, my little Cole-man. This has been a long day and I miss all of you and yes, Marietta, I'm even thinking of poor little Pepper and of course, I'll always love my little Buttons. I hope that I fare as well at his age as he's doing. God love you all and God bless you all. Goodnight.

SOUTH AMERICA ENCHANTMENT

January 28, Monday

Lima, Peru

Wow! If I said I slept well, it would be just in my imagination. Between the camaraderie going on in the other rooms, well into the wee hours of the night, and my obsession with getting up early enough to get to the airport on time, it deprived me of any restful sleep. However, I'm up and no, I don't take a shower. Its cold water and I'm still quite tired from the road of the previous days and although I don't mind missing a bus, I definitely don't want to miss this plane.

Knowing that I have to face that spiral staircase, I can only say "Thank you, God, for relieving the discomfort that I've been experiencing the last few days about my left knee." I thought that I just banged it, but it's still quite painful. I am so grateful to God for letting me do the Inca trail without this discomfort, and I don't think I would have achieved the success I did if I'd been on the trail with my knee feeling this way.

Now I have to face the spiral staircase, and feel like a turtle with all my gear on my back, as I carefully descend. Even though the ceilings are sixteen feet high, people of the by-gone era were short, and the doors are equally so. The first time I go through, of course, the walking stick tied to my backpack is an antenna that will not bend. I almost go head over tea kettle with my flashlight looking at the ceiling rather than the floor. I soon get the knack of balancing things, and eventually I'm successful in getting to the main entrance.

At this hour, the 'bastion' is still intact. The doors are sealed with the heavy grates that protected us from the untouchables of the outside world. I pity any late-comers wandering the vacant streets without knowing where to knock, so that the proprietor could look through a peephole in this heavy fortified premises.

As daylight breaks, so does the stringent security and the doors start to open and the first shades of light appear. I check outside, to see what the day brings and to my surprise, Pablo is already there, sitting in his vehicle. I approach him, and he's very grateful to see that I'm ready with my gear. We go to the airport without much of an incident. The city is just starting to awake and traffic is modest.

Lima is not a city that I feel deprived by not having spent more time there. Yes, there are museums and theaters and with a population of millions involved, there are many things to do. However, it's not a very pretty city in comparison to some that I've seen in South America. I'll always be biased towards Rio de Janeiro, and Buenos Aires is the nicest city that I've ever been in South America, and Montevideo in Uruguay equally commands attention, to say nothing of Santiago. But Buenos Aires has got the jewel that holds the crown.

I read that the airport was about twenty kilometers away, but the ride was comfortable, and we were soon at the airport. Pablo does not speak much English, but I was able to gather that he's had an operation on his leg. I don't know how serious it is, but one thing I am sure of, if my knee hurts; his must be in pure agony. He can hardly move it, let alone walk on it, and it's stiff. At first I thought it was an artificial leg, and I didn't expect him to carry my pack or anything like that. He's got a little note that was written by Roberto, my agent. It said that he had to stay three hours at the bus last night and he's upset that he had to wait that long. I give Pablo some money and I was hoping that people would be kind to me at his age.

We say our goodbyes and I make my way to the air terminal and, I guess one good turn deserves another. I'm a little apprehensive having only a scrap of paper with a couple of numbers written down on it, but with some help, an attendant points me towards the reservation desk. I'm confirmed on the 9:00 a.m. flight and I'm there at 6:15 a.m. So, talk about being early!

I stand in another queue, looking like a luggage department on wheels and they confirm that yes, I have my ticket. "Do you have your passport?" again efficiency. I've gone through

SOUTH AMERICA
ENCHANTMENT

two hurdles and I stand in this long queue, waiting patiently as it drags itself endlessly, inch by inch, through the check-in counter, only to be stopped at the final leg of it by an attractive young lady saying, "No, no, no." And I'm saying: "Iquitos." And she's saying, "Yes, but later." What I gather is that it's not time to check in. This is probably one of the few airports that I've ever arrived at too early.

It's now about 7:10 a.m., time to check in. I don't really care what time the plane leaves, I'm just anxious to get rid of the humungous weight on my back. The young lady that's checking in my luggage looks at my walking stick and says, "Hmmm, what about the stick?" And I said, "Well, I don't mind taking it on the airplane but I don't figure you'll let me take it on the passenger part." She smiles and I said, "You know, I walked on the Inca trail with it." No problem, so my stick has its own private label and bag.

Now I'm thinking I'll have a nice breakfast. Wrong! Out of the three *restaurantes* in the airport, they're all fast-food places. I end up having some kind of bun with chicken in it and a purple drink for around seven *nuevos soles*. It's not the money. It's just not being able to have a good breakfast, which I was really hoping for. I was going to try to get caught up on my notes, before I forgot any moments of importance, but with the long days that have preceded today and this early morning, I could barely keep my eyes open.

Finally it is time to make my way through security. The first leg of security is a piece of cake. They check your passport, scan the ticket and if it's validated for that day, your next step is the baggage security. As I pass through, I empty all my pockets and think I've done everything right. Thank God I did this early. They stop me on the other side and a security man, in limited English says, "You have a fork." Puzzled, I repeat, "A fork?" And he says, "An eating fork." Then it dawned on me. I know that I've taken the pocketknife out to put it in my large case, but I probably do have a fork in my belt that I carry my camera and other essentials in. I dismantled the small pack, and he retains the 'weapon' before I con-

157

Robert F. Edwards

tinue on. I don't think I'll be known as the "terrorist from Canada" that tried to hijack a plane with a fork.

This was an old souvenir of mine, a Lufthansa fork from a by-gone era when the airlines still served with metal utensils. This fork was unique in the sense that it served both as a fork and spoon. One of the stewardesses had given it to me, in a goodwill gesture when I raved how great this would be for eating peas with. Anybody that has ever been served peas on a flight will understand; just try and get those little devils into your mouth. It is quite a challenge and this particular fork with its German technology; I had carried all over the world because of its dual use. The security guard recognizes the stamp of Lufthansa and gives me a naughty shake of the hand. I try to tell him that it was really given to me. I'm not a terrorist and I'm not a person that steals either. Anyway, I've had my weapon confiscated and I'm told that I can get it at the service desk upon arrival in Iquitos.

I make my way to the waiting area and have a cup of coffee. I can't believe the coffee works out to almost US $2.00. Airports all over the world know they have a captive audience and the chance of you coming back is really irrelevant. If you come back, you're still a captive audience. So, prices are only competitive to what your wallet can bear.

The flight is on time and we board. The weather is overcast, but pleasant and off we go into the wild blue yonder, a little late due to something with freight and the young couple behind me. Our first stop is a city en route to Iquitos, just for getting rid of some of the passengers and cargo and taking on something that's far more important, and that's fuel, for the last leg. It's in excess of two and a half hours before I get to Iquitos.

The landscape is taking on a new phase. The mountain ranges that I've enjoyed and trekked through in the last month are now diminishing into more rolling hills with lush vegetation. The rivers are brown and look like a snake that has either indigestion or is in agony as it coils in and out of the terrain. Far below, I see thin pencil lines drawn over the

SOUTH AMERICA
ENCHANTMENT

rolling hills and these dirt roads during the rainy season would be nothing more than a memory of better forms of transportation.

As the plane continually heads towards Iquitos, there's no doubt in my mind that I'm starting to enter into the massive Amazon basin area. The vast tributaries are the highways that have been used long before records were kept and are just as active today in this region. In many ways, this is the only means of transportation other than air.

I was told that from Cuzco, it would take anywhere from ten to twelve days to get to Iquitos by boat. I would have welcomed that trip if I hadn't had a quest to see the Nazca Lines. As we're approaching Iquitos, I start to see the change of landscape. The small farms below are not terraced like the ones in the Andes or around Cuzco; they're small plots of land similar to conventional farming standards. Also, as the plane continually makes its final descent, I can see the lush jungle terrain ahead and the palm trees are starting to appear. I can't help but feel that I've been transported to a totally different environment. As we approach the runway, I now feel that I'm in a tropical environment. After the plane lands and I walk from the tarmac to the terminal, the first humid heat of the mid-day is present and once again, I realize that I've entered a new phase of this adventure.

Upon arriving, I'm one of the first off the aircraft, so I go to a tourist information facility and gather some information about hotels. This is going to be a moment of exuberance in my life. I'm going to upgrade from some of the lower hostels that I've stayed in to at least a three or four-star hotel. I do this periodically just to, I guess, give myself a little bit of luxury, and it's due. I've first experienced this reward when I was in India and I've done it ever since. I love backpacking. I prefer it to any other way of traveling. However, once in a while, I just need an upgrade and today, due to the long duration of travel and the conditions I've traveled under; I'm going to treat myself accordingly.

Robert F. Edwards

I decide on the Victoria Regal Hotel, and the information bureau tells me that I can probably barter a discount because of the season. He also told me that this particular hotel provides transportation back and forth from its location. I would probably have to pay US$50.00 for transportation from the airport to the core of the city and back, so this is taken into account.

I meet a young man; his name is Clever Sinazahua who is representing the hotel. He's similar to all the agents that I've experienced throughout this trip – eager to please, and gain your business and can almost do anything but magician's tricks. I tell him that I've got to get my luggage and to retrieve my 'weapon' that has been seized by the authorities (better known as the "fork").

So, I start to barter with him a bit. I must admit, these people are exceptionally nice, but they're no match for the training that I've received from other skilled barterers throughout the world. With hardly any effort on my behalf, I've managed to get him down to $35.00 a night. I'm sure I could have succeeded in achieving a much lower rate, but this particular hotel has a swimming pool. God only knows why I've chosen one with a swimming pool, as I am not able to swim. However, I think seeing that inviting pool in the Nazca Hotel when I was waiting for the bus has put this idea in my head.

I collect all of my belongings, including my walking stick, which has fortunately traveled without being splintered into toothpicks. The ride to town is quite extensive and there are three of them and one of me. Clever has not stopped pitching since we've gotten into the vehicle. He is telling me about the jungle tours, the city tours, and every other kind of tour that could be toured upon.

I try to be polite, but I am very tired. There's no two ways about it, with being up at an early hour today, plus staying up late last night, and not getting much sleep the previous two or three days, I am not in full form. I tell him, from what I've heard and read, that around Iquitos there are a lot of *turista* jungle ventures but not as authentic as the expeditions that

160

could be achieved in other parts of the Amazon. I have to give
this man full credit, he admits this is true. However, it
doesn't deter him. The pitch becomes more feverish as we get
closer to the hotel because like any time frame, his is running
out. He then tells me that these tours can run anywhere from
fifty to a hundred dollars U.S. a day and he asked me, once at
the hotel, to at least give him the opportunity to show me pictures of the facilities that he has access to. They were quite
nice for jungle accommodations, but I've been living in very
similar conditions for the last month.

I now want to upgrade to the *turista* level for at least a day
or two, and did insist that I have a double bed. True to his
word, there is a small swimming pool in the internal part of
the complex. The hotel is also right in the downtown core. An
extra bonus, I have television with over a hundred channels
and CNN is one of them. There is air-conditioning and the
room warrants the three stars that it's commanded. I assure
him that if I decide to do anything on a tourist basis, I will
phone him first.

Now, I am going to have a rest. I no sooner check in than I
notice there's almost an evacuation of people leaving the hotel. I'm so tired that I'm not overly concerned by all these *turista*s running into vans. I just assume they're going to visit
the jungle or some other tour. I am elated with my room. It's
small but first class, and it's exceptionally clean. I take off my
clothes, but I just can't bear to put my dirty body on the clean
sheets that I plan to use for the night. So, with a feeling of
pure ecstasy, I have a long hot shower to remove not only the
dirt, but to re-energize my ailing spirits and fatigue. With
that, I welcome this double bed to have a long overdue *siesta.*

Not surprisingly, I slept very soundly, for about three hours
to four hours. I forced myself to get up and dress, to see my
new surroundings. It's about 4:30 p.m. and I want to famil-
iarize myself with the city's layout during daylight hours. My
first recognizance is to the bank and there's a huge line-up,
waiting to exchange currency. On my way down, about four
or five blocks away, I had passed a lot of moneychangers. Af-

Robert F. Edwards

ter I get to the bank, I use my Visa and to my surprise, once I put the card in, pushed the button for English, followed the instructions, instant US$100.00 – two fifties. Feeling quite proud of myself and reassured that now this plastic card can produce magic from what seemed mystical in ancient times, I have money in my pocket and look at the line. It is slowly inching forward.

I thought I would try and see what the moneychangers would do. I know they always want a considerable premium, but with some haggling we settle on a rate of 3.5. If I had a larger amount to exchange, I probably could have gotten 3.7. However, for my first attempt with moneychangers, 3.5 was adequate, especially when he started at 3.4. He tried to get his premium back by shorting me twenty *nuevos soles*. I don't say this is a good way of exchanging money. But if you're going to do it, the first thing is to find what the rate of exchange is. Second; try to ask for a bit of a premium when you're dealing with the black-market. You have to be careful of counterfeit currency. I have to confess; I wouldn't really know the difference. If you're in a hurry, you'll probably pay the premium rate anyway. Regardless what currency it is, I know enough to make sure that the bills are new rather than worn out and dirty.

Feeling quite satisfied with my financial transactions, I make my way to a restaurant. I order a beer and ask the waiter, a Hungarian young man, about the different types of fish. I order a local fish, like a catfish and soup, which the menu describes as Creole. He brings me a small glass of what looks like milky water and I take a sip. It's quite hot (as I told him I do like my food well-seasoned) and also a bowl of corn that's been roasted. With the two combinations, along with beer, I must admit that it's very good. This drink reminds me of clam juice or the broth from the mussel. Shortly thereafter, my *sopa* is served and it's a different type of Creole than I'm aware of, but absolutely delicious. There's a pasta or spaghetti as one of the main substances, potatoes, and there's even an egg on it, olives; but it's the broth that's seasoned just right. As Goldilocks would say, "It's not too hot and not too cold, it's just right", and the spices were just right. It's sure hitting the spot. I no sooner finish it, and the main course is served, an absolute delight. The fish is on a large platter, lined with a banana leaf. The fish has a remarkable taste, with some peppers, onions, and other seasonings. There's a pile of what looks like white fluff and I ask him what it is. It's the shredding of a certain type of plant in the area, which is very bland, but it's seasoned with orange zest and limejuice. It has a unique flavor and a taste in my mouth that I've never experienced before. The fish is absolutely delicious, and the best meal I have ever had in Peru. In fact, it has to be one of the best meals I've had on this trip. I am having minor orgasms of gastric delight with this whole experience and I guess my facial expressions are portraying it to the waiter.

It's unfortunate, as most of the *turistas* have evacuated to the jungle. My waiter confirms that the place is going to be closed down and the city, as far as that goes, for the balance of these two days, which is really too bad. He explains to me that he's got to go into the jungle for the next two days also. I guess, when you don't want to be around, the best place is to

Robert F. Edwards

head for the hills. He gives me an address of where to check into taking a riverboat and also a small town that he said I would probably enjoy. The price of the whole meal is so small that I give him a 50% tip. At first, he is quite aghast by the generosity. When I tell him that I really enjoyed not only the service he has given me, and the meal that he has provided, but also the friendship, he accepts it. I guess you might say if you are a Star Trek fan, "I've gained a friend."

From here, I return to the hotel, check for some e-mails, and yes! My friends of the world have honored me and blessed me with some correspondence, to say nothing of my wonderful and endearing wife with hers. In her e-mail, she has mentioned the snow. Usually in Vancouver, it only snows for a day or two and then the rains wash it back into the ground, but for some unknown reason, this snow seems to be staying on in abundance.

I now ventured off into the *piazza* and take some pictures of the region and the buildings. One of the unique things about Iquitos is that there are very few vehicles, but there's a huge abundance of motorcycles. A good portion of these motorcycles have been converted. The front part of them remains the same, but the back is where there are extra seats. This is how you get around in this town, on these motorcycle taxis. This is just the reverse to what the people on the border of Bolivia and Peru do, as on their bicycles, the front is the taxi. These converted motorcycles race up and down the one-way streets, which prevail (unless somebody else is going the other way, in which they give quarter to).

I think a Harley Davidson enthusiast would have mixed feelings of gratification. One, that finally the mighty motorcycle has dominated and overtaken the automobile; and on the other side, he would have the dilemma that his beautiful hog that he probably cherishes is now being hacked and channeled into a taxi, which would make any Hell's Angel feel that he has really gone to hell.

SOUTH AMERICA
ENCHANTMENT

Iquitos has a population; I've been told, of around 350,000. It's the largest Peruvian jungle city. It's also the capital of the department of Loreto. The only way that you can get in to Iquitos is either the way I've gone; by air, or on the Amazon. It's the largest city in the Amazon basin without road links. The Jesuit missionaries founded it in 1750 and in the 19th century, the rubber boom played a significant part. Today, there is still the possibility of oil discovery, but the *turistas* play the most important role, in their quest for jungle excursions.

The accommodations and 'jungle lodges' are quite 'touristy' and the gentleman from Vienna showed me pictures of where they went. Of course, you get to see the crocodiles and some monkeys and birds and if you're lucky, a pet python, maybe even have a swim in one of the little waterfalls that's in the general area. It's an illusion to what real jungle conditions are; but by all standards, for somebody that has never been in a jungle environment, this is probably as close to the real thing that they'll enjoy, with the safety and comfort of civilization giving them the taste rather than the endurance.

These lodges are usually on stilts in the rivers and the only way that you can get to them is by riverboat. Obviously, the more luxurious ones cost more and you're taken there by Yamahas and Toyota outboard motors. If you're staying at

165

more budget-conscious place, you'll be taken in by some slower mode of transportation. The prices ranges anywhere from US $50.00 a day to whatever your pocketbook will bear. I'm not overly enthusiastic, at this point, to take part in it due to the fact that from even my first conversation with Clever, I decided that it's too *turista* for me.

The evening has now subsided over the city, and being this close to the equator, darkness comes about 6:30 to 7:00 p.m. and by 8:00 or 9:00, its pitch black. I've wanted to see the restaurant known as "Maloka Restaurant." It was mentioned in The Lonely Planet as one of the most expensive. My curiosity hasn't diminished and over the years, when I've used the Lonely Planet book as my traveler's bible, I've always found their information not only to be accurate, but worth pursuing if they mention a particular place to eat. So with that, I'm going to make the quest of finding this place.

Without much difficulty, I do find it and there are maybe no more than two people in there – the waiter and the waitress, and I'm sure there is a cook, so there are three for sure, maybe somebody else, but the place is empty. By now, it's about 9:00 p.m. and I really fail to comprehend at this moment that I'm probably one of the last, if not the only *turista* left in Iquitos. However, I sit down and the waiter is very friendly and I order a beer. I ask for a large one, he says, "We only have a small one." So, that's fine. He goes over the menu and he tells me that they even have crocodile to eat. His English is relatively good. He's obviously not very busy; as I'm the only guest in the place. So, I have my own private waiter now and with that, a little further conversation.

The woman comes over and there's literally nobody else around. So, I invite them to sit down and then finally say, "Why don't you have a beer with me?" For the next two hours, we talk about everything and anything. Her English is probably a little better than his, but they're both limited and my Spanish pronunciation is so bad that everybody, by the time they understand what I said, it's back to English. I am having a delightful time learning about these co-workers; he's a real ladies' man and has a wife and five children. She's no longer married and she has two children, one now a man in his thirties and a younger girl in her late teens. The evening progresses and the three of us are enjoying the company.

It's now about a quarter after eleven and behold, another person appears and it's approaching closing time, which is fine for me. With that, I settle up the bill. But before I leave, the lady tells me that she really likes to cook and for the next two days, she's going to cook and stay at home, while the man is going into the jungle to enjoy himself doing whatever he wishes. She asks me if I like chicken and I said, "Why, I like any type of food." "Do I like spicy?" "Yes, I really do like spicy." So, she invited me for lunch the next day, which I think is absolutely great. She's quite adamant to make sure that I've got the time right, that at noon she'll meet me at the hotel. With that, I say "*Adiós*" and "*Buenos dias*" and off I go.

As I head back towards the hotel, I see a grocery store and I'm one of the last customers to get through before the big mighty wooden door is closed and it only opens to let people out rather than in. It's well stocked with an abundance of different types of food and a variety of sundries products, (anything from shampoos and soaps and toilet paper) to fresh meat and produce which has been pretty well picked over, not that I was going to buy any meat. However, I do pick up some pop, water, biscuits, and chocolate bars and make my way to the front.

As I'm doing this, I noticed a T.V. cameraman filming different people and lo and behold, he starts to film me for some reason. They say that "fools rush in where angels fear to tread" and I have to use that expression with myself. I wouldn't say I'm naïve, but I'm often in a world all of my own. I didn't think too much of it, but have to admit that I thought it was rather strange that a T.V. camera man would be taking pictures of people buying food, but my whole attitude towards the city closing down was strange.

All I want to do now is get back to my hotel. By now, the streets are quite sparsely populated and it's not my agenda to be out at night, even in my own city walking the streets. It's a rule that I've made long before this trip; that safety is behind doors at night, and let the people of the night do their evil deeds without me.

I'm soon back in my pleasant little room with my food supplies, happy as a clam, and I'm looking forward to a good night's rest. To you, my beautiful and dearest little wife, I miss you dearly and I really thank you very much for all your wonderful e-mails. I can hardly wait to be back with my little family, to my daughter and Cole. I really hope that you're enjoying your holiday in Mexico as much as I'm enjoying this adventure. Goodnight one and all and God bless.

SOUTH AMERICA ENCHANTMENT

January 29, Tuesday

Iquitos, Peru

I get up at about 6:00 a.m., record some of my thoughts of the previous days, and again, have a wonderful shower. If I sound so enthusiastic about hot water and a shower, you can only imagine the other conditions that I have been in for the last month. I'm watching television, and of course CNN, as I'm obsessed with news and information. To have access to this media that I've been deprived of over the previous weeks is really a treat.

By about 8:00 a.m., I decide that I'd like to have some breakfast and go down and have toast. I don't know exactly how to describe it. It's *pan* or bread, about the normal size, and I don't know how they've done it, it's dry - it's Melba. As soon as you bite into it or God forbid, use your knife it will shatter into pieces like you've driven a spike into glass. Anyway, I have some coffee and papaya juice as well. The waiter asked me if I'd like anything else and I suggest I'd like to have some eggs, and he asked me about whether I wanted ham or bacon or sausage. This rather surprises me, so I end up with ham and scrambled eggs.

This is my first introduction to what events are actually taking place. A large protest had been planned, and I'm not going to try to exaggerate it, nor minimize it as a non-event. During the night, and into the wee hours of the morning, a great deal of military police and army, (as well as the patrol police that drive these luxurious land cruisers), took over strategic spots in the city.

Obviously, there are areas that protestors would be more concentrated in than others. The waiter told me that I could probably go down to the square and that that general area was safe. To go more than two blocks in the other direction was very dangerous, that the police were using tear gas to control the situation, as well as turning people back. He also

169

Robert F. Edwards

advised me to be very careful, that people are in an angry mood, and that they could take their frustration out on tourists. So, if I was to go outside, be careful.

Not the best start to the day, but I put my camera in my bag and venture outside. There's a mist about, the sky is overcast, and I soon detect a smoky aroma in the air. As I walk a block away from the hotel, it's my first indication that it wasn't like this the night before. There are large piles of tree branches burning in the street. The streets are literally empty.

I eventually spot two men, one with a camera and the other one trying to phone on a pay phone. So I approach them and ask if they speak English and the one that's not on the telephone says, "A little bit." I find out that they're reporters from Lima covering this event. So it's a little bigger than what I anticipated as just an ordinary strike or a protest. The whole city is deserted and closed down. The only people remaining (with the exception of this one *turista,*) are those staying in the five-star hotels, which are somehow morally obligated to stay open. The people are exceptionally angry and really want to get their point across. Even the airport is closed. Everyone in the city is behind closed doors, or out of town. It is quite an eerie feeling.

When the cameraman gets off the telephone, he shows me pictures he's taken of the night before. These fires were blazing, and people marching around waving flags, in their strong

protest. This was not a *fiesta* or a carnival, by any stretch of the imagination. This was, in the strongest terms, civil disobedience. From what I can gather, the Japanese Finance Minister, Alberto Fujimori, is now the president, and he's enforcing some stringent rules on the people, and many suspect corruption in the government. This particular region has told him no, they didn't sign the agreement, they're not going to honor it, and this is their way of expressing their views on his decision-making.

I walk down the four blocks to the square and it's like a deserted city. There's nobody on the streets for the first three or four blocks; and when I do get to the square, there's police, and the odd person just observing. It's an eerie feeling, and in the short time I've been here, now I fully comprehend the evacuation by most people. Today, there are only people that have nowhere to go, or the reporters, and a very strong military presence.

I go back to the hotel and to my amazement there are two young Canadians that have just checked in with their guide.

Robert F. Edwards

They're originally from Winnipeg, Manitoba, but now living up in the new territory that Canada's just distinguished, Nunavut, and he is with the CBC. He's making long distance phone calls, to see if the CBC wishes to cover the story, and he's trying to get a camera and so forth. Once he gets off the phone, I introduce myself to David and volunteer my camera. We find out about an hour later that no, CBC is not going to cover the story or get involved in regional conflicts. The couple leaves, as they have their own agenda today, but I hope to see them later.

By this time, it's twelve o'clock and I'm wondering if my newfound friend will be taking me for lunch or not. I hang around for the next hour and just when I've given up, and decide to go in the restaurant to order, this woman comes with her daughter. She's got two different trays, they're really well done, and Tupperware would be delighted to take the patents off this. They're two small trays connected together with a handle on them, and in these she's brought the meal.

I ask the waiter if we could sit down in the dining room area. She explains to him what she wants done with it and he is more than accommodating. I give them the menus so they can order something of their choice. This lady and I have a beer, her daughter has a Coca-Cola. Her daughter's eighteen years old, and a very attractive young lady. The woman explains to me that she tried her very best to get here at twelve, but there's no transportation whatsoever and they had to walk the great distance.

This is so typical of these South American people. Their word is their bond. Their commitment to another person becomes their quest or their fulfillment in life. No obstacle is too big, no inconvenience is even considered. I just admire and really enjoy being with these people, not for the sake that they're doing something for me, to which I'm more than grateful, but for the attitude that they have and the respect that they have set their standards. I can't help but think everyday of the two Argentinean ladies, and their moral standards that

SOUTH AMERICA
ENCHANTMENT

my generation was brought up with, are still flying high and strong.

George Bush talks about his quest for a safe and just society, which sounds very noble, but his two children have been brought up more than once for underage drinking; his brother's daughter has been charged with securing drugs from a pharmacy through fraudulent acts. Not the quality of standards that this lady and her daughter (although poor) have. These women have much higher standards that they have set for themselves than the president of the United States has ever set for his family and his country. These people have morals; they have ethics; and they have honor and respect, both for themselves and for others. I speak well of these people. They have earned every word and more.

Back to the meal, it's well done. Very nice tasting rice, potatoes and chicken in an orange sauce that's very pleasant, not overly seasoned. I thoroughly enjoy my meal. The ladies ordered some kind of meat (very salty) and plantain, often a basic preference that is just used for everything. This particular way it's prepared, it's baked and then rolled into a ball. It's very dry, and not something that I would've ordered.

I kept on telling her that I enjoyed the meal that she's prepared for me better than the restaurant meal. Both of them seemed to enjoy their meal and we talk for a while over lunch, before I was feeling somewhat tired, and I said, "I think I'm going to have a *siesta*." Before I leave them, I have some photographs taken of the three of us. And a funny little thing happens at the very end. As I go to give the young girl a kiss on the cheek, we get mixed up on which side of the cheek I was going to give it on, and I am bobbing back and forth as all three of us are laughing immensely. Finally we both give each other a little peck on the cheek and I give her mother one as well and exchange e-mail addresses. A wonderful experience and I'll always remember the meal, and the enjoyment having it. With that, I go back upstairs and yes, it is the rainy season. There's nothing like the sound of rainfall to give you a good afternoon *siesta.*

After a good rest, I watch some news on television and catch the first excerpts of CNN, the world at your doorstep. The coverage of CNN seems more global once you get off the North American shore. They provide short excerpts of everything from the weather to sports and, of course, news events that are taking place. One that caught my attention was a plane flying from Iquitos that crashed in the Andes. When I saw the people at the airport crying and in shock, and think that we seem to go from one moment of despair to another with these events; and flying over those mountains just yesterday, my heart goes out to all these families.

It stopped raining, so I get dressed and go downstairs for another long invigorating walk. There are a few venturous people that have opened up their iron doors and have the tenacity to show that the leaders of this resistance are not intimidating them. But generally speaking, the streets are deserted and there's an unusual amount of debris. I still notice the police, if they're not on every corner, they're driving by.

I wonder whether it's the calm *before* the storm or the calm *after* the storm. Being an optimist, I'm inclined to feel that it's the latter. I feel like Charles Heston in "Planet of the Apes," as the only person around this deserted city. It's such an eerie feeling, especially knowing that under normal conditions, this would be a very bustling metropolis.

I work my way back to the hotel and tired of surfing the T.V. channels, I decide to surf the Internet. There's just nobody in this city and there's nobody to speak of in this hotel, probably less than five of us. I try to get some information about getting to the border. From my little map, I thought Iquitos was the border city; it isn't. It can be anywhere from

SOUTH AMERICA
ENCHANTMENT

two to three days, to get by river to the Brazilian border. There's also a small military airplane, with passenger capabilities of eight to twelve people, and depending on the weather and the military and the mood, it flies.

This is one of the first experiences I've had in being marooned, or at least contained. There is no conceivable way of being able to get out of this area today. Without the airport available and the riverboats not moving, I can only say "Thank God for Visa!" As long as my credit is available and I can continue signing my name to my bills, I have a beautiful room and an abundant amount of food and T.V. and air-conditioning to appease me. There isn't much left to do but return to my abode and prepare myself to rest. It's always in the way you look at things. No, I wouldn't have planned this, but then in some ways this is probably God's plan to give me the rest to re-energize my body and prepare for the next part of this adventure down the 4,000 miles of the Amazon. I've been feeling in good spirits and good health. The only discomfort I'm having, which I have no explanation for, is that my left knee is still extremely painful. I'm more than grateful that I'll be going down the river rather than the Inca trail, which at this point, I would have not accomplished that feat.

With that, I would like to say goodnight to my beautiful little honey bun and thank you very much for all your wonderful e-mails. It seems I always feel so much closer and have much warmer thoughts of our long relationship in marriage when I read your e-mails in far-off places. I miss you, my beautiful wife, and my wonderful companion. And Cole, I hope that you have some good experiences and good stories and I love you both. Goodnight one and all.

Robert F. Edwards

January 30, Wednesday

Iquitos, Peru

Just about the end of the month, I've had a restful sleep, and have caught up on my notes, lying in bed, just being what my beautiful little wife calls "a sluggy bug." I have to say that, at least this opportunity has given me a chance to keep these journals up to date and maybe, just maybe, being able to put more depth into some of the events that I've experienced. Whatever, time is on my side.

I get up and go downstairs and meet David and his wife, the Canadians. We talk a little bit about everything and nothing, and exchange cards. It's rather interesting; out of most of the people I've met, other than some of the agents, nobody has any kind of business cards. Sure enough, as Canucks, organized as we are, David has a business card that has CBC printed on it.

In our discussions, I learn a little bit about him and his wife, and their enjoyment of living in the far north of Canada. This has inspired me to ask Marietta if she might wish to take that adventure into Nunavut, and see that part of the world. David tells me that, "No, there are no roads." I am getting used to that down here, as well. He tells me that we can leave by plane and snowmobile, if it's a small region, from one point to the other.

I check for e-mails and to my delight, my wonderful wife has sent me another one. It's snowing, even in Vancouver. She has managed to get out of the driveway at last, and our two dogs, Buttons and Pepper are sleeping together now. I love it! I'm glad we got a male and a female. It's a warm feeling to know that even the dogs are getting along together.

I have breakfast, and decide that I'm going to venture out and take some more pictures. There's a place called "the iron house" or *Casa de Hierro*, down in the *piazza*. I don't know how I've missed it before. This particular house was built dur-

SOUTH AMERICA
ENCHANTMENT

ing the rubber boom and the construction and design was by none other than the man that built the Eiffel Tower.

The streets seem to have a little more activity and the fires from the bundles of wood and palm trees haven't been cleaned up, but there doesn't seem to be any fresh ones and nowhere near the amount of smoke in the air. I guess, people got tired of being out all night or maybe the beer ran out, who knows? But there seems to be a feeling of calm and less tension in the air today.

I find the building and no wonder I missed it! It could have been the tin man's house in the Wizard of Oz. It's anything but attractive, so I didn't take a picture of it. It's got a red roof and looks like tin sheeting throughout, not very attractive, I'm sorry to say. As I walk around, there's still a strong police presence, but more people are venturing out and I've noticed the odd person with a motorcycle taxi.

I start to walk along the river stonewall. This city, I really like it. It's most unfortunate that I've come here under these conditions, because I think it would be a very vibrant city. It has a flavor of what you'd experience in Louisiana and the Creole-type of one-storey buildings. The whole city seems to be built on riverbanks, which have tremendous fluctuation in seasons due to the water level. The river rises three to four meters, so the buildings are two-storey at the best, and certainly no high-rises, modern or otherwise. During the rubber boom, a lot of different nationalities came running in and built their mansions in the style of their culture. So, it's a very interesting city, with a strong colonial appeal to it. I hope some of the pictures that I've taken will do it justice.

As I walk along the cement wall that protects the city from the rising river, I take some pictures of the floating homes just scattered throughout. It seems rather a unique way of living, these boathouses. I'm seeing one fellow fishing right off the raft that secured his home. With all due respect, you wouldn't describe them as what some people in North America would think as a floating home. It's more like Huckleberry Finn's extension of his raft, with a shack on top. To me it's quite

177

Robert F. Edwards

unique, but by global standards, it's a shack with a thatched roof. Also, the little wooden boats that commute back and forth to these floating homes are nothing more than planks that are put together with tar and caulking that makes them waterproof. In this shantytown of Iquitos, yes, these are the poor people, there's just no two ways about it.

When I'm walking along the promenade, a young Peruvian gentleman wishes me good day. This, incidentally, is very common. These people are exceptionally friendly and pleasant to each other. So, I acknowledge him and he speaks English quite well. We talk for a few minutes, his name is George, and he works as a guide. In Vancouver, these 'guides' would be considered unemployed, but know the city exceptionally well and rather than begging, they provide their services of seeing the city and they describe the unique parts to tourists in hoping that they would receive some form of remuneration.

We haven't gone very far and he tells me about seeing some *iguanas* and I go back and take a few pictures with him. From him, I learn about the church that I've taken pictures of, the Church of St. Augustine, which is also a seminary for young men studying for the priesthood. As we go then in the opposite direction towards the floating city, he tells me about the different historical buildings along the way that were made by Italians or Germans. Most of these now are occupied by the military. He expresses (and I agree with him,) that these historical buildings should be converted to museums rather than to military operations.

The more I walk in this city, the more I realize it's very easy to get around it. It's pretty well the grid system, streets in straight lines being intercepted by other straight lines. This city seems quite modern compared to the confusing large circles, and small passages of other cities, including Cuzco.

It doesn't take us very long to get into the market part of the city. Unlike so many places in the world, a block or two here makes a vast difference between a high standard of residential living to a very poor community. On a normal day, the market place would be a bustling metropolis of trade and commerce, with everything from produce, fresh meats and fish, to consumer goods. I watched an old man pedal his sewing machine, as anywhere else in the world that doesn't have a continued source of electricity, and here the cobbler repaired a pair of shoes.

We get further into the market, which is not complying the complete shut down and solidarity that persists in the rest of the city. I stop by a corridor in this market place renowned for selling remedies for what ails you, similar to the one in La Paz. This is where shamans and medicine men and women made their own concoctions, and would fix up a potion promising that you'd recover. Probably not so far from the truth, as throughout the Amazon, research scientists are now asking natives to show them some of the plants that they use in their medicines.

At one of the booths, a small Peruvian woman with a warm smile describes to George what the different remedies were and is only too eager for me to sample one of them. "This one gives you a lot of energy," and from a bottle the size of a 26 oz. bottle of whiskey, unscrews the top, pours the potion into the cap, hands it to me. Over the lips, down the throat, there it goes. It does give me a nice warm glow. I don't know whether I'm energized, but it doesn't taste bad for a tonic.

Now that she feels she has got a fairly interested audience, she starts showing me some more of her wares. After I've had my shot for the day, she takes another bottle off the shelf, and goes into a long description. George translates for me, and I understand that the general concept is this is for mosquito bites because I pointed out that I've managed to accumulate  or have been inoculated by some of the mosquitoes. This will do it. He says, "All you've got to do is drink this stuff down and it's the best repellant in the world." And believe me; I would have bought a bottle of this for the trip if I'd just had a choice of quantities. This one is in a huge 26-ounce bottle. I am offered another sample. This one doesn't have a flavor that you'd want as a sipping drink. However, she said it's good for three to five days. I'm sure once your body had this smell on it, most mosquitoes and probably your friends, wouldn't want to cuddle up to you, let alone bite you. I can't help but like this woman and I sincerely would have bought a bottle if it had just been smaller. I'm not saying I would have drunk it, but I would have bought it. With that, I ask if I could take a picture, and just the difference – these people just love to have their pictures taken. So, she and I have are beside the counter with all these magical potions and George becomes the photographer.

While I have the camera out, I've taken a picture of the many huge bundles of bananas that are present and accounted for. There's an abundance of bananas in the market, and this is a basic food here. They don't have any Chiquita stamps on them, believe me, and they're not uniform in perfection, but they really are tasty bananas.

We continue our adventure down these muddy lanes. He's showing me where the water comes up and I ask him, "Well, you know, they've got little shops here now. What happens when the water rises? He says, "Oh, they use them to store their boats." This makes sense. They just convert the roads into canals and Mother Nature provides the motivation to row your boat ashore. It's a poor area in Iquitos. Like so many underprivileged places that I have been in, these people are very industrious and creative, "true survivors," and their adaptability will guarantee their survival. There is just a real lack of money, as well as incentive to try and improve. I didn't ask George, but I probably could assure myself that most of these people are illiterate and locked in to this lifestyle.

We make our way down the long pathway leading to the floating city of Belén. I doubt very much that if I had a vehicle, even a four by four, I could get it down this particular trail. We walk on planks that are maybe one meter wide towards this floating city, and George tells me that next month, they're actually going to have their first election and will be appointing a mayor. Up until now, these people have had no representation, but they don't have to pay any taxes either, when they live on the rivers.

George asked me if I would like to take a boat trip on the river for a half an hour and go up and down and see some of the floating homes. Without any hesitation, I quickly respond by saying, "Yes" and then the pertinent question, how much? It is only five *nuevos soles*. The three of us start working our way down the river, and I notice on the other side of the river, there's a church. During the season of high waters, they'd tie these boats in a row and the children would walk across them to the church and into the school. The river rises three to four meters, judging from the stairwells on this particular church and school. Of course the homes that are not on stilts, but are actually on the river, just float up and down to the river's height.

As we sail past the floating homes, I couldn't help but say to George, "These people are happy", and they are. They are poor and let there be no mistake, but they're only poor in ma-

terial things. In all other things, they're rich beyond the North

SOUTH AMERICA
ENCHANTMENT

American dream and probably a lot of Europeans. These people have an attitude and quality that Ministers and the Pope try to express to the parishioners. They're washing their clothes with soap in the river. They're clean people and it brings to mind something my mother said when I was growing up, "You can be poor but you don't have to be dirty" and these people are not dirty, they're just poor. The homes are made out of wood slats and thatched roofs and from what I can see, the inside is very sparsely furnished.

But they have something about them that I love. We're coming into an area where some people are washing their dog and I smile and wave. Of course, they wave back and they want me to take a picture. They make you feel at home. Their home is much warmer than a lot of castles. I am thoroughly enjoying this riverboat ride. I only wish in my heart of hearts that I was an artist. I would love to paint these remarkable sights that I'm seeing on the river.

We pull up alongside a boat and the gentleman has just managed to catch more than his share of the food chain today. There's about six or seven different types of fish, and George points out some of them are bottom feeders with tentacles. I actually get to see my first piranha of the Amazon. Not that big, but it has just as ugly a mouth as the ones that I've seen in aquariums.

We return to shore and George asks me if I would like to go over to see his girlfriend, who lives in the neighborhood. I said "Sure, fine." George tells me that often when he's taken other people down here in a group, in many cases they say, "Oh George I can't go any further, the smell, the dirt!" He questions me, "How do you feel about it?" and I said, "I just think I'm in a beautiful place, with some beautiful people." I'm not naive enough to say that this isn't poor and that I don't recognize the poverty, but the quality of people are beyond any description I can give. Again, he asks, "It doesn't bother you?" and I said, "I'm not saying it doesn't. No, it doesn't bother me walking through here or being a part of it.

Robert F. Edwards

It bothers me that these people aren't able to share a better standard of living."

We continue walking up a hillside and come to a group of

women cleaning fish, scaling them, cutting them and preparing them for market. They're doing it while the market's walking by. I can't help but enjoy their friendliness and their openness. People are curious the world over and I'm as curious as anybody you'll ever find. And when they see that I'm as curious about what they're doing as they're curious about me, there's a bonding and I ask George to take a picture of me with two women cleaning fish. This is a very rich day in my life. I'm enjoying being alive and I'm enjoying sharing my life, this moment with these enjoyable, friendly people.

With that we make our way through a maze of mud, stones, and even sandbags, to his girlfriend's house. I meet her mother. I don't know whether she's out, or whether she doesn't want to come out. They just have a cloth blanket hanging over the door, and I'm in a very small room just by the entrance, sitting on a little wooden chair.

I take a picture of one of her sewing machines, which requires only a strong foot and no electricity, mainly because I'd

SOUTH AMERICA
ENCHANTMENT

like to show Marietta that her sewing room is an upgrade

compared to this one. This woman and her mother make their living by sewing garments. While I'm there she's brought a client in, for some adjustments to a blouse she's making.

Shortly thereafter, George comes back out and the weather has turned 180 degrees, from being quite humid and hot to foreboding skies, preparing to rain. I suggest to him that we get back to the hotel before it starts really raining down and the distance is about twelve to fourteen blocks. We haven't even gone halfway before Mother Nature is giving us a downpour. There are only two seasons here: The rainy season and the dry season. I happen to be in the first season.

Back at the hotel, George is still highly motivated to the idea that we'll do something tomorrow. I'm also highly motivated that I'd like to move on. But, we'll see what tomorrow brings and with the afternoon rain, I promise myself I am going to the restaurant to have a beer. I also order spaghetti in a cream sauce, some bread and for dessert, bananas with maple syrup. I'm fully satisfied. I do a bit of e-mails and the rain says we're not going out this afternoon, so I have my afternoon *siesta*. One thing, with all the events that are taking place, this has been a good chance to rest up for the second half of this adventure.

At around 5:00 p.m., the weather has improved and I venture out on the street. There's a lot more activity going on and the police seem to be everywhere, even around this hotel area. Four blocks away, I see what looks like a gathering for maybe a protest march. So, I take my camera and start to work my way down.

On the way, I pass by a middle-aged fellow that has obviously spent the day drinking. He signals for me to join him, with his family sitting beside him on the stairs. There are more and more people gathering now, either taking part in the protest or looking on from a bystander's point of view. After I take a few pictures, I joined this happy-go-lucky drunk, and sit down to have a drink with him. I take a sip of what's he's drinking and boy! I'll tell you, I thought some of the vodka in Russia was rough, but this stuff I sure wouldn't want to have matches around it. I humor him along, but he doesn't speak English and I'm not really in the mood to be the translator.

I start heading back the other way, which now is in full swing of protest marches and quite elaborate; anything from

SOUTH AMERICA
ENCHANTMENT

flags, to some costumes, to beating of drums, and many banners are being waved, with pictures of Che Guevara who fought the revolution with Fidel Castro. There is much raising of hands, and before long, I find myself doing it, also. I don't try to get involved in things but needless to say, before long, the protestors are smiling and giving me the thumbs up. One of the protestors motions for me to join them, and I get him to take a picture of me holding one of the banners and actually carrying one of the flags, and so forth, but I hope I'm not on the 6:00 p.m. news. I might not be allowed to leave Peru as being one of the agitators of a protest.

All is going well and I noticed that even though the police have their plastic shields and riot gear out, they are being very passive. I imagine, as long as there is an orderly type of action and no real violence, "Ah, let them blow off steam and they'll get up tomorrow with a headache." I think this is probably a very good attitude. The police presence is more than accounted for, it's very visible, but it's non-aggressive. If I were naïve about the circumstances, I would probably think it was some kind of parade. When things start to heat up a bit, and there are a few more men that have been drinking, I think that it's time for me to say, "I've had a great experience and a great moment and I'm glad I've shared it with you, but I'm going back."

When I return to the hotel, the other Canadian contingent has just arrived. They spent the day seeing the floating village and also a butterfly farm owned and operated by an Austrian lady in her mid-forties. I enjoyed some conversation with them, and then had dinner, which were rice and a nice river fish.

I asked the hotel manager if he's had any more updates about boats, planes, or anything moving to the border. He says, "No, but the planes only fly on Wednesday and Saturday", so that eliminates leaving tomorrow by plane. The boats won't do anything tomorrow, just the torpedo boat, which takes ten hours. It leaves at something like 6:00 a.m. in the morning. But tomorrow, at 9:00 a.m., hopefully this adventurer can continue his trip to the border and beyond.

I watch a little bit of television and for some unknown reason; CNN is now off the air. There is not much else to do, but say goodnight, sleep tight, and I sure hope no bed bugs bite.

I love you dearly, Marietta, and I really cherish our e-mails, and especially the ones that you're sending me and making me feel very important in your life. I love you dearly. And Wendy, I hope you're having a very good holiday and you and Cole are enjoying every moment of it. Goodnight, one and all.

SOUTH AMERICA
ENCHANTMENT

January 31, Thursday

Iquitos, Peru

It is the last day of the month. I've slept well through the night and I've now developed a habit of going to bed early and rising with the sun. Today is no exception. I'm quite wide-eyed and bushy-tailed at quarter-to-five in the morning. Today I really hope to accomplish some direction on my adventure down the Amazon. As I watch CNN and some of the other channels, I try to prolong my stay in bed, but to no avail.

I'm wide-awake, so I prepare myself for the day ahead, as well as getting my gear ready. I have no idea, at this point, whether it's going to be another day or even, God forbid, and another week before I resume my quest. However, by 7:00 a.m., I go down and have a modest breakfast of buns and coffee. The staff at the desk knows me very well by now. The young man told me repeatedly, both last night and again today, that he really can't find out anything about the military airplanes, until at least 9:00 a.m. We don't even know if the airport's open.

However, the streets have resumed the hustle and bustle of everyday life and the continual humming of motorcycle taxis and other modes of transportation fill the air with a new sound. It's comforting to know that the city has returned to normal. I can't help but smile when I see all these motorcycle taxis line up at the intersections. When the light changes, they rev their motors and proceed down the road. Every time this happens, I can't help but think "Start your motors, get ready, get set, and go!"

Most of them have canopies, and when the rain comes they bring up this plastic shield, so the drivers have maybe two or three inches to look out as they're wheeling these taxis up and down the streets. There are very few automobiles and what do persist are mostly small pick-up trucks, but no heavy transportation. The odd bus is how people commute to their jobs, but no heavy motor transports because there are no roads directly to and from Iquitos. The big coach buses that are so prevalent throughout the rest of South America don't exist here.

I walk the streets in every direction, and continue to explore the possibilities of a travel agent to give me the information that I'm really hoping for, which is a seat on a boat or plane. I realize that I have to achieve a ticket before I can be guaranteed passage. It isn't just showing up on stand-by. Though the people are friendly, the travel agents are null and void of even a *pequeño* amount of English. Neither discouraged nor distraught by it, but somewhat disappointed, I continue my quest of seeking out information and also looking for something that might be very unique to this area. I've been told more than once that most of the products and the garments come from Lima. Other than bananas and papayas, there is very little that's homegrown here.

I walk until about nine o'clock and come back to see if my faithful attendant has had any success with the airlines. He informs me that "no, the line is consistently busy" and I have no doubt in my mind this person is trying vigorously to break through the system and that the line is completely congested.

I check the Internet and to my pleasant surprise, my good wife has sent me an e-mail bringing me up to date on what's happening in Vancouver. There's snow on the ground, the dogs are okay, but she has a migraine. I just hope that everything will go well for the next month until I return. I also get a very rewarding e-mail from my fencing master, Roy Suzuki, telling me that they not only miss my fencing, but they miss my discussions.

Once again, I venture out. It's a nice day and I've found that in the short time that I'd been a resident of Iquitos, "to make hay when the sun shines, Nelly." I walk back down into the promenade area, and probably the only thing that I really don't like here are the turkey vultures. This particular scavenger bird is I have to say, offensive to my eye. These black birds with their long red necks meet all the criteria of a vulture, though the residents have assured me that they're good eating and I'm sure that I would far rather eat them than have them eat me. I would sooner not see them in my presence.

Other than that, the day is pleasant and the people are in full recovery of trade and commerce. The stores are open and there's a real hustle and bustle amidst the streets. Even the tires and debris that were being burned in protest are quickly being cleaned up and replaced by the insatiable amount of

motorcycle taxis with their humming sound of bees revving up their wings. Believe me, the *turista* is probably the last person that actually travels any great distance with these. It's the locals that use them consistently. Traveling on them is anywhere from one to five *nuevos soles*, depending on where you're going.

Once more I'm on my way back to the hotel, only to find out that the morning showers are starting to make their presence felt. I'm only a few doors away from the hotel and by now, the rain is changed from a drizzle into a downpour and I happen to notice a travel agent's office. I pop in and ask if anybody speaks English. A young man called Victor said that he could speak a little bit of it. And with that, I start asking him question about Santa Rosa and the border between Brazil and Peru. He is well aware of the situation but he doesn't know where you're able to purchase a ticket for the boat. I keep running into this enigma; everybody knows what has to be done, but nobody seems to know where it can be achieved.

At that moment, Clever, the first agent that I met at the airport, comes in. He doesn't look that well and he told me that he'd been feeling stuffed up, and said he'd spent most of his time in the last few days in bed. As luck would have it, he knew where the boat agency was and he said when the rain let up, that he would escort me there. I also tell him that I would give him some penicillin for his bad cold, headache and fever.

I quickly ran back to the hotel, secured my documents and money. It is going to cost me $50.00 to get to the border on a high-speed boat. Without too much further ado, I return. The rain has subsided to a heavy drizzle. Clever signals a taxi and we head down to the designated area where these tickets could be purchased. The first place I go to, which has facilities for the better boat, doesn't have one for Friday but could have it for Saturday. I ask if there's any other available, she says that there's another one down the street, and Clever tells me that it's nowhere near as good, smaller and so forth.

However, it's only ten or twelve hours on the water and I'm anxious, to say the least, to get this part of the adventure back on track. It's not that I don't like Iquitos; it's just that I'll feel much more in control and not so isolated in a remote part of the world, once I get to Manaus. At the next place, yes, they do have accommodations and I fill out the forms and purchase the ticket. Clever asked all the questions, and is a good interpreter of what's requested.

That completed, he assures me that this taxi driver, for five *Soles*, will show up at no later than 5:30 tomorrow morning, because departure time on this particular boat is at 6:00 a.m. I ask if the taxi driver would be good enough to take me down to the boat earlier, to make sure that I'm on the right boat.

SOUTH AMERICA
ENCHANTMENT

He interprets my needs, and before I leave, the young man has written down my name, the hotel, my room, and the time.

I'm always a little apprehensive, but I can assure myself that these people seem to have a good response to following through with their commitments. I feel that by giving myself sufficient time, that if all else fails, I could get another cab driver with the help of the attendants at the hotel, and get down to the designated port of departure.

With that out of the way, I give four days' supply of penicillin and some instructions on what to do, also to put some Vicks on his chest and in his nose. He's got a lot of congestion and sinus problems. We part company and I feel quite elated to having this major decision behind me.

I returned to the hotel and put my documents away. For the first time, I opened up my hammock that I've brought with me to see the fundamentals of how it's assembled and figure out how I'm supposed to secure it. I have to admit that I was impressed when I bought it. I'm equally as impressed on how to use it. And though I'm not holding bated-breath on using this, I'm very grateful that I brought it, compared to some of the hammocks that I've seen hanging in the ferries. Those hammocks are the conventional type with knotted ropes that you would find in backyards.

The one that I have is quite unique in the sense that instead of getting in from the top; you get in from the bottom. There's a Velcro strip that fits on the bottom so once you secured yourself inside the hammock, you can seal it up. The top has high density netting for mosquitoes and any other little insect that wishes to visit you during the night. I'm sure, if money were no object in this part of the world, this style hammock would fast replace anything that was available at this point. You have got to give us Canucks full points. This creation has been made on Gabriola Island, British Columbia. It also has another great feature, a tarp that will protect you against any amount of rain while you're hanging there in this cocoon. I have to commend the ingenuity of this creative person.

Robert F. Edwards

Now that the rain has subsided, my adventurous nature takes hold once more. I felt it would be prudent to make my way back down in the general direction of the boat disembarkment just to make sure that if the taxi driver that's been designated doesn't show up, that I know that the other taxi driver is going in the right direction. I walked the better part of nine blocks and knew that I've got part of it right but wasn't quite sure of all the directions.

I've also gone past the square in which the *Casa de Hierro* is situated. Unfortunately, when you get up at some ungodly hour, by eleven o'clock lunch seems to be appropriate. I manage to hang off until the bewitching hour of high noon, and go upstairs on the terrace to have a beer and *papa fritas*. I'm thoroughly enjoying these and savoring them as the activities and traffic below provide the entertainment.

Now that I'm sitting inside the Iron House, I thought that the Eiffel Tower looked like a Mecano set. This engineer, Eiffel, whom by trade was a bridge builder, loved steel. This thing is bolted together with steel panels, and is anything but attractive. Even in the glory days of the rubber explosion, it must have been an oddity, certainly unique to the area. The panels could easily be fitted on to tanks for armor protection. I chuckle and yes, it's known throughout the world as the Iron House; to me, it will always be the Tin Man's house of the "Wizard of Oz".

I'm just about ready to depart, when I ask the gentleman at the bar if he speaks English and lo and behold! He's from Birmingham, England. His name is Michael, but he goes by Mick, his friend with him is Phil and the other fellow is Papa Dan. I spent the better part of an hour talking to them, and could easily write a book just on these three unique characters. These adventurous individuals have left their homeland to seek a sanctuary, and have found a common denominator of enjoyment.

Mick was an insurance salesman in Birmingham, and a hundred-thousand pound a year man. Phil Duff had spent most of his career in the consulates of the British Empire. He served in Africa, and remote parts of the world, but now was in the British Consulate in Iquitos.

Papa Dan is a legend of his own. He is in his eighties and he was one of the few Americans that were serving in Singapore at the time of the Japanese invasion. He was captured and was in a Prisoner of War camp during the Second World War. This man has all his faculties. He's an interesting individual. I wish he had more time to talk to me, but he has just come out of a bout of malaria and is still weak.

I have a few more beers with Mick and Phil. Mick's stories are just part of the interesting people that you meet when you have an adventure like this. He knew Vancouver very well, and he was there for the Expo in 1986. He had originally visited Iquitos to do some fishing. When he returned to England, he had made up his mind that he was going to leave his wife and return to Iquitos. One evening, they were watching T.V. and he asked her if she would like a cup of tea. She said yes, she would. When he came back from the kitchen, he said, "I'm really sorry, luv, but there's no milk. And this woman always has milk with her beverage. He said, "I'll just pop out to the local store and pick some up." And three and a half years later, he said she's still waiting for the milk.

Phil has been here now for seven years and has that British Consulate air about him, but a delightful man. We exchange cards and he tells me that if for any reason I need his services, he looks after the Canadians and Australians, as well as the British as a consul.

Mick had found a niche for himself here, amongst the tourists that come for the fishing. He's very much the salesman. His first love probably was selling and his last breath will be one. Before going out fishing, the guides would always say, "You need boots, nets, fishing gear, and so forth." So, he opened up his own shop about a year ago and supplies all this equipment. Tourists have a choice of either buying or renting them and inevitably, they rent them because when they're finished with the jungle expedition, it isn't the equipment that they really will be using on the streets of the large metropolises that they live in. Obviously an entrepreneur by trade, Mick is doing well.

Mick and Phil are both in their early fifties, and were quite amazed that I've managed to see 60, and they said to me, "We really thought you were our age." Oh, it's very nice to hear. The hours move by very quickly and the stories that are told are numerous. One that I remember is when Papa Dan and Mick had gone out fishing one time. Papa Dan had brought his supplies, which was a cooler full of whiskey and beer, but no food. All three of these men are outpost material; drinking and smoking is the order of the day. Papa Dan was just about ready to fall asleep and Mick started singing "Oh Danny Boy" and he got through the first two verses of it when he felt a tap on his shoulder. Papa Dan turned to say, "Don't sing anymore, please." And there were tears running down his face as he said, "My mother used to sing that to me when I went to sleep at night after my father died." Mick told me that this man has experienced what few men have read about in these interment camps in the Japanese occupation and some of the things that this man has endured in his life has made him hard-boiled, and yet, this hit his heart strings. For all of us, there's always something that can bring up a memory that you can't recall without the shedding of tears.

On a brighter note, a couple of Australians sought Phil out for British Consulate advice. They're from Melbourne and we enjoy a bit of rhetoric about the meat pies and all the things that go with the steak down-under. Mick again mentions some of the nostalgia of what's available in this city for the British taste buds, like steak and kidney pie, and bangers and mash. I find that when you meet a person that is from an-other part of the world and they've been away for a long time, they still cherish memories of their fatherland. Mick and Phil are British stock. There is no two ways about it. Though they probably wouldn't spend a fortnight in England for the rest of their lives, here their memories of the enjoyment of the past still lingers on.

SOUTH AMERICA
ENCHANTMENT

Before Mick leaves, he tells me to drop by and make sure that I get some information from him on the border. He has a friend in Leticia, Colombia that will help me with my passage. Phil and I continue to talk for another half hour, about anything and everything. This has been a rewarding afternoon, this encounter with some unique men and their experiences. All of them love Iquitos and have found a little piece of paradise that they say they hope the world won't discover. Each and every one of them has said that this is one of the best-kept secrets in the world and I have to agree. Phil has probably summed it up the best when he said that because it is difficult to get here, it has eliminated much of the colonization along the way, and prevented a large portion of the unsavory people from making this place their home.

I return to the hotel in more than high spirits and enjoy a little *siesta*. I have a bit of difficulty relaxing when I noticed an extra guest sharing my room. Up on the ceiling was a very large spider, I don't think it was a tarantula, but wasn't too eager to find out. Feeling unnerved with this visitor above me, on the ceiling, I decided that my fencing career should be re-activated and took my walking stick from the Inca trail. Unfortunately, I'm much better with the saber than I am with the walking stick when it comes to making my point. Somehow, this spider now is on the floor and I guess I'll just be careful that when I get up I don't walk on him, or he crawls on me. Anyway, just to share "that not everything is peaches and cream in this world".

A bit later, I go down to settle up my bill with the hotel that I'm staying at, the Victoria Regal. I highly recommend this place and their staff, which through these words I hope have expressed my gratitude and appreciation. I was saying my goodbyes, and the desk clerk that had been so helpful to me with flight arrangements remarked that he had seen me take part in the street demonstrations on the previous night. I don't know what I do so differently, but I'm not one of the silent minorities. I'm spotted in a crowd and people seem to remember what I was doing and where I was. I can assure my wife and anybody else, maybe the world sleeps, but they don't let anything go by that I'm doing without being recorded or made public. I was quite amazed, because I only stepped into the parade maybe once or twice, three times at the maximum, but this young man witnessed my participation in the protest. I hope it is not on the 6:00 p.m. news.

Now that I am leaving, I'm hoping to spot Mick and get some information about his friend in the border town of Colombia and send one more e-mail off to my beloved wife before I depart to Brazil. I find Mick in his shop, called Mad Mick's Trading Post filled with a collage of items, from rubber boots, to fishing lures for this particular area. We have a bit of a reunion and he apologizes for being somewhat distracted. He points to the big puddles of water near where we were standing. He tells me, "It has already started." It's the *fiesta* or carnival time in February. A common practice amongst the people here, young and old is to fill up water bombs and drop them on people. As I'm talking to Mick, I watch a motorcycle taxi go by and by a fraction of an inch, a water bomb splashes below missing it.

I've noticed this with children throwing water when I was in the Belen Market the other day. I just thought that they were being naughty, but I guess this is a tradition, which starts during the carnival period. In South America, carnivals are a much bigger event than Christmas, and they last a lot longer than our few days followed by the New Year. Carnival means celebration, or feast of the flesh and this is done quite a few weeks in advance of Lent and then is followed by Easter. Most of these places are of Roman Catholic faith. I guess the idea is to stock up on all the bad things you do, before you have to serve penance during Lent.

Mick gives me Ivan's brochure and some information on the area I'm heading into. This is a tri-border location of three cities; Peru's is Santa Rosa, Brazil's is Tabatinga, and Colombia's is Leticia. These three towns all congregate in a central region in the jungle. I'm given to understand that you can pretty well go from one village or city to the other in these

SOUTH AMERICA
ENCHANTMENT

three countries; but when you're ready to leave, you better have your documents properly prepared and it's no different than any other border. It has its requirements and you have to comply.

Also, I ask Mick, "What about a place to eat?" I really believed the other night that I hadn't gone to the right place that the Lonely Planet had suggested. After talking to Mick, I realized yes, I was in the right place and yes it was as expensive as I thought it would be. Of course, with Mick still having the British desires, he recommends the place right beside it, which has 'bangers and mash'. Not quite what I came all the way to the Amazon basin to have, British sausages and mashed potatoes. Anyway, I politely thank him very much for all he's done, and set off on my merry way.

I take a stroll, for a last look "down memory lane", and really do enjoy Iquitos, and the people. What a difference a day makes! This city is very active tonight and it has well over three hundred thousand people. I would say not everybody's out, but there's a lot of activity going on. The one thing that seems to be substantially absent is tourists. I'm sure they're around somewhere, but they're not very visible. Of the foreign visitors staying at the hotel, there were three or four women and I'm sure they're from somewhere in South America.

As I walk the streets, it's a nice night, but this *is* the rainy season. You can have the rain coming down in a torrential downpour, lasting anywhere from ten minutes to half an hour, depending on the amount of rain that wishes to depart from the skies. Right now, ten minutes is about all that it feels that it can contribute to the ground and I continue walking through Iquitos.

It's about 7:30, 8:00 p.m. I'm actually looking for a restaurant that has more people in it than just the waiters and me. As I walk along the promenade or the stonewall I decide that I'm going to sit and just rest for a few minutes. A woman in her early forties approaches me. She is selling cigarettes and chewing gum from a little wooden box that she carries, and asks me if I want anything, and I said no. So, she sits down

199

on the bench beside me and starts to talk in Spanish, of course, and I'm talking in English. But, we were getting along pretty darn good. She's interrupted periodically by people buying just one cigarette from her and she tells me that she has three children. They're all boys and I guess the oldest one is a teenager and the youngest one is about six.

We're making some small talk when some teenage boys come over to ask me if I want my shoes polished and I said, "No, thanks." I've never been much for crowds and especially when they're hovering around me. Before long, there's about four or five of these boys and one of them asks, "You're Canadian?" And I said, "Yes". Another one is trying to sell me some thongs, and makes not a threatening gesture, but an unpleasant one. He wants me to buy the thongs or he'll slit my throat, that's the interpretation that I've got. I've heard and read that sometimes you can get set up, with young people wanting to rob you. I've just had too many great memories of Iquitos and of this journey, to allow six or seven young people to ruin my memories. With that, I say goodbye to the lady and that's the end of the incident. Maybe my imagination is beyond any real comprehension or maybe I've just avoided a situation I didn't want to get involved in.

I start to check out some more restaurants. Even by 8:00 p.m., there is still nobody in the restaurants. I don't know how these people make a livelihood out of the situation here. By now I have decided to just go back to the first restaurant that I went to, with the Hungarian waiter, and have a good meal. I'm not overly hungry right now, but tomorrow I'm going to be on the water all day and should have something more than a beer and *papa fritas* in my stomach.

I find the restaurant and the Hungarian is off for the night, but an equally as nice Peruvian serves me. I have fish soup with garlic, and the main course is another local fish, pan-fried, with rice, and a beer. The soup is delicious, a clear broth, but believe me, I love my garlic and I could ward off a gang of vampires with this. With the fish, it's adequate, a pleasant white meat, and again this is the second fish I've had

SOUTH AMERICA
ENCHANTMENT

from these waters with no bones. I don't have to eat the fish like I was dissecting it strand by strand. I don't know whether these people know how to filet a fish with a skill unbeknownst to the rest of the world, or whether they're a much larger fish than the ones I've seen being caught. The only thing that doesn't really appeal to me is the way that they've prepared it, and it's fairly oily and the seasoning does not (of course after eating that much garlic) have any salt.

I finish the meal and return to the hotel, only to find the manager still present and accounted for. We talk for the better part of three-quarters of an hour about some of the places he took his wife to on their honeymoon; Niagara Falls, New York, Buffalo, and Florida. We talk about anything, from some of the Peruvian lifestyles, the past Inca, right up to North American Indians. He is a very nice man and really somebody that I've enjoyed talking to.

I get up to my room and make my final preparations for the early morning tomorrow and make sure everything is packed in its proper areas and only have to make slight modifications after I've prepared myself for the day ahead. I watch a little bit of CNN and nothing particularly newsy on that. I'm not

Robert F. Edwards

extremely tired, but 4:30 tomorrow morning is going to come early enough and over and above that, there's a fair amount riding on this. I've got to hope that the young taxi driver will show up and that I can get on the right boat, of course, and let the adventure continue.

My little honey bun, I really hope that all's going well with you and I miss you very much and I worry a lot about you, especially when I'm in places that few North Americans know where they are, and even fewer have ever been here. You seem to have such trials and tribulations at home and I just hope that your migraine is gone. I love you very much and I hope you're gonna be better tomorrow morning. Wendy, I guess this is the last day of your holiday, so you and Mr. Coleman shall return to the snows of Vancouver. And with that, I would like to wish each and everyone a very good night.

SOUTH AMERICA ENCHANTMENT

February 1, Friday

Iquitos, Peru

Everybody has had "one of those days", and it means that you were not in-synch with the world, or the world didn't want to help you make it through the day. Well, I would just like to assure each and every one of you, "No, this is not one of those days. This is one of the greatest days I could possibly have."

Once I depart Iquitos, it's like the point of no return. I'm going to have to keep going forward until I get to Manaus. My documents have to be in perfect order or the Customs and Immigration on the Peruvian side will send me back to Iquitos to have them properly verified and put in order. Over and above that, once I've cleared Customs in Peru, I have to meet all the requirements with the Brazilian side and I have to clear customs in Tabatinga. The border town in Colombia is Leticia, and the Peruvian is Santa Rosa.

As soon as I've got passage on a boat going to Manaus, I have to again clear Customs at Benjamin Constant in Brazil. These are quite strictly observed in this region. One of the things the Brazilians are adamant about is to have your yellow fever shot which I should have no problem with. I feel confident that all my papers are in order. However, I've had some unpleasant surprises at borders in the past, and being in this remote area of the world, I'm going to have a bit of concern until I am through.

I've managed to secure passage on a speedboat. Normally this trip takes from Iquitos to these borders anywhere from two to three days and longer if you're going against the river. This boat is only supposed to be about ten, twelve hours. So, I've picked up a day. However, when I arrive at the border towns, the passenger-vessels/cargo-ships making their way down to Manaus in Brazil, can be anywhere from two to four days waiting for passage. This is providing that there are sufficient facilities and that the captain will take you.

Robert F. Edwards

Adding to these two anxieties, there's the fact that the better part of this world speaks the regional language, which is often a dialect of Indian, and the second language is Spanish. Once I cross over the border into Brazil, it not only becomes a different country but it becomes Portuguese and I need to have a dictionary in Portuguese, and it is one language that really escapes my understanding. In Spanish, even last year, I was able to grope with some of the words and requests, but with Portuguese I don't have the same advantage. It's going to be hard to make sure that the captains of these boats realize that I have to clear the Customs in the different countries and that I have to have my documents in order, plus I have to get a boat. Some questions yet to be answered.

Anyway, the morning starts early for me and I can say to one and all, it was a very restless night. In so many cases, when I'm getting up exceptionally early and there's a lot at stake, I have a very restless night and this was one of them. So, along with an early morning, I could probably say a sleepless night, I'm prepared and in full form by 4:30 a.m. and make my way down the dark corridor with my huge backpack and the other little one that's gaining the weight of stones as each day passes by.

To my surprise, the shower is lukewarm this morning, instead of a real hot one. I'm a bit superstitious that this is not going to be the greatest day, and little do I know what is yet to transpire. The lobby is in total darkness and I wake up the attendant that's on duty, stretched out on two chairs. We make a bit of small talk and it seems like eternity is ticking reluctantly forward, but finally at quarter after five, true to his word, the taxi driver shows up in his mighty Honda taxi. We put the gear in the taxi and he heads me down to the boat.

This is the beginning of a great day, believe me. This young man obviously knows what boat I'm going on. He also knows that he is to help me take my gear down to the boat and make sure I get on the right boat. So, off on the right foot for a remarkable dance ahead. We get there considerably early, more like 5:30 a.m. instead of quarter to six. The boat is supposed

SOUTH AMERICA
ENCHANTMENT

to depart at 6:00 a.m. There's a lot of congestion around this harbor and of course, there's a lot of looming hands that will take your luggage, maybe forever, but more likely just to carry it down for a nominal fee. However, the taxi driver and I manage to lift my unbelievable amount of weight to the boat. I was told also that for anything over fifteen kilos, I was to pay about two *Soles* each. It doesn't seem to be a concern. My only worry is that my huge backpack doesn't crush the ceiling as they're putting the cargo and baggage up on the roof.

It's a very small boat and even in the dark, it looks like I'm going to be on the waterline for the next ten to twelve hours. However, I get a seat behind the captain, and sit quite patiently as other people get on board, and the cargo loaded. Everything's going, including the bottom end of an outboard motor. We wait until they have loaded these huge plastic containers, there's got to be at least a hundred liters or more.

There's a lot of hustle-bustle and activity going on, but yes I'm on the right boat. There's another boat behind us, a huge ferryboat with the hammocks slung across them. This type of boat, I imagine, is the one that's going to take two to three

Robert F. Edwards

days trip that I'm going to try to accomplish in ten to twelve hours. However, let's see what transpires.

When I look at the river, I'm thinking it would have been an interesting experience if I'd chosen the latter and taken the two days trip down the river. Choices have been made, decisions have been done, and I am now just waiting to be cast off. This boat has a metal hull and one very large Johnson outboard motor on it.

Sure enough, about quarter after six, we cast off. There's an expression that motorists say, "putting the pedal to the metal." Well, we haven't even left the harbor and this boat is ready for take off. Believe me, they're just putting it right to the box and we start speeding down the river. It's starting to show daylight and it looks like it's going to be a nice day. Surprisingly enough, not a rough ride. The river has got a bit of current to it, but it's not a fast moving river, probably due to the exceptional width. As daylight takes its full command, the boat continues at top speed. We're just zooming along the water, almost close to a hydroplane.

The first hour is fairly uneventful. To my delight, we are going close to the shoreline, and I am able to take the odd picture of these unique little settlements, with the houses constructed of boarded planks for walls and thatched roofs. Just what you'd expect Jungle Jim to come upon in a clearing, along the thick lush shorelines. The vegetation is very thick, all tropical trees and ferns that I am not familiar with.

The waters of this great river are the *only* way of transportation in and out of this area. We have gone a couple of hours before we stop. There is a siren on this boat to announce its presence as it comes in to dock. There is a priest traveling with us, and spends some time giving the villagers the spiritual guidance that they are seeking. He speaks a small amount of English, and I would think he's about my age.

We also seem to be the mail carrier as well. We stop at little hamlets along the way, dropping off mail and supplies, and one of these huge containers of fuel. It's interesting to watch trade and commerce take place in this small outpost. Other than using the modern high-speed motors, I'm sure it's not much different than when the first boats supplied these people with the necessities that they request. How these people make a living out here to secure money is beyond my limited imagination. With only fishing, and eating the fruits and wild life in this area, it's a paradise all of its own.

As we continue down the waterway, to my pleasure, I'm served a hot dog bun with a piece of cheese and a bit of meat in it. It's fresh and most welcome, along with a cup of coffee that has milk and sugar in it. By now, it's almost 8:30. I've spotted some of the boats that are used in this region, the wooden dugout boat that I have only seen before in "National Geographic." Some are quite large and they now use outboard motors. The leg of the motor with the propeller, I'm not exaggerating, it's got to be at least a meter and a half, maybe two meters long. I'm sure there is a rationale for everything and I just don't understand it. Earlier in the day, the motor leg was tilted so the small steel propellers were just hitting the water. It might be that when they get into deeper waters that they lower the leg. I have no idea, but this is very different than any outboard motor that I have seen in other parts of the world.

Robert F. Edwards

Some of these dugouts are only large enough for two people and the catch of fish. It's still the old biblical nets casting upon the water to get their rewards. That method was successful thousands of years ago, and is still successful today.

There is a lot of debris on this river; dead-heads, flotsam and jetsam, lily pods, and I have no idea of how deep the water is or where the sand banks are. Mind you, I'm not at the helm either. We keep motoring along and we hit a log. It is full speed ahead even after we hit this dead-head. It's interesting to hear people chatter back and forth when you have no way of knowing what they're saying, but I still understand instructions from the command bridge to second in control, full speed ahead.

Our next stop is at a military base, where they dropped off the other two large containers of fuel. After some conversation, the assistant gets undressed to check the bottom of the boat and the propeller shaft. At first, I thought that some of the steering mechanism had been dislodged; but no, it's still intact and after a lot of conversation and crescent wrenches being produced, we're back on our way.

Around noon, our next port of call is a police station/customs point. They have to check that I'm actually a Canadian, and have a current passport, but no real setbacks or anything else. The good priest gets off at this point. It's about a five minute, ten-minute stopover. I feel quite comfortable taking pictures and I watch people having their early meal in a small café. There's another little outlet that has all their clothes laid out, open-air shopping at its best. It's very peaceful here. I don't think there's an expression that goes further than 'being laid back', but if there is, this people certainly know it. If high blood pressure is present in this community, it's strictly because of the heat and the humidity, not by pressure.

While I am having my documents checked, one of the policeman has a nice smile to him and I ask him if he'd let me take a picture of us together. I probably have more pictures taken of me with police on this expedition than I have in my entire life, but I can't stress enough the different attitude. I have not had the same kind of experience with police since my years in England with the British bobby, who gave the impression that they were a public service rather than a police state. These men are downright friendly. They're anything but intimidating. Not to be misconstrued, they do their job to the maximum of the law, but still have a nice attitude about doing it.

Back on the boat and we haven't gone too far, when the siren blows again. There's a woman waiting on the edge of the bayou and we stop for an exchange of goods that she has ordered. She gives the captain of this vessel a couple of bags, fruit, I guess, as payment; a much easier lifestyle than Wall Street. And with that, we're on our way. The assistant takes the helm and the captain takes one of these fruits, just bangs it, whacks the living daylights out of it, and cracks it open. There is a white pulpy substance inside with seeds. The seeds are large, about the size of a thumbnail. I tried it. The pulp is very sweet, and the seeds are almost like an almond, quite crunchy.

Again, this reflects another example of the attitudes of these people. When they have something, they share it. The captain breaks open three or four of them and passes them down; everybody is enjoying this very nice fruit. No sooner is that done and the woman behind me passes me another fruit, all peeled in its pleasant form. It is orange in color, and it's very dry. It's a nice fruit, but would be enhanced by lemon or limejuice. I'm told that's exactly what they do, when they have other citrus fruits available.

Robert F. Edwards

Before long, out comes another one. This one is about the size of a small acorn squash. However, it's again a fruit and the captain informs me that it makes you strong. Now, I'm not sure in Peru if strong has the same connotation as in Asia; but when men raise their arms in Asia, 'strong' means that you have a very strong sex drive or sex member. I didn't ask him to elaborate on what he meant, but the fruit was just as tasteful. People are laughing now, both the women and men, at the way I am devouring this stuff. I guess it's always nice to see a foreigner enjoy something that you take for granted.

I was sitting near a little boy and his Peruvian mother. She informs me that she's Peruvian, the little boy's father is Colombian, and he's about maybe three years old. A cute little fellow and we start playing a game. At first, he pokes me and the mother is very mortified that he has done this. I know he's just touching me, more or less to see what I'm going to do. Since I'm a foreigner, and I've got white hair, he probably hasn't seen anybody quite like me. With that, I play a game with him with my fingers and he's laughing, another one of those great moments of enjoyment that I have received on these adventures.

I know my good wife has always mentioned to people she doesn't know how I do it. I don't speak any other language but English, but here's a little boy that I'm having a lot of fun and he's having equally as much fun with me, and his mother is just delighted. In addition to this woman and her son, there's also a Colombian woman and her daughter (about eleven years old), and some men from Peru and the captain. All of a sudden, people are talking to me, talking to each other, and it is party time. I am so grateful that these people accept me and I think one of the most wonderful experiences that I have on these adventures is because of the people. They want to help me whenever it's possible. They go to the four corners of their imagination to try to communicate with me and to understand what I need, what I want, what I'm hoping to do, but above all they just want to share my life and

SOUTH AMERICA
ENCHANTMENT

be a part of it. I've always said to people that I'm a very rich
man and it is because of moments like this.

These people are by far the most enjoyable people I could
possibly hope to travel with. We're very cramped, and there's
no standing up, or walking around on this boat, I'll tell you.
So, this little boy calls me 'Grandpa'. Probably the only English word he's ever heard. Anyway, I'm having a great time
and I'm taking my share of pictures. We stop to take off more
supplies and that's when I ask the Peruvian mother if I could
have a picture of her son and myself. She is more than delighted and she wants to get in the picture as well. So, Cole,
there's another young boy that calls me grandpa. You better
look after me when I get back home.

As soon as we leave, we're served a hot meal of beans, rice,
and potato, and a piece of chicken. I gave my chicken to the
Peruvian mother for the little boy because they only get the
one meal. The day just toddles along and the shoreline fluctuates, as we pass some large islands in the river. The boat
continues full steam ahead, until we get caught in a heavy
rain, which does slow it down a little bit. This is best described as two seasons here, the rainy season and the 'not'
rainy season. I'm definitely in the rainy season and I don't
really find it that offensive. Mind you, I come from a very
rainy climate myself, so keep that in mind. Generally speaking, these heavy downpours are short lived, and the sun
comes out, and it gets very hot.

What I've noticed with people who live here, so it's not just
myself, everyone perspires. More times than enough my shirt
is just soaking wet. But then, when I look at other people, the
perspiration is running down their face as well. Our afternoon shower subsides quickly and we stop again. A few people get on and, "Oh my God, the boat is packed!" The man
that's sitting beside me is close to being a giant. A nice quiet
man, but his body needs both our seats and I feel quite
squished against the side of the boat. I happen to glance over
at the Peruvian lady. Both her son and she are also cramped
up against the other side of the boat, with another Peruvian

211

Robert F. Edwards

man that could easily lose 100 pounds and still say that he was quite well fed.

Another hour passes uneventfully, before we stop and these men, thankfully get out. In the meantime, a few more men get on. The captain and the men are conversing and their rhetoric is leading to merriment. I wish I could understand some of it, because there's quite a bit of laughter.

It's about 3:30 p.m. when I see a large village up ahead. I turn to the man beside me and ask, "Santa Rosa?" And he said, "*Si.*" I am amazed that we've arrived so soon. I was hoping that we would arrive around 6:00 p.m. or at least before dark so I could find a hotel. We're making good time; though on water, it's deceiving as you can see the land a long way off.

Once we get closer to the shoreline and Santa Rosa (Peru), we can see on the opposite side Leticia and Tabatinga, which looks like a sprawling population. Santa Rosa is just a very small village. We stop on a military police barge to clear the port and none of us get off, only the captain. I guess it's for checking the bill of lading and the documents. Within ten minutes, I see him thanking the guy and taking the documents and putting them in his briefcase again. So, that part of it is done.

Then, we go to what looks like a Polynesian advertisement, these houses on stilts with open-air walls, a thatched roof and the people are just sitting around on mats. At this point, I have to get off and the lady behind me tells me that this is where they check our passports. So, I and two other people head up this long walk towards the Immigration building.

It looks exactly like everybody else's house. However, nobody's there. I have a little twinge of worry, with all my gear still on the boat and now I haven't got anyone to check in with at Immigration. As I am looking around, hoping someone will notice me, I see a woman next door. I happen to be not a nosy person, but a curious person and take a good look in. Their houses are rectangle, and this one has some kind of masonry walls on the outside, still on stilts. There is a big double bed inside, a hammock and a crib, so I guess that must be the

SOUTH AMERICA
ENCHANTMENT

bedroom I've taken a peek-see at and it looks quite comfortable. This may be one of those *residencias,* as there are no accommodations here.

Some people come in, and find the Immigration officer for us. He doesn't look much like an Official. He does have a cap and a shirt that says "Immigration" on it, and escorts the three of us into his office. One of the fellows doesn't have his documents filled out correctly. He looks at mine, and stamps the Exit Visa for me. I ask him if he speaks English at all and he just smiles at me. Again I ask, "*Pequeño?*" and he smiles again and says, "*Sí*", and I said, "Santa Rosa?" he said, "*Sí*". He stamped the passport, says "*Completo*" and "Peru?" I said, "*Sí*". So, now I have the first step of accomplishment, with clearing my documents from Peru.

Getting back on the boat, the next stop is the Brazil side, which is my destination. With no further problems, we dock. From the water level, it looks like the Inca stairs all over again, at the Isle of the Sun. Huge steps, but these are more like a retaining wall that is built for the different levels of the water as the river rises.

213

Robert F. Edwards

As soon as I get off the boat, I'm surrounded by a bunch of people yelling, "Taxi, taxi, taxi." They're not taxi drivers; they're people that will take you *to* a taxi for remuneration. There is no conceivable way that I could lift both bags up these steep steps. So, I hire a fellow to take the one bag and even by heaving it onto our shoulders, we find it staggering to lift it up. We eventually get to the top and another man that was on the boat approaches me and he asks, "You want to have a hotel?" And I said, "Yes". He said, "I'm going to a hotel. It's just up the street." I said, "Well, I'll have to take a taxi." So, we join forces with another fellow, Roger, and all agree to get a cab.

At this moment, my thoughts returned to Canada and the young man that I fence with. Sam had asked me if I was religious and I said, "I believe in God." Now, when I get back, I will be able to tell Sam that "Yes, I am religious", and "Yes, I have a great deal of love and commitment to God." I've said to people in somber moments that when I try to do things, nothing gets done. When I let God do things, everything is completed at an unprecedented speed and accuracy. I don't say this lightly and I don't say it with tongue in cheek. I say it with true, unequivocal devotion to God. This next episode relates only too well that when you let God do it, things really do get done. I can't strongly enough express my gratitude and devotion to my God.

Roger, his friend and I get out of the taxi, which happens to be a vintage Volkswagen, not the new bug. I strap on my huge backpack and carry the other small one up, again, a very steep stairwell. We look at the rooms and from what I can see, they are more than adequate, with air-conditioning that actually works. All this, and Roger tells me that it's about thirteen dollars a night.

I mention to Roger that what I really hope to achieve, is to get to the Consulate, and check in with Immigration. I'd like to find if there's a boat going to Manaus, and since I've got the hotel, maybe change some money also. He talks to the manager and, yes there is a boat leaving tomorrow for Manaus.

SOUTH AMERICA
ENCHANTMENT

They can't tell me if there are any facilities available, but we could get a taxi to go down and check. At best, I'm thinking this is going to take place tomorrow. Within about ten minutes, the taxi is here and bang! My first quest, to go to Immigration. In this particular case, the police do Immigration services as well as protect society. They check my documents, bang! He even fills out the entrance form for me. That's done, I'm in. So, it's ready, and he says, "We've got you in the computer now".

I thank him, get back in the taxi, go to the boat, and my eyes just about fall out! It's not a large ferryboat, but it's new and clean and beautiful. That's the word; it's got to be called beautiful. Yes, I can get on the boat. The crew-member that's in charge says, "You can come back at 2:00 p.m. tomorrow." And I'm saying, "No, no, I want to buy the ticket now." So, he fills out the passage ticket, makes sure that I have a passport in order and stamped by the Brazilian government.

We, in North America, think that we're so efficient, with our inflated egos. Yes, maybe the offices are cleaner, and the computers are faster. But we have the biggest problem, it's our attitude. These people accomplish things and they know what's going on; probably because they communicate with each other, just like this police force is also part of Immigration and Customs. This person in charge of the boat is wearing a T-shirt and cut-offs. No, he isn't in any uniform; no, he isn't wearing whites and first mate cap; but he knows that you have to have the documents in order before he's going to take you on as part of the passenger list.

I'm ready to pay for my ticket and put my money down which is U.S. and he says, "No, no, no. This is Brazil. I want Brazilian *real*." So, the taxi driver takes me to the money-changer. The rate is not that good, but then I'm not taking my life savings and converting, I convert $100.00 and I get two hundred and thirty five Brazilian *real*, but she will take the Peruvian money. So, I save one ten *Soles* as a souvenir and give her the rest. This was much easier to do business

215

than with the bank in Peru that wouldn't take the Chilean currency.

Sometimes free enterprise and government do blend very well together. Here's an example of a police force that's integrated with Customs and Immigration and probably does a better job than countries that have separate operations. And here's a woman that knows the Peruvian currency, is charging a good premium, but is pleasant about it. She doesn't cheat me and doesn't give me a bargain, either. A lot easier than standing in line in a bank, only to find out that no, they won't do it.

With that behind me, back to the boat and "Yes, here's your money, here's your ticket, and you have to be back at 2:00 p.m." I say, "Well, if we come back at 1:30 p.m., is that okay?" He starts to laugh and says, "Yeah, no problem, done." I go back to the hotel. In record-breaking time, less than an hour, I have completed all this. The only thing that puts a bit of a dent in this story is that the boat cost me a hundred Brazilian currencies. The taxi driver watched and I gave him thirty. He definitely gouged me. I looked at him two or three times and said, "It's too much." And he made a bunch of gestures back and forth, but he still wanted it. In my heart, and that's probably where it sits, I know that he charged me more than he should have. But, if I put in my perspective that if I'd hired somebody to do all this, I probably would have had to pay about the same. It's not the money, it's just I wish that he treated me a little more fairly.

Once that is done, I go back upstairs and ask the young lady about how much to pay, and so forth. She doesn't speak any English and doesn't really understand me much, but when I say "the internet?" she understands and points to where the Internet is. I have an e-mail waiting for me from my beautiful wife and she tells me that she misses me a great deal. I wish she would do this more often when I'm at home, show her feelings for me. Our marriage would be so much closer and our love would be so much greater.

SOUTH AMERICA ENCHANTMENT

I write her a bit about what I've accomplished. I really believe that I've done Mission Impossible. This boat is only going to take two, two-and-a-half day's maybe at the most, to get to Manaus, instead of eight to ten days. With all due respect though, I'm running with the river and so I'm taken advantage of not only the current but also the rainy season, which is lifting the river and its flow. So, Speedy Gonzalez here, better known as Rapid Robert, is going to make progress.

I've returned to the hotel via cab. Most of the people I've met are just very nice people. Unfortunately, this taxi driver decided that he needed a tip. He would have got one with my blessing. Now, he's just taken one with his greed.

I'm not exceptionally hungry at the moment, but sooner or later, I should have something to eat. And with that, I take a stroll up into the intersection. There's a band playing and there are three girls who have got more energy in this heat than I do. They're really dancing up a storm and the music has got the samba beat to it. I'm back in Brazil, that's for sure. I watch them for a few minutes and enjoy the music, before returning to a disco bar and yes, have another beer. I'm starting to find that I can't get diet cola, and beer sure seems to cut the grit out of your mouth. The way they serve beer is rather unique. They put it in a thermo Styrofoam container to keep it cold. The more I travel, the more I realize that throughout the world, people overcome the inconveniences that they feel they're having and here, cold beer is something that hits the spot, whether you're a foreigner or a domestic. The Styrofoam keeps it chilled, and as the Brits say, "I'm chilling out right now." Some of the locals are dancing to the swing of the blaring loudspeakers in this disco. I don't see any food being served and though I'm not famished, I feel that I probably should have something before retiring for the night.

I head up the walkway and it's like an open-air market or bazaar. The people are serving chicken and sausages and other kinds of meat on a shish kebab with rice. There is also what I think is ground corn that's the other accessory to this meal, and of course potato. I now have a coke, full body, and

217

Robert F. Edwards

the meal. The meal is not something that you would brag about for cuisine. I have a sausage, rice and cold potato. But boy! The price is right, including the pop which is always a premium when you buy a global brand like Coca-Cola. It comes to four *real*.

On the way back to the hotel, I stop in for one more beer to wash this food down and bring on a little bit of fatigue. I can't help but think what a remarkable day that has transpired. Even in my fondest wishes, let alone dreams, I don't think I could have accomplished a portion of this achievement two days ago, in my mind's eye. I am completely amazed at how much has transpired. I will definitely have a lot of time to be able to explore the jungles around Manaus.

With that, I'd like to say goodnight to my beautiful wife. Love and the word itself don't describe all the emotions that I have in feelings for you, my beautiful wife. I wish in some ways we were more of "birds of a common feather", but believe me, where we fly together is pure paradise. I love you, my dearest wife. For my daughter and my little grandson, I imagine your vacation is now completed and I love you both very much. To each and every one of you, I hope life is giving you one of these days like I have just experienced - one of receiving achievement, accomplishment, and exhilarating beyond your dreams. Goodnight, one and all.

SOUTH AMERICA ENCHANTMENT

February 2, Saturday

Tabatinga, Brazil

I've not had the most congenial sleep after the long enduring day yesterday. However, it was spasmodic and no complaints. The hotel that I'm staying in is not a five-star, but then I'm not requiring the quality of a five-star hotel. I'll always be grateful to Roger. There's a knock on the door, and Roger asked if I've had breakfast and I said, "Give me ten minutes", during which I clean up and prepare myself for the day ahead.

For breakfast, I can't believe that I actually have an egg, cheese, bologna, some bread, and coffee is also included in the meal. It might be cold, but it's the largest breakfast I've had included in hotel accommodations on this trip.

Roger and I make a bit of small talk and get to learn each other's lifestyle a little more. Roger is in his early fifties, and his friend accompanying him are both pilots, not of an aircraft, but pilots of the river. This is a very important job. I know very little about the pilots and their qualifications, but I do know that they rank above sea captains. When you enter into their charted waters, the captain has to turn over the command of the bridge and the ship, to a pilot. So, both these men have qualifications that are not only rewarded in financial situations, but also have a reward of respect throughout the naval community.

Roger is going on to Colombia and does some exchanging of money and I ask if I can tag along. So, off to Leticia, Colombia we go. It is the most progressive and developed of the three countries in this juncture on the river. I also read that it has the most conveniences for the traveler, including hotels and restaurants. Once I'm here, it's a nice community and there are some super stores. No, it's not the big-boxed wholesalers like Wal-Mart. They haven't found this place, thank God!

If I had to spend two or three days waiting for a change of transportation, I would prefer this as first choice. The *peso*,

Robert F. Edwards

which is used in Colombia, is about twenty five hundred, three thousand *pesos* to the U.S. dollar. As I said to Roger, "Go for lunch and spend a million *pesos* and become a millionaire." We had a little chuckle over that one. I spend some time talking to a gentleman that is part of the shipping lines and operator of the transports that Roger and his friend are involved in. He speaks exceptionally good English and also informs me that he is the manager. Roger and his friend had checked in and have to be back on this side later, to take the boat through this channel. We finish our visit and I take a picture of all of them, including myself.

We then go over to the moneychanger. Obviously, Roger and his companion have done business with this moneychanger before. For whatever reason, they've found that he's probably either the most satisfactory, or legitimate. After the renewal of friendship and the introduction of me, the money changing takes place. Both Roger and his fellow pilot exchange about US$50.00. I'm prepared to exchange US$200.00. The man quotes me a rate of 2.38 *real* to the U.S. dollar. I type out 240, and he says, "Oh, no!" like almost a gasp of like "where are you in the real world? I just couldn't possibly do that." When I tell him the story that I've had my training with the Berbers in Africa, we all get a good laugh at it. I don't get a better rate, but at the end of the transaction, he gives me two extra *real,* as well as Roger, one for him bringing in business and one for the amount that I've contributed. Also, I guess it's a new two-dollar paper currency.

We spend a little time in Colombia and then take a taxi back to Brazil and the docking area. We take a few pictures and buy some fishing hooks. These things look like a gladiator's mini-weapon, rather than fish hooks. It has three prongs with a long extended shaft that you'd wrap on to a stick. Probably if you're proficient, you can get three for the price of one, quite a brutal-looking piece of equipment. If I can't get a fork through Security at an airport, I will have to make sure this is in the checked luggage being transported back to Canada.

SOUTH AMERICA
ENCHANTMENT

Roger and the other pilot have bought a large supply of frozen meats and other supplies to take on board the ship. As they're stocking up, I look around a little more. There are pigs here; I've just heard a squeal. These particular two pigs were very unhappy, as they were being pulled in the direction that was opposed to their enjoyment of eating. Yes, it's a lifestyle that is different. I don't think I could live indefinitely here, but it's got its rewards and interests. As I see more of the mosaic way of life here, I have to wonder who's winning the advancement on civilization. It is a free easy lifestyle. Shorts and T-shirts, and when the sun's out, enjoy it; when it's pouring rain, get out of it; pretty simple rules to learn.

I go back to the Internet and send off a couple of e-mails to my wife and daughter, and have received some from my ever-loving wife. I decide that I'll stroll down, not memory lane, but any lane that is available and enjoy the sights and sounds of this interesting and remarkable society. High noon is fast approaching, and I find the restaurant that I had my eye on the night before. I ordered a beer and a bowl of soup. The soup came in a pot the size of at least four to six servings. No, I wasn't able to consume the entire bowlful, but I savored this delicious cuisine. There were little bits of meat, potatoes, some noodles, onions, peppers, and seasoned broth. It would make anybody start to salivate just listening to me. Along with that, the rice was absolutely delicious. It was fresh and flaky. Uncle Ben, you better watch out, your days are numbered. I thoroughly enjoyed myself, watching the traffic as the entertainment going by. I had two bottles of large beer, rice and this enormous amount of soup for sixteen *real*, which would convert to about US$7.00. No one can get a decent hamburger in the United States for that.

I return to the hotel to make my final preparations before the taxi arrives to take me to the boat. I've just about completed the final preparation when the phone rings, and the taxi's there. It's a little early, but reliability. The more I travel in this part of the world, the more I really appreciate and enjoy the people's commitment and their follow through. There's

Robert F. Edwards

no reneging, there's no renegotiation, and you don't need five documents for the lawyer to complete the transaction. And it would be so much easier if I would conform to the spoken language of the day, which now will be Portuguese.

I load my heavy weight of cargo into this poor little Volkswagen and off we go. Incidentally, the fare, including the entrance fee, is six *real*. I'm not going to dwell on it, but I did pay a premium of about eight *real* to the previous taxi driver and unfortunately I probably would have given that to him as a tip, rather than him extracting it. Anyway, this gentleman gets me there, makes sure that I'm on the boat, makes sure that my tickets are in order, and "*Vaya con el Dios, Señor.*" A young boy is more than eager to show me the boat. I want to get my heavy backpack into a storage area, but I've been given the understanding, "No, you just park them where you park." So, I make arrangements to have my big bag go into the holding area.

This is a very nice boat. It's steel construction throughout and it's either very new, or well-maintained, maybe a bit of both. It consists of three floors above the storage area and the engine room. On the main deck, there are some hammocks and eating quarters. The second level is the primary occupation area of the passengers and there is a huge dormitory in which to put your hammocks. There are some cabins available, from as much as twice what I paid, two hundred *real*, and right up to four hundred *real*. The third floor is a little cafeteria or bar, and the outer deck is where you can sit and enjoy the river.

With my tour completed, I string up my hammock. It's the first time I've done this, and I've certainly got a hammock that nobody else in town owns. Canadian issued, Canadian designed, and unique to its construction. In my particular hammock, you enter from the bottom and there's a Velcro strip that closes it afterward, with mesh for mosquito protection on the top. I strung this up to the best of my ability and before this day comes to a close, I'll know if I've done it right.

For the next hour-and-a-half, I spent the time leaning over the railing. The dock work is all heavy manual work. They're unloading goods from one of the barges and it's all done by manual labor. I have no idea what the sacks hold, or weigh, but the men load the heavy burden on their heads and walk the better part of maybe fourteen meters and then laboriously stack them on pallets to a significant height. South Americans are not tall in stature, but very strong, and these men are proving their worth.

I also noticed an incredible number of propane tanks, (standard size) they're stacked six to eight high on this barge. They were too numerous to count, but I would think that probably a thousand or more would be acceptable. A truck arrives on the dock, with a complete load of bricks, all taken off manually and put on the barge. We just take for granted the forklifts, cranes and other mechanical devices, but the industrial revolution hasn't turned its full corner of success down here.

Once we depart, the river expands and contracts, and I'm enjoying the continuation of lush jungle foliage on both sides. It's interesting to see the homes of the individuals that have eked out their own little space. One can't help but feel the tranquility and total attunement that these people must have, with not only their surroundings, but also nature and God. What a simple, non-stressful life. It may not have the financial rewards that the majority of you would be rushing to exchange for, but by the same token, this lush, beautiful countryside with the endless forests and the slow moving river must induce tranquility and peace.

The day wears on and around 6:00 p.m., we arrive at the Brazilian port of Benjamin Constant. I know that this is another checkpoint for proper documentation. I feel confident about my visas and permits. However, the one thing that hasn't been examined is my medical inoculations. I've read that Brazil is very strict on making sure that people are inoculated against yellow fever. This stop takes the better part of two or two-and-a-half hours.

I thought we were making good time, but the barge that had all the bricks and the propane tanks has arrived about the same time as we have. This port-town looks fairly large, with a fair amount of facilities. The entrepreneurship is evident again. I see a woman with a small barbecue set up, cooking shish-kebabs of different types of meat, probably some of fish, and doing a fairly brisk business.

A couple of guys have taken their motorcycles off the main deck of this boat and have arrived on either their home turf, or a place that they're going to be easy riders. The traffic flow is busy, going back and forth on this boat. You'd think that it was more of an exodus of refugees than passengers. I would think about ninety percent of the people on board are Brazilians that are making this voyage, and the other ten percent are people from Colombia and Peru. There are no Argentinean or Chileans that I'm aware of and only one North American, a Canadian, me. I'm not sure if I am the only person who speaks English on this boat, but at most, it's a very small minority. Sometimes you can be in a crowd, but you're still very much alone.

The night has come to this region of the world and I'm still wondering if Immigration is going to examine the documents.

SOUTH AMERICA
ENCHANTMENT

However, we cast off and I feel that *completo* is in order. As we go down the river, there's a huge light that is on board the ship, and it sweeps back and forth across the river to make sure that there is no debris in the darkness. This is a very safe and controlled adventure so far. I wander the decks and look out at the shoreline, where I see the odd flicker of light. Somebody's burning a kerosene or propane light, since no electricity or cables go in these parts of the world.

It's peaceful and there are some stars out, so 'the big guy' must be giving us a bit of the heavens above to gaze on. I happen to smile, and start talking to a man in his thirties who's from Colombia. He's heading down to Manaus also, and he's the first person that I've met on this ship that speaks any amount of English. I'm not concerned in any shape or form, but I am somewhat surprised that there are no foreign travelers.

The young Colombian and I venture up to the canteen and have a couple of beers, and a snack. It's a combination of egg, cheese, tomato, and hamburger patty squished together in a bun. It's hot, and I'm not going to elaborate on its cuisine or its nourishment.

It's relatively early, by South American standards, about 8:30 p.m. and the Colombian fellow and I are finishing off our beers. He's telling me that around midnight, we will stop and there will be a police inspection and Immigration. I have no reason to doubt him. From what I've read and understood at this point, I was expecting it at an earlier period. However, it doesn't really matter. If it happens, it happens.

The dorm that I'm assigned to; talk about standing room only. I take a picture, and really hope that it turns out. It is wall-to-wall hammocks and when I do climb into my hammock, I'm touching two other people. I guess it depends which side I turn, one's a young lady and the other is a young man. So, at least I'll never get cold in this place, and it's quite humid. Even though you wouldn't know it, there's supposed to be an air-conditioning system that's in force.

225

Robert F. Edwards

By 9:00 p.m., I'm struggling with my hammock to try and find a way to sleep in it with any degree of comfort. Getting in to my hammock is challenging, but I'm starting to get the hang of it. It's a very unique piece of equipment and once I find how to appropriately use it, I'm sure that I won't leave home without it. Throughout the night, I'm having difficulties maneuvering in it and have some kind of concern that I'm going to end up on the floor, rather than swing like a banana in the air. That's what it looks like in this dormitory, an infinite amount of bananas hanging from stems. Or else, bats instead of hanging from the wall, we are draped across the room. Maybe it would more appropriately gigantic cocoons waiting to expel their first butterfly. I had no idea that it would be this congested. There's got to be in excess of a hundred and fifty people. This is very tight quarters. Now I know why the price is right. This is a comment, not a complaint. I'm still grateful to be on this boat and I'm also thoroughly enjoying the experience.

True to the Colombian's word, at quarter to twelve, we're rustled out of bed, (hammocks to be more precise), and about eight to ten police do a very thorough inspection of the docu-

SOUTH AMERICA
ENCHANTMENT

ments and in most cases, of luggage and bags that are strewn in abundance on the floor beneath the hammocks that contain each passenger. They have a stern look about them, but they go through my documents and hand them back. That's the beginning and the end of that situation.

This is a good time to conclude this day's adventure. I'd like to say to my wife, I miss you very much and I really can't express my sincere gratitude of your being able to express yourself so well in the e-mails, of your love and your devotion for me. Believe me, my beautiful wife; it's equal on my side. To my daughter, I'm glad you're back in Vancouver and that Cole had a good time. I'm more than interested to hear of your adventures and I love you both very dearly. To the rest of you, I'd like to thank you all and pleasant dreams and wishes. Goodnight.

Robert F. Edwards

February 3, Sunday

Amazon River, Brazil

Not really much to get up for, but then I haven't slept much either.   So, at 5:30 a.m., I make my way over to the washbasins and brush my teeth and clean up a bit. I have a cup of coffee and what looks like a Ritz cracker but tastes more like a biscuit, which is the breakfast of the day. I've read that you should bring something to appease your appetite. In the cafeteria, there is an abundance of beer and Coca-Cola, as well as some food that can be obtained for a price, but should be consumed only when extremely hungry.

The river here is very dirty and it is evident that the Rio Negro is heading into the main channel of the Amazon. The day continues as so many other days that I've experienced now that I'm in the jungle area: rain in the morning, clearing, and more rain, clearing; that's why it's called the rainy season. I meet up with my new Colombian friend and we talk for a bit. He's got another friend from Colombia with him, and then

228

SOUTH AMERICA
ENCHANTMENT

we're joined by a third person. Only Roberto speaks any English, and he keeps me involved in the conversation.

When I went back to get something from my belongings, there is a young lady who is reading the Bible (it's Sunday) in her hammock. With at least a hundred and fifty hammocks in this one dormitory, the majority of people are either sitting in their hammocks or letting them swing a little bit. There seemed to be numerous young women (less than twenty years old themselves) who have young children. With all these babies, you don't hear any sound out of them. They must be either contented with life, or have a much better personality than our sugar-fed hyperactive children of North America.

I also see something that is, to me, more rewarding than if I had attended an uplifting sermon in church. I'm sitting on deck when I notice a butterfly (or moth) and the wingspan would about 3". It had landed on the deck and was upside-down. There were two people standing nearby, and I thought, "Well, as soon as they're finished and out of the way, I'll try and at least lift it up and see if it's alive." Somehow, by its own endurance and preservation of life, it lifts itself up but because the wings are wet, flying is almost impossible. While I'm struggling with an idea of what to do, a man approaches it. I'm thinking, "No, no, don't", but to my delight, this gentle person picks the moth up and tries to get it to fly again. Unfortunately, the wind drafts that the boat is creating don't let the moth take flight. After three or four attempts, he carries it over to the railing and makes sure that it gets airborne. This is what God must hope for in the development of mankind. This kind deed shows full respect for Life itself. I'll never know this man's name and will never see him again after this journey, but his moment of kindness will be in my heart forever.

I try to get caught up on my journal, but it's difficult to concentrate on this cruise with the number of people that are present and accounted for. Every time we stop at another port of call, we don't take anything off, we just add to it, and the people are the number one commodity. When we started,

229

there was probably seventy-five to a hundred. It's now closer to two hundred. I did a quick count of the hammocks on my deck, I've got a hundred, and the lower deck is equally as crowded. It's amazing to see so many people play the role of a sardine, and yes, this is a steel ship, so we're in the tin can also. The only thing that's lacking is any sauce.

When I move in my hammock, I bump into three other hammocks, one above me and two beside me. Talk about being close! However, the mood is congenial, and everyone is friendly and enjoying the camaraderie. The ship itself is well maintained, but there's no luxury. This is a 'bare bones; take it as you can' cruise. Even the seats that are available on the upper deck are steel. This boat is made to last. They do have good showers and toilets, and they are all very clean.

The food is good. It's much better than I anticipated, but a little repetitious. The mid-day meal is served early, between 10:30 and 11:00 a.m. There's spaghetti, beans with some pieces of meat, and rice, of course. These are always the main ingredients, then served with another meat, mostly chicken. I think I've eaten more chicken on this trip than I have in the last couple of years. For Peruvians and Brazilians, one of their main meats is chicken. All done in different ways, but still comes out as chicken. The evening meal has a salad with it, and the same three basics: rice, beans, and spaghetti. The food is well prepared and meals are organized. With this many people, they do it in shifts, so they make sure that everybody sits down, eats all the portions, then all those people leave, they clean the tables, put brand new plates down, and the next wave comes in.

The ship seems to be on the River of No Return. It's endless. With the width of this river, I feel that the scenery is moving by rather than us. Of course, the shoreline changes, but the color of the river remains consistently dark brown. When I wash, whether it's my hands or have a shower, I don't know if I am cleaner than I was, but it's cool and not as cold as some of the showers I had on shore.

SOUTH AMERICA
ENCHANTMENT

About mid-day, I happen to spot a person that's a lighter shade of brown than the majority of people on board and to my surprise, he's a German. So, there are at least two foreigners amongst this ship of Peruvians, Colombians, and the livelier Brazilians. All of the people are congenial to each other, living in these tight quarters.

I spend most of my time on deck in between the heavy bursts of rain. During a moment of pleasant weather, a unique insect drops in for a visit. It's huge, with long legs and a square little head. Its wings are 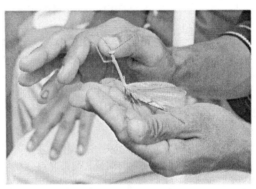 about 2" to 3", with distinct markings in the middle that look like two eyes. With my limited knowledge of insects, it looks very much like a praying mantis. One man picks it up and it walks all over his hand, before it bounces back on a pole. One of the Colombian men tells me that it's quite a rare insect and I could pay a great deal of money if I was to purchase it dead in the shops.

Watching the river go by is becoming rather tedious, to say the least. There's a group of about four guys sitting around a table, with about three tiers of beer cans. Beer is extremely cheap, at about a *real* and a half, and pop is one *real*. I am starting to gather that a lot of people are going to the carnival in Manaus. I was thinking, "Oh well, at least, I'll avoid the grandiose carnival in Rio de Janeiro," but of course this is celebrated throughout Brazil and every city takes the lead in its approach to the carnival.

I've got a couple of days before I really have to make a decision on this. I've been told now that we will probably be arriving some time on Tuesday. Roberto, the Colombian, thinks that we're going to be arriving around 2:00 in the morning. I

231

sure hope that he's got it wrong and that it will be more like 2:00 in the afternoon. Who knows? Just have to take one day at a time.

We've completed the dinner meal, which is served at 5:00 p.m. The day seems extremely long, due to the fact that there's very little to do. There are a couple of pool tables and there is television, which most people on my deck are watching. I don't want to watch television, since I haven't traveled a huge portion of the world, just to watch "The Lion King". However, when it rains, there is a herd mentality to get inside and I'm no exception.

By 7:30, 8:00 p.m., I've reconciled to the idea of 'bed', not so much because I'm tired, although I didn't sleep well last night. Tonight, I'm hoping to find a better approach. I've watched other people lay in their hammocks and there's a lot of diversification on how to sleep in one of these things. I feel if I can somehow manage to lie on my side, not all my problems will be solved, but my sleeping habits will have improved immensely.

With that quest in mind, I'd like to say goodnight to my beautiful wife, Marietta. And all I can say, my wonderful wife, is that I'm glad you're not here. The heat is stifling and the cramped quarters would leave you distraught. So, I can assure you, my beautiful darling that you may be a little lonely but with Pepper and Buttons as your companions, you've chosen your domicile much better than I have tonight. I wish you a wonderful rest and goodnight.

SOUTH AMERICA
ENCHANTMENT

February 4, Monday

Amazon River, Brazil

Oh, it was a much better night, sleeping in my hammock. I found some of the routine, and positions that you can maneuver in these banana peels. Also, it rained all night and this hot-blooded human being had a much better night's sleep with cooler weather. All things being said and done, I got a fairly good night's rest in my new mode of sleeping.

When I got up, it was still raining, and not too many other people were getting out of their hammocks. It's a new experience. I just cannot believe the number of people that can be crammed into one given area, sleeping at different levels in these hammocks, again, like peeled bananas hanging. But now, with this being my second day in the hammock world, I am impressed with how quiet the children are and some of the women stay in there all day. Other than getting up and having something to eat or going to the toilet, they lay in the hammock. There nothing likes sleeping the distance and the landscape away.

This early bird starts his day around 5:30 a.m., and there are a few others that get the early cups of coffee. I am getting to be known by, I wouldn't say everybody on board, but without a doubt, I am the oldest person here. If I do have any competition in that sector, I'm the only one that has white hair.

Shortly afterwards, Roberto gets up and joins me sitting out on the deck. The rainwater coming off the ship is pouring down a spout near us, and I made a comment that it looks like a shower, its coming down with such force. I rushed down to get the camera, but wouldn't you know it, by the time I got back up, the torrential rain had stopped. It was now just a drizzle and my beautiful waterfall has now become a dripping tap. There's not a great deal to do on this boat. Maybe that's part of the reason why people stay in their hammocks.

233

Robert F. Edwards

They just try and sleep through it. However, I'm not one of them.

As the day wears on, it seems that one of the great events is food time. I do have to give these people full credit. Though the meals are repetitious, they're tasty and well done. Considering the number of people that they feed on the two levels, my full compliments for the remarkable job they do, and the quality is more than commendable.

At lunch, I meet up with Alex, the German. He informs me that he hates the rain so there's no point in him spending much time outdoors today. He's probably going to be one of the banana peelings that are spread all over the decks. We return to the upper deck where the little cafeteria, the television, and those monstrous speakers are. The music is pleasant enough and I don't know whether my ears have become accustomed to the volume, as it doesn't seem to be as loud today.

There's a fellow that's joined our merry group, a Brazilian, with his wife and their beautiful little baby. She's six months old, and just looks like a Kewpie doll. I start making gestures and laughing, and she responds by giggling. She's only got two teeth, starting to come up from the bottom and the rest all gums, and laughed like anything, she's just a delight!

I noticed that children are never left alone, the parents are always present. Nine times out of ten, they're with the mother. I imagine growing up, especially in the primary years, always having the parent within your sight must give a security and a feeling of well being. This is different than the childcare centers and the baby-sitters in North America, where the parents are both working. These parents enjoy their children and have fun with them, and both are part of each other's lives. It's a shame that we've given away this wonderful gift of life for a few dollars and unnecessary possessions. As I walk around this ship, the children are either asleep or just sitting very contentedly. When my mother was a child, from strict British stock, she was told that children were to be seen but not heard. These children are seen all the time, everywhere, but

234

SOUTH AMERICA
ENCHANTMENT

they're not heard, and they're happy little people. I wish children in North America could enjoy their childhood as much these young people are. Being poor is only in the eye of the beholder.

On that note, we've managed to get past high noon. The scenery is consistent, and we see a lot of little boats, nowhere near the size of this particular one, but passenger boats going back and forth. Another interesting part about traveling in these waters is the difference from our tugboats on the West Coast, which always pull the barges. For whatever reason, these people push their barges, and it must have something to do with the navigation up and down the river.

We pass numerous small settlements and boat-people fishing in wooden dugout canoes. It's very peaceful and tranquil, although the average person would not want to spend days on end here, just because of the facilities on board, but sailing on this wide, awesome river is something that I'm very grateful to be experiencing.

We fellows have decided that since it's the last night, we're going to buy each other a round of beers. It starts off with about four or five of us that are going to celebrate the last night. There are lots of women aboard this boat, but most of them, even though they're very friendly, stay amongst themselves. However, this one girl breaks tradition and starts talking to some of the fellows. She's from Tabatinga, the border town in Brazil, and she's going to be visiting her sister in Manaus. She is nice young lady. I find out later that she's twenty-four years of age. Throughout the day, her little group seems to have gathered some steam. I think she's quite lonely and quite homesick. I saw her walking around the deck very despondent and now she's got about four other women that she's hanging around with. When people have their own little group, it helps take the mind off a lot of things.

For us men, our minds are now focused on dinner, which is fast approaching, at 4:30 p.m. in the afternoon. Like people that are either famished, or have nothing else to do, we bolt to try and get in line first, only to find out that we're in the second sitting anyway. With the meal finished and 6:00 p.m. fast approaching, one of the fellows of my little merry group decides that it's beer time.

So, we take our beers and sit outside. It's a very nice evening. The camaraderie starts to take place. The girl and her little group end up joining us. Other people start dropping in, and spend some time making conversation. The young lady from Brazil is Therese, and the other one was Violet, and then Maria, and Margaret. Violet was thirty-seven and she thought I was forty, and I said, "I can't thank you enough for the compliment." She was probably a bad judge of age, but just the same though, it was nice to hear. This is happening on a consistent basis. I think it's primarily due to my white hair, but people of all ages and gender ask me how old I am, and gasp, as if I was one of the ancients in their presence, but still competing with them. I'm beginning to wonder if that water in Cuzco's ancient temple does have powers for youth or longevity, or rejuvenates the cells in your body, because I'm feeling exceptionally well. The only thing that is bothering me a little bit is my knee, but other than that, I'm feeling in top condition.

SOUTH AMERICA
ENCHANTMENT

The night wears on and the merriment becomes more bois-terous. At about ten o'clock, Therese and I put on a little bit of a show. I guess I started it off, hamming it up with a Tarzan yell because we were in the jungle. That's a wonderful part about being old, I am not intimidated or trying to impress anybody, and therefore I can be myself. I don't have a lot of inhibitions to be politically correct. I just want to have a good time and have everybody else enjoy themselves as well.

The high spirits seem contagious. I guess there's a bit of Jungle Jim left in me, and as I let out my Tarzan call, every-body is clapping and the women are laughing, and giving me the thumbs up sign, which is very predominant in Brazil as "way to go" or "first class" or whatever. My group renders a song that comes on and Therese and I do a little pantomime (she is actually singing but I am pantomiming the words) and everybody gives us a big clap and there's a standing ovation when we're finished; so much for to-night's entertainment.

We finally settled down to the guys seriously drinking and some of the women are as well, but certainly the women are not as enthusiastic about drinking beer as the fellows. I swing over to orange juice and buy a few rounds. The only deterrent to enjoying the beautiful night out on the deck are these bugs. Without exaggeration, they're the size of my thumbnail if not bigger. These huge bloody things are hitting the decks, and once upside down, they crawl around and there's just no way of getting them back to being airborne. Actually, when I was dancing, one hit me right on the nose and it does hurt. It didn't bite me; it just smarts from the im-pact.

The night starts to clear. It's a beautiful night for stars and I just can't help but wish that I was with Marietta and we were looking at the stars together. I really miss her, and I love her very much. I know this isn't a place that she would enjoy at all, and it would be very difficult, even if we have a cabin, be-cause of the heat, and the food, to say nothing of the smells, it would be her concept of going to hell. But the sky and the beautiful stars remind me so much of some of the wonderful evenings I spent with my true love.

I spent a little longer with the rest of the group. By now, they're really into a party mood and everybody is buying beer. I'm trying to shuffle mine to anybody that would take it off my hands, as I have switched to orange juice. I've made up my mind, when this is finished, I'm going to say goodnight to one and all. Even though I'm not really tired, tomorrow's going to be a very invigorating day in the sense that we will hit Manaus. I say goodnight despite a lot of, "Oh, don't go yet, it's early" and with all that, I depart down into the holding tank, which is really unbearable.

Down below, which is supposed to have air-conditioning, it is actually worse. If they just left all the windows open, the breezes of air would be much cooler than this imitation of comfort however, enough complaining. It's just extremely uncomfortable in here. My Canadian-made hammock is nowhere near as porous as the hammocks that are made down here, and with the netting on top, which protects me immensely from insects, also works against any kind of cooling agent.

I would like to say goodnight, my wonderful wife and I miss you a great deal and I love you very much. Wendy, welcome back. Looking forward to hearing from you. I wouldn't mind a little bit of communication break. With that, I hope, Cole, you're getting back into the routine and that you're giving your mom a little bit of the rest that she didn't achieve on her holidays. I would like to say goodnight to each and every one of you, and see you tomorrow.

SOUTH AMERICA
ENCHANTMENT

February 5, Tuesday

Amazon River, Brazil

I can't say I got up early. I could almost say I never went to bed. Between drinking beer and this insatiable heat that has permeated this deck and the hammock swing, I felt like either a ping-pong ball going back and forth or one of those toys that you hit the marble or the ball bearing and they all just keep swinging back and forth in perpetual motion. I'd like to say I slept, but I'm not sure when.

I finally realize it is 5:30 in the morning. I've endured as much of the hammock as I can tolerate and with my continual up and down, I might as well stay up. I go down on the lower deck and what a difference! Of course, the motion of the boat has produced its own wind and it's much cooler down here. So much for man's intervention with nature.

I sit down in the forward part. One of the fellows with our group had a cabin, incidentally, and he paid four hundred *real*, four times what I've paid. We do the ritual that we did the day before; coffee and some of these little biscuits that are the size of a Ritz cracker, and get on with the day. Yesterday Roberto, the Colombian, helped me locate where they had stored my large packsack, so I don't have any anxiety as we approach Manaus wondering where the large packsack is. It's in one of the food storage compartments, which has helped put my mind at ease.

I do the rituals of shaving and toiletries. I even have a shower which, to my amazement, does make me feel better, even though I know that the river water is as dirty as I am, or maybe even dirtier, but mentally I feel somewhat cleaner for it. There's not even a hum in the compartments. The sleeping hammock babies are just sprawled in all different angles in their sleeping modes. Finally, about 9:00 a.m., people start to rustle and stir and get their days in order.

239

Robert F. Edwards

It's a beautiful day. There's no other word for it, and there's an air of excitement, knowing that we are getting closer to our port of call. I also noticed that there is a lot more activity on the river. There are lots more passenger boats and small powerboats. I love the way they drop passengers off. These little power taxis with huge outboard motors come drifting up along side, passengers unload, and they buzz off. It's a lot of fun in this part of the world. The things they do and the way they do it - it's more than interesting. It's downright delightful.

People are in a joyful mood, and coming up and wishing each other well. I hope my pictures turn out; they'll spin more than a thousand words. These girls, still teenagers, are making me feel like some rock star. They can speak hardly any English, and I don't speak any Portuguese, but they get some guys that can interpret that I'm the "disco man" and "Am I going to go to the disco soon in Manaus?" and "Will I be dancing in the discos?" They really honor me and they want to have their pictures taken with me, and one girl said to me, "You look like a Hollywood star." Boy, if I had an inflated ego, these people would have put it into the stratosphere. I'm just having a ball, and meeting some of the nicest people I've

SOUTH AMERICA
ENCHANTMENT

ever met in the entire world. I can't help but think of those two wonderful Argentinean ladies that I trekked through the Inca Trail with. Also Camello and his father Michael, but these people are equally at the top of the mound. I told some of the young women that I feel like Peter Pan and these people are sure encouraging me to keep going my merry little youthful ways.

I can't help but recall my sister-in-law's comment, a few months ago, when I was playing a videogame of her son's and I won it. I came running up the stairs to tell everyone and I was quite excited about it. She said, "You're a real kid at heart." I think that sums up what this adventure is becoming, that these people have let me expand, without being inhibited, my youthful attitude. To my gratitude, they've shown me encouragement and enjoyment of my behavior, and God bless these beautiful people.

There's a real excitement in the air. The men are trying to point out Manaus to each other and we're still at least three, four hours away from it. But now seeing more barges and larger ships pass, this makes us feel a lot more aware that we're no longer in a very isolated part of the world, but we're

rejoining civilization. There's scurrying on the deck as people are assembling their baggage and starting to prepare themselves for disembarkment.

By about 2:00 p.m., we actually reach the Rio Negro, which means black river and yes, it is really black. I've been on juncture points of the Indian Ocean and the Atlantic. I've been many rivers carrying a lot of silt and have seen the direct contact with clear, fresh water. But this one definitely has a strong dark black line between brown water and black water.

Now, for the first time, we start to see some of the refineries, but we are still about eighteen to twenty kilometers from Manaus. The activity becomes like an anthill under stress, baggage being checked and unpacked. I can't believe how big these holding rooms are now that the mesh of hammocks has been removed. Everybody is very excited about reaching Manaus.

Roberto, from Colombia, and I have decided that we'll tag together and he's got access to a cheap hotel room in Manaus and we're going to be a pair of backpackers together. Manaus is now coming into view. It's a very large city. Roberto says that it's around two million and I have no reason to doubt him. We first approach the harbor where most of the container shipping is located, and soon a lot of the river ferries become evident, commuting both ways on the river. As we get closer to this area, it becomes very colorful. A lot of small *turista* ferries that do excursions up the two rivers to different resorts are present and accounted for. It does remind me a little bit of the activities that go on in the Aberdeen Harbor in Hong Kong to Macaw.

We are being escorted in by the coastal patrol. There are little water taxis running around, scurrying here and there, as we get closer and closer to where the large docking for the riverboats are. Now coming into view is the market place that was built during the rubber boom in the Brazilian period and their contribution to rubber. The docking facilities for our boat are right in the downtown part of the city. As we approach, some other riverboats are very large and take a greater number of passengers down to Belém.

As we start to get closer to where we're going to be docking, it's the first hint of a problem for me. We're going to have to cross over three or four vessels before we actually hit the dock, and then make our way up to the landing area. I've got my gear already and I try to explain the situation to Roberto. I asked him for some assistance and he took my small backpack, while I carried the large one on my back plus the walking stick.

As we scrambled from one boat to the other, this makes the Inca Trail feel easy in comparison, after climbing quite precariously up and down different levels of boats to get to the dock. I'm very grateful that I ended up having the walking stick as a stabilizer. Once we are on the wharf, it becomes evident that nobody really knows what's going on. There is a lot of conversation between my new friends, but it's rather difficult in the sense that everybody's speaking a different language than mine.

However, as my backpack becomes excruciatingly heavy and we seem to be standing around waiting for further instructions from anybody that happens to be in the vicinity, I take it off and just stand by all our gear while Roberto scours around trying to find different people to get specific information. With that, I put my huge backpack back on and I try to insist that I'm taking a taxi, but still we have to walk quite a distance on this wharf before we reach the streets of Manaus.

We do rent a taxi and we don't go a great distance (which Roberto was right about). The cab was ten *real*, I thought it would be about one or two. After a long discussion with the taxi driver, he still insists on his ten and reluctantly we both paid the piper. We go into the hotel and I guess seedy might be the best word for it. We both want to check the rooms out, so Roberto checks his room first and then he stays with the gear while I go up and check my room. The first impression is deceiving, the rooms are actually much worse than the seedy

Robert F. Edwards

appearance of the entrance. I have no intentions of staying in this hotel, no matter if they were paying me.

There are three or four different hotels along the way and I suggest we check them out. Roberto finds one down the street that is run by a woman and doesn't seem too bad. I mount my gear back on, and return with him. I guess when you've seen the worse, even second or third worse looks pretty good. With that in mind, I check in for two nights. The room doesn't have a television or air-conditioning. It's a very old building and the room is small. Actually, the floor is the best part of the whole room, a beautiful inlaid hardwood, and probably the original. I would think that they could easily account for about a hundred years or more in their endurance of the different lifestyles that have been present and accounted for. I don't think that this particular hotel was what it's presently used for. It probably was some luxurious residence. The ceilings, incidentally, have got to be at least twenty feet high. With that description of my humble abode, Roberto and I decide that we'll go out and do a bit of an exploration of the city. The time is now close to 5:00 p.m. I'm quite prepared to have something to eat very shortly.

Our first quest is a travel agent. It's just at the other end of the block. To my surprise and delight, this man speaks English. Roberto wants to get a flight tomorrow for Rio de Janeiro and he's bartering on that, while I'm trying to gather information about the jungle and Manaus itself. And wouldn't you know it, Mr. Carnival himself seems to always manage to get in to Brazil during the carnival time and yes, next week is the big carnival. This is celebrated throughout South America and even Portugal, but Rio de Janeiro is *Uno* or number one. I was there last year, but I also took part in some of the smaller towns, so this is a big event throughout Brazil and Manaus will be part of this event. I'm also told that the ship that they're aware of will continue down the river to the mouth of the Amazon and leaves once a week, but there might be other boats available, and this particular boat leaves on Tuesday. I just arrived on Tuesday, so Manaus might have a foreigner

244

SOUTH AMERICA
ENCHANTMENT

known as Bob Edwards for a week in its presence. With that, we say thank you.

Both of us would like to get to the Internet, which isn't a great distance away and Roberto was given a map of the region. We end up going into one of the main streets, if not the Main Street, in Manaus. It's a large street, about four lanes going in each direction, with a large boulevard down the middle. It's surprising, I haven't been in a very large city for a long time and it's quite overwhelming to see the amount of traffic and congestion and motion of all modes of transportation, including people walking. However, after some directions, we end up finding the Internet and I actually have thirty-eight e-mails waiting. A lot of them are just business and information, but my beautiful wife's e-mails are present and accounted for. This makes traveling, especially in the way I do, so much more enjoyable. To be able to communicate and keep an ongoing account of both what I'm doing and what's happening on the home front, I still feel in tune with home and my loved ones. Thank God for the Internet.

After the better part of an hour is spent, now it's dark. I've indicated that I'm quite hungry, but Roberto says that all he needs is some *citro,* which is juice. He still wants to make a phone call and yes, we get a special card and then we have to go to another place that allows international phone calls. It's unbelievably expensive. One hour with the internet is three *real,* and two-and-a-half minutes on the phone to Bogotá, which is just a short distance compared to what I would have to do to talk to Marietta in Vancouver, was twenty-two *real.* Not only is the Internet a marvelous communication system, but also it's exceptionally cheap. No wonder young people grasp hold of it with a newfound delight.

With that out of the way, we decide to do a bit of walking and we come across a beautiful *piazza* with little kiosks set up for eating. I really would like to have a steak and some potatoes, but they don't even have *papa fritas* or soup. So, we end having *suco* which is juice served in crushed ice. I have to admit it's delicious. It quite easily puts milk shakes in jeopardy of being extinct.

Roberto is a great talker to the locals, but I don't think their Spanish is up to speed. He doesn't speak Portuguese, but he's a quantum leap ahead of me in communicating. English, after a few words, becomes limited. We decide to go to the *Teatro Amazonas*, a famous opera house in Manaus and designed by Doménico de Angelis, who built this remarkable building during the rubber boom of 1896. A lot of the material was imported from Europe and it is an Italian Renaissance style of building. It's closed now, but just the outside commands the attention that it dutifully deserves. Also, there's a huge *piazza* in front of it, with a large statue. The building is over a hundred years old, but in remarkable exterior condition still.

It's getting exceptionally dark; although it's only about 7:00 p.m., but I don't like walking the streets of a strange city at night and haven't developed a good enough feel for Manaus to know whether I feel completely at ease. A large city and not really knowing where I am, I'd prefer to get back to the hotel. I am quite persistent that I'd like to get back and I can tell, just by the way things are going, that Roberto isn't the best guide of the city. He's having some problems reading the map and distinguishing where we are. We do work our way back and get lost a few times, but in the end, we locate our hotel. He asked me two or three times on the way if I wanted something to eat but my primary concern was to get back. I feel much easier now, after checking the gear. Nothing has been molested or touched and I'm more than grateful for that. The room, also, hasn't improved much either.

Now, we both decide to get something to eat, even though he said he wasn't going to. There's a restaurant across the street, quite a nice one. Its forté is meat, and you just eat as much meat as you can consume. It is much on the same principle as the Argentine Feast of the Meat that I've salivated about ever since I left Argentina a year ago. But Argentina will always have (at least, in my taste buds and mind), the

SOUTH AMERICA
ENCHANTMENT

best tasting meat of the world. Still, this is good. I also have a couple of beers. The popular beer in Brazil is sweet, but a very nice light beer and in this hot climate, it quenches your thirst. I have to admit that I'm not a big beer drinker, but this seems to quench my thirst much better than my number one favorite drink and that's diet Pepsi.

We complete our meal and return to our rooms. Roberto asked me to wake him up at 7:30 a.m. and I said that would be no problem whatsoever for me. That concludes today.

I miss you very much, little honey-bun and I'm so grateful to have your e-mails. As much as I love you dearly, where I'm staying and enduring some of the parts of this adventure would not be in your interest at all, let alone your survival mode. I love you very much and I miss you a great deal. Goodnight little Wendy bird and Cole man. And to all of you, goodnight and God bless.

Robert F. Edwards

February 6, Wednesday

Manaus, Brazil

At least, the air-conditioning works in my room and actually quite well, considering everything else. I have slept well because it's the first night away from a hammock and the sardine effect. However, upon getting up in my room, I've not been alone. There's bugs and spiders and I'm having mixed feelings of staying here a second night. I guess first things first, get cleaned up and tackle the day that is present and accounted for. I start to prepare myself for the day, but I've got to get my laundry done. I'm down to the last T-shirt that I've brought and shorts.

I gingerly knock on Roberto's door. He says, "Give me half an hour" which is fine and I go back to the insect haven. Soon we are both ready, I've got my little side-pack full of dirty laundry, the camera and the few other things that I felt that I might need during the day. We venture off for breakfast and to my surprise, we find a little place that serves a good cup of coffee. Roberto orders, (what looks to me) like an egg McMuffin but far superior to McDonald's . It is a nice egg with a piece of cheese inside a bun. These people seem to have the obsession that everything should be squished together, with these presses. They did it with the food on the boat, also. It looks like a big waffle iron, for making grilled cheese sandwiches. Very tasty and we both have a Coca-Cola, three *real.* In this part of South America prices are reasonable and just to do a quick conversion, three *real* for the two cups of coffee, two egg buns, and two other plain buns (or a dollar-and-a-half U.S., the global currency).

We return to the travel agent and in the meantime, Roberto has managed to find a cheaper price on a ticket to São Paulo, but then he'll have to bus up to Rio. After a lot of negotiations and time, he gets a ticket to Rio, which leaves at noon today. I get rid of my laundry which empties my back-pack out, but

SOUTH AMERICA
ENCHANTMENT

it won't be ready until tomorrow morning which surprises me with the length of time, but when in Rome, be a Roman.

Off we go to see the adventures of Manaus. It's still quite early and Roberto has some running around to do, so I agree to stay with the Internet. To my happiness, there is another e-mail from my wife and I send her one off. Shortly thereafter, we both decide that since he's got about two hours before his flight that we will go back to the theater.

It's open now and the admission is five *real*, the best money I've spent. Inside, it warrants every quality that the European opera houses have and these rubber barons brought a culture to this part of the world that has been both enduring and rewarding. I've taken quite a few pictures of the inside and they've got some staff members, two young ladies and a gentleman dressed up in period costume. Our guide takes us up to the opera boxes and private rooms used for viewing performances. They're rehearsing now, but to my

249

disappointment, there are no performances until April. From the very grandeur of this building and listening to the orchestra that's practicing, I know the people in Manaus support this well-earned art. The guide tells us the iron columns that support the terraces of private rooms were brought in from England. Also the huge curtain is the original, and it has never been folded. It rolls itself right up into the dome above, so that it hasn't deteriorated, and even after a hundred years, it shows that people had the right idea.

As we enter one of the rooms, I get a picture of two young ladies (parlor maids) dusting. The men would sit in this room smoking their cigars and drinking their brandies, and on the other side, the women would fan themselves and make conversation. Segregation of the sexes was the order of the day during this period. Down on the main floor is a ballroom for dancing and the frescoes on the ceilings are quite remarkable. One of the frescoes depicts a woman with her arms stretched out. She seems to follow you throughout the room, even when you go the opposite way, her arms follow you; and the optical illusion continues when you go behind her, she's turned around with that arm stretched out for you. The sexual con-

SOUTH AMERICA
ENCHANTMENT

text is even more apparent in another fresco, of a woman with no clothes on; her arm goes up and down. These people had not only a lust of the flesh in those days, but they also had the knowledge of optical illusions. The floor the ballroom is cut in diagonal designs, a work of art in its own right, with many different inlaid woods from all over the world. In the theater itself, there were four distinct frescoes on the ceiling describing the elements of art, such as tragedy, comedy, musical, and high-end opera. Also, there were masks of all the great Greek performances. The walls of the corridors are covered with a fabric, but during the military occupation of Brazil in the seventies, the building was neglected. They covered the frescoes that are still underneath, but they not in pristine condition. I bought two CDs of the musical performances recorded in this building, as the acoustics are works of art in themselves. As an example of how much thought was put into this, the builders of the theatre mixed up a rubber compound to use at the entrance, so that late-comers in horse-drawn carriages wouldn't disturb the performance because

the carriages obviously would make a noise on the cobble-stones. We think we have some great ideas today, but these people weren't slow and when they wanted something done, they overcame the obstacle.

Across the large *piazza* facing this building were a lot of the land barons' homes. So, if you were rich enough, you didn't have to take the carriage to the theater, you just walked over. The large statue in the square indicates, by use of two different types of stone, the two rivers, the Amazon and the Negro, (the Negro being the

251

black stones). With all this knowledge, both Roberto and I
head back to the main centre. It is 11:00 a.m. and we say our
goodbyes, and he reminds me, "Please send me the photographs". So I am back on my own, once again.

One of my first priorities is relocate my belongings and myself to a different hotel. Right across the street from the
Internet and where all the buses seem to stop are quite a few
rows of hotels. I just thought that at random, I would start
with one called The Imperial Hotel. Not a bad choice, for a
name at least. I went in and it's between night and day, compared to the one that I'm staying in. It's not a five-star but it
has some star rating compared to subterranean (the one that
I've been staying in). I ask the price and its ninety *real*, compared to twenty, so almost five times the amount. The clerk
at the front desk is an East Indian fellow, born in Bombay. We
make some small talk about his homeland and his city of origin. It's nice to talk to somebody that has a larger command
of the English language than most people here. Already, he's
discounted it to seventy-seven *real* and I'm almost tempted to
take it but out of prudence, I said, "I'd like to check around a
little bit and also I'd like to look into some tours first."

He mentions the person next door that has a little tourist
booth. Lady-luck and myself entered the domain of this very
kind person that's named Harashi. He doesn't speak much
English but makes up for it with great energy. He starts to
show me the amount of conventional accommodations that
most of the tourists go to. He produces a map and with a lot
of gestures on both our behalves, he shows me some of the
areas in the north that I want to take part in. I asked him
about the carnival, which he tells me starts at the Convention
Center. I learn more about the city itself, and most importantly, about the boats continuing their voyage and my quest
to the mouth of the Amazon.

I just really like the fellow and he'll do anything but push
you on the ideas. He's made about ten or fifteen phone calls
to confirm the information he is giving is correct. For all this
kindness, I ask if he would be interested in joining me for

SOUTH AMERICA
ENCHANTMENT

lunch and he said, "No, no, that's fine" and I said, "No, I really insist. I would really like to take you for lunch." He mentioned a small restaurant that he knows of and the food is good. So, I get to be on my first city bus ride, for about seven kilometers from the hotel. I know taxi drivers throughout the world have a reputation for being bad drivers in the sense that they drive fast, reckless, and try to get from point-A to point-B as fast as any race car driver. However, this is the first time I've been on a bus that performs in the same way. These people believe that the pedal to the metal is the only way automobiles or any other form of transportation, including this large bus, performs. Last night, I just about got run over by a bicycle (not a motorcycle but a bicycle); and it's not that they're out to pin pedestrians to the asphalt, it's just the way they drive and you really do have to be careful. This bus is just rocking, and they're all standards, so these guys are just shifting gears all day.

We get off the bus and walk less than a block. From the outside, this doesn't even look like a building, let alone a restaurant. It just looks like it could easily be, if it had been at ground level, a carport. However, when you go down a few steps, there are little metal tables with fold-down chairs and a plastic cover over the tables. Any person not knowing this area, or being from out of town, let alone a foreigner like myself, would have walked by this place without even giving it a second glance.

We sit in the outside part, and this man asked me what I'd like. He describes some of the fish, the specialty of the restaurant. I decide on a white fish, quite nice. In the meantime, lots of people are coming in. This whole neighborhood is in need of restoration and improvements, and if this were in North America, it would be just bulldoze over and start fresh.

With the meal, I ordered an 'Arctica champagne' which is a pop made from the granada fruit, or passion fruit. The fruit grows locally here, and seems to have many uses, as a remedy and tonic, and in a soda drink that's very popular down here called Barreiro. This is an alcoholic beverage, made with the

253

Robert F. Edwards

passion fruit, cream, sugar, and *cachaca*. The fruit is harvested after it falls to the ground and it looks about the size of a papaya. The seeds inside resemble eyes, and there's a legend that one of the first native Indian origins comes from this fruit. For many of the fruits grown here, the natives of the Amazon have used them to cure diseases. Botanists and researchers in pharmaceutical companies are now trying to learn from the different plant extractions how to improve the global contribution to health.

One of the legends I was told was of two brothers and a sister living in paradise. The sister is tempted by the snake to have sex and is cast out of paradise. She bears a son and when the son grows up, he begs her to take him back to have these special nuts that were in paradise, which they do, and of course, he gets such a craving for them, he decides to return again. The bird that was protecting paradise is replaced by the monkey. The monkey kills the boy, shooting him full of arrows. The mother buries him and from his left eye, I guess, grew one virtue, and out of his other eye grew goodness and kindness, and so forth, and this is how this fruit's legend is put into effect.

Now back to the meal. Believe me; I've tasted fish all over the world. I'm not a connoisseur of fish, but I have had my share of both delicious and exotic. This fish has a place in paradise, along with the fruit of the legend. Every mouthful of this fish I'm savoring and even thinking about it, my mouth is watering. The preparation is very simple. It's a large fish and the steak-sized filets are just pan-fried, sometimes with lime or lemon on it. Along with it, I have beans and rice mixed together and there's also a pepper. This hot pepper makes the Tabasco sauce pale by comparison. Once you get the pepper into the pores of your tongue, it's literally impossible for liquid to cool it down. However, I manage after quite a few gulps of different things to subside the heat. I won't do this one again. This gentleman just looks at me as if he has watched a performance done by an immortal. He does insist, "No, I don't like hot food." When I popped the pepper into my mouth, his eyes bulged. Maybe mine did too, I don't know. This meal is the best I've had in Brazil and it may very well be the best fish I've ever had in the world. I am just elated by the experience.

We walk back to his office, and he has the patience of Job. I was asking him about the hotel. I said, "It's sort of expensive." He said, "Would you like to go?" He makes a phone call again and about six, seven blocks away from this Imperial Hotel is another one. I was considering this, as it was only thirty-eight *real*. However, I have decided to stay at the Imperial just for the location and access to his office. Though I'm familiarizing myself with the city very quickly, and it's not a very hard city to get around, the Imperial is my first choice. We check out two or three other hotels and fifty-five to sixty

real seems to be the price chiseled in stone, no matter how many days you wish to stay.

After he makes a few more phone calls for me on other things, I decide to do a bit of strolling, and have an afternoon to do nothing and see a lot. I stop into a liquidation place, try on a pair of shorts, didn't like them, but again people are very easy going here, more than helpful. When you say this isn't what you want, it's, "Oh well, too bad. I wish I could help you, but maybe next time."

As I continue along, I happen to see a barber shop and my hair is getting exceptionally long so, I felt, "Well, I'll get a haircut." The young fellow that cut my hair is in synch where the beat rolls on. He's sporting a two-tone hairdo and some unique side-burns. Most men here have their hair cut very short, and especially the young men almost have G.I. Joe haircuts. However, this G.I. Joe just wants a regular haircut and with a bit of explanation, I sit in the chair and watch huge tufts of white hair hit the floor and mingle with the black hair that has already gone before it. The fellow knows what he's doing and just gives me a really good haircut. It's a joke that when I can't speak the language, I can get a better haircut than when I'm sitting in the barber chair in my own neighborhood. Another thing, he points to my eyebrows. I've always been very reluctant to have them cut, but he makes a gesture and I figure, "What the heck? I've had it done once before, why not?" Boy, when he gets finished with me, I do look a lot younger and feel more 'uptown'. Its five *real* (about two U.S.), I give him a tip and he just can't believe that he gets more than the going rate.

I continue strolling up and down different streets, just enjoying myself and spending time thinking about my next moves in the week ahead. It's now close to 5:00 p.m. and I'm back in the general vicinity of the hotel. So off I go to the Internet, my favorite mode of communication. I send my beautiful wife a couple of e-mails and head back to the Imperial Hotel to see if this gentleman from India is on duty. Nobody seems to know, so I explain to the girl at the front desk (who speaks little or no English) that I'd like to stay at their hotel but I'm not prepared to pay the ninety *real*. She says, "Oh, I'll give you seventy-seven." I say, "No, I'm sorry. That's not good enough. All the other hotels would go down to at least fifty-five, sixty." So, she comes back in a minute and says, "Well, the very best we can do is sixty" which was only five more *real* than I was hoping to get in the first place.

It's dark now, about 7:00 p.m., and my feet are hurting. I've walked a lot today in sandals, which isn't my first choice of footwear. The *piazza* is now buzzing with activity, and many kiosks with these shish-kebabs of meat and again, rice and beans, and a little bit of a salad, which I order. The girl has trouble changing five *real*. When you are doing what the locals do, boy! It's really cheap living here. This meal ends up being about a dollar-and-a-half, I guess, U.S. I order a large beer and sit down and just watch the activities taking place.

SOUTH AMERICA
ENCHANTMENT

Lots of people are hawking goods, anything from jewelry to kids trying to sell Chiclets. I give two little kids some money without even getting the Chiclets. I'm not really a big gum chewer. One fellow comes over with butane lighters. One caught my interest, and he wants forty-five *real* for it, which is ridiculous. I said, "Ah, *mañana*", but he knows that a sale now is worth a dozen sales tomorrow. So, I finally give in at twenty *real* which is probably twice as much as I should have paid, but it's well done, and I hope that Marietta likes it.

I decide that my feet have done as much walking as they want to do and I'm going to venture back to the hotel. Once I entered the room, I know I made the right choice by moving. The room is full of bugs. I don't know what kinds are on the floor but I've got rid of as many as I could see. Also, there are spiders and three different types that I'm aware of, and God knows what other creepy crawly things are lurking in the dark or hiding under the bed. I'm not going to get on my knees to take a look, that's for sure. I watch a bit of television and then reluctantly turn the lights off to sleep. It's not a very peaceful sleep. During the night, probably my vivid imagination, but it felt like something's crawling on me and half a dozen times, I got out of the bed and turned on the light. It's not the first time I've slept with bedbugs or other insects and it's not my preference, so I feel much better that I'd made the right choice by moving on.

With those sobering thoughts, I'm going to say goodnight. Goodnight, little honey-bun, and I would far rather have Buttons on the bed than what I have here. I love you very much and I hope that you had a good day. Wendy, I haven't heard from you on the e-mails and I gather you and Cole are busy; I love you dearly. To each and every one of you, God bless you and have a good night's sleep.

Robert F. Edwards

February 7, Thursday

Manaus, Brazil

Well, I make it through the night with each and every companion, either in hiding this morning or not. I get cleaned up and get the balance of my things packed. It's early and I'm off to the room where they serve breakfast, which is one bun and a cup of coffee. Then, down to the Internet. Unfortunately, I find that in this particular case, the early bird doesn't get the worm. The worms aren't up yet. So, the Internet isn't open and neither are most of the shops. I have to wait for the Internet, and the laundry doesn't open until 8:30 a.m. So, I've got a bite on the day but I'm just going to have to be patient.

As I walk around, it's a nice day and people are starting to get their shops open for the business of the first trade and commerce. I work my way down into the market area which is where the old plantation buildings are. It's very interesting, with lots of small stores and every conceivable choice of goods. This city really doesn't cater to tourists or to the great souvenir quest of bargains. This is a working city. However, it's interesting to walk around and see the different shops with their choice of survival in the trade and commerce world.

I'm pretty convinced I'm going to try to go into the jungle and preferably up into the northern parts, so I probably need something lighter than the heavy wool hats that I bought in Peru. I have an idea of what I want, but to obtain it is something else. I do happen to find a hat shop, and for five *real* I end up buying a cap with "Yes, Manaus" written on it.

With that done, I go back to the center core of this market, where there are Indian crafts. It's not artifacts by any stretch of the imagination. These are working crafts, anything from headwear to complete outfits that the natives wear. They are made from some type of dried bark. The headdresses go right down to the legs and some of them have pants to them. Some

258

of these costume-attires also have a large erect penis built in, and so it's very easy to identify which is the man's and which is the woman's. Throughout the world, I've found that mankind seems to be obsessed with erections and this culture of Indians is no exception.

The woods used are really interesting. Some of the masks are made up of a very soft, balsam wood, and some of the other carvings are from beautiful rich mahogany. Many items, anything from large headdresses to small ones, and armbands are made with different bird feathers and local nuts. To say that the craftsmanship is primitive would be both naïve and incorrect. The materials used are all natural, the shells of the nuts and plants, along with feathers, have been integrated into the crafts. There are hats that are woven out of a fiber similar to straw, but much stronger, as well as baskets. I just wish that I had more space in my baggage. However, I just can't let this opportunity go. I purchased a fraction of what I would like. I limit myself to one small mask, an antique hardwood carving, plus a few small pieces of jewelry with the feathers in it. It's now about 9:30 a.m. and off to get my laundry and start my trekking back to my new abode.

Back in the neighborhood, I see the travel agent that I met the first day is open. I found the old adage of 'check, check, and then check again' seems to be a good rule of thumb when you're traveling and I still use it consistently. I ask them about the carnival, but nobody seems to know too much about what's transpiring. Also, I haven't seen any shops displaying a lot of costumes, either. But these men tried their best and they suggest, "If you really like to go dancing, there's a club" and the fellow was good enough to write it down. You can either go with just your underwear and a bunch of sparkles, for thirty *real*; or you can spend sixty *real* and get a shirt and a bandana. He also said that the young fellow next to him in the travel bureau is going to go and I can go with him. People are very friendly and sincere about it. So, I said I'd let them know and I was laughing. I said, "Well, I sure don't want to go where I'm half-naked, because I've got an old

259

body." Phil says, "How old are you?" I say, "Sixty." He laughs gets up, and he says, "I'm only forty-five and I'm fatter than you." He wasn't really; he was in fairly good shape.

Next, I pick up my laundry. God, I knew I had a lot of clothes to be washed but I didn't realize what a big bundle. Back at the hotel, I make my first reconnaissance. I'm not going to be able to take all this stuff in one haul. So, with my laundry, my hiking boots back on my feet, and my smaller bag, off I go to the Imperial. With my first load of goods arriving and myself, I check in. It's not exactly the same room I saw, but it's quite large. In fact, it has a bedroom and a small sitting room with a fridge, television, and oh yes, the air-conditioner. With that first load, I go back to the other hotel. The woman said, "Are you checking out?" I said, "Yes." I put my huge backpack on, and with my trusty walking stick from the Inca Trail I make my way down the six blocks to the Imperial Hotel. With all my goods now in the newer hotel, I feel quite vindicated.

I go back to see Harashi, the travel agent. He's consistently in good spirits and I told him that I am now ready to book some of the programs as I have figured out roughly what I want to do. If everything goes to plan which, why not, tomorrow I am going to take a tour into the jungle and go up about one hundred and fifty kilometers north of Manaus. On the ninth is when the carnival starts and I'm hoping to go to the Community Center where they have a platform of chairs. To the best of my knowledge, you get a seat, especially if you pay for it. The next day is a day of rest, Sunday, and I have full intentions of going to church before taking part in the carnival's activities.

I did take part in the carnival last year in Rio de Janeiro as well as in some of the smaller towns along the southern coastline. I've been told that the spirit of the carnival is best felt in the northern part, due to the population mix. The Portuguese brought in a lot of slaves from Africa; and between the Indians and the Africans and the Portuguese being interbred, they not only produced a very beautiful race of people but they blended a lot of the African superstitions and culture into a religion. The carnival is in anticipation of Lent. In Catholic countries, during the forty days before Easter, you give up meat and other things as a penance. Whereas the Moslems that practice Ramadan have their fasting from morning to sunset. So, on Sunday, I might do both, be a true Roman Catholic and go to church; and become a pagan at night.

Hopefully, on the eleventh, I am going to take a two-day expedition into the jungle for what they call treetop camping, where you stay in the canopy, high up in one of these huge trees so that you get the full impact of Mother Nature. The next three days I will be going to a floating campsite. If all goes well and weather permitting, we'll stay put; if the weather is uncooperative, we'll just pull camp and go somewhere else. This is where we take dugout canoes and torches at night, and wake up the animals so we can see them. Nice bunch of tourists. Good attitude on nature at its best and mankind at its worst.

So, that will take me up to the fifteenth, or a week tomorrow. I don't want to plan too far ahead because things do change in the life of a traveler. This is what I tentatively booked for the next week. Tomorrow's trip is (in monetary interest, ninety *real*; and the tree-top adventure for two days is one hundred and thirteen U.S. dollars, international currency of the world; and the Green Planet tour of floating campsites for three days, I am quoted a special discount of one hundred and fifty dollars. I started with a student's price of one hundred and eighty, and told him that I was student of life but definitely not a student in age. He sounds like a very nice man over the phone and by the time we got finished, he dropped the price to a hundred and fifty. I know this is the low season with a lack of *turistas* anyway, so maybe I'm just getting a good price.

With the better part of the morning behind us, I tell my agent that all I could do was keep thinking of the fish I had yesterday and would he be interested in a meal again today? He said sure, he would be happy to and with that, I toddle off to the Internet and do a little bit of checking. I got a few e-mails from my good wife and a bunch of other e-mails from some of my friends.

The weather, of course, has its moments of tears from the sky and then the sun comes out and blesses the earth once more. At noon, one of his friends is joining us and we return to my restaurant of first choice in Manaus. His friend is a lawyer, a very nice man, and one of the few lawyers I've ever met that has good humor. Maybe he has an advantage by not speaking English.

I choose a different type of fish today. It's a smaller fish. In fact, the head and the tail have joined the rest of the body on the plate. This is equally as tasty, but nowhere near the texture of meat of the large fish yesterday. We also have the rice and beans. The lawyer shows me a more civilized way of having the pepper. He takes a very small portion of the pepper, and with a spoon, pulverizes it into the plate. Then you take a little bit of this juice (which is similar to Tabasco sauce); add a little bit of oil and by choice, some salt and most importantly, the better part of a lime. And you've got a flavorful, peppery sauce. Nowhere near as pungent and demanding as just popping one of these deadly little chilies into your mouth.

About an hour-and-a-half later, we return to the office. Harashi and I sit around a bit and talk. I tell him that I'm going to try and get some money at the bank and just do a little bit of running around, only to find the banks are closed. The inter-banking systems don't work for foreign cards and with a lot of help from the locals I gather the best bank for international transactions is the Bank of Brazil. All these banks favor their own banking cards and even the ATM machines are of local banks. I recall that the last time that I was in Rio de Janeiro, that Brazil prefers MasterCard to Visa, and I had trouble finding a bank machine to accept the currency. I return to the office, five banks and an hour later without any success.

The agent, Harashi, informs me that he'll be coming with me tomorrow, which is a sheer delight. I really enjoy his com-

SOUTH AMERICA
ENCHANTMENT

pany, just an easygoing person to be around, and polite. The people of South America remind me of Canada about fifty years ago when people had this wonderful attitude. They were polite, thoughtful, generous, and good neighbors, kind people. You might say that we're influenced by the Americans, but we seem to be taking on habits that are not commendable. In North America, we seem to be going through an adjustment stage and it's not for the betterment of civilization. Developed countries seem to be both impatient ignorant, demanding, and rude; maybe not in that order, but in that priority. In this country and this city, people are still the good neighbor. They're actually what biblical times described as the Good Samaritan. They help each other. They help strangers. They're kind and they're poor. But above all, they're rich in all the things that have made humanity prosper and grow as a civilized species. I enjoy very much being around these types of people. They've rejuvenated many of the attitudes that I grew up with as a boy and want to continue as a man.

This man, Harashi fits into that category of being helpful to me and will do anything. He's concerned about the Convention Center and the carnival and he asked if I'd like to go on the bus and see where the Convention Center is. With that, we both cross the street and get on the bus and it is again another ride for your life. I'm amazed at the speed they travel and without having major catastrophes. One thing about these buses, you enter them from the back, where a conductor takes your fare as you go through a turnpike. Quite a different system of being organized than the transit systems in Canada and the United States.

These buses are also diesel or gas buses, and boy, do these guys ever drive, and I'll tell you! They weave in and out with these huge vehicles as if they were a sports car. While we are waiting for the light, I just can't help but think of somebody with a checkered flag waiting for them to change because as soon as they get the signal, its pedal to the metal and bang! They're off, and it doesn't matter what living creature's in front of them. And I should warn anybody, look both ways

263

Robert F. Edwards

and look again and then run like hell because whether it's a bus or a taxi, to say nothing of those motorcycles and bicycles that wheel around and try to get you, pedestrians are not the chosen people. As we're barreling down the roads, for some unknown reason the thing starts to hiccup and he informs us that there's something wrong with the bus, so we all have to get off the bus and get on a different one.

The Convention Center is designed as an amphitheater, very modern and extremely high. Along both sides are the bleachers. The whole construction of this center is open air and concrete. There's a small group of people at the main entrance and my good friend asks a lot of questions and translates the best he can, on what areas are free, what is charged for, and about the seats in the semi-circle part of this construction. It's got the most magnificent view because the parade will be going right down the center of the amphitheater and you'll probably be able to see the whites in everybody's eyes in the parade.

However, I'll be happier than anybody that's attending this parade if I get to sit down as this is an all night-affair. It starts about 8:00 p.m. and goes right until 7:00 a.m. I can't picture twelve hours or more standing, no matter how enthusiastic I am. We are just about to leave when a gentleman whom we had been talking to, comes over and offers us some cake and Coca-Cola. This fellow gives me this piece of cake and it's absolutely delicious. There is a big hunk of pure chocolate on top. Both the upper and lower molars developed a sweet tooth in each and every one of them. There are about eight or ten people grouped around the table, all happy and very friendly. When I make the motion of discoing, young and old alike light up like little Christmas trees and give me the thumbs up, smiles, and laughing and cheerful.

It starts to rain. It's funny here, people generally don't like the rain and they only have two seasons: rainy and non-rainy. However, they seem to have a strong feeling about it. When it's raining here, it starts gentle, rains hard, and then eases off, and goes away. Not like where I live in Vancouver,

SOUTH AMERICA
ENCHANTMENT

Canada where you get a drizzle for two or three weeks and the only time you know there's sun is when you see a weather report from some other part of Canada.

We make our way to the bus station and we have to wait for a bus called *Centro* to take us back downtown. Harashi takes me back to the hotel and wishes me a good night, just a fine man that gave me a wonderful day in my life. I return to the room, and watch a few of the bands setting up in the streets. There's a massive crowd gathering about two blocks away.

I make my way down and yes, the carnival has officially started. This is more what the carnival is all about, bands sprouting up either on the streets or the *piazzas*, and mega-speakers producing the sound that is music to Brazilian ears. The sambas, the rhythm, and just the party atmosphere are alive and gyrating. This is more what I'd experienced last year in some of the smaller centers. Even in Rio de Janeiro, if you knew where to go, there were these street dances where the locals really have a good time. They drink lots of beer, eat shish-kebabs and dance the night away. And when I say "the night away," I literally mean the entire night! Sleep by day, play by night. My feet, though, are absolutely killing me and I'm just a little too tired to take part in anything other than admiring their stamina.

So, with that, I return to my room and say goodnight to my beautiful wife and I miss you dearly. I love you very much and someday, somehow, I would love to take you on a trip to see the little critters and the birds and bees that you love so dearly. I hope those dogs in your life are looking after you, rather than you looking after them. Good night, little Wendy bird, and Coleman and all your dreams come true. For all the rest of you, get a good night's sleep. The carnival is just around the corner.

Robert F. Edwards

February 8, Friday

Manaus, Brazil

I got up at 6:00 a.m. and at 7:00 a.m. I was supposed to be picked up. My friend Harashi showed up at on time and at quarter after eight, we were still sitting in the lobby. After numerous phone calls he was assured that the vehicle was on its way. If my friend, the travel agent, hadn't been able to come, I would have thought that there had been a mix-up of hotels, or that they'd missed me, or I'd been late, or something had happened, and the latter would have been the truth. Something had happened; the vehicle had encountered a traffic jam due to an accident. So, I guess, all these racecar drivers do have collisions like everybody else. We finally do get picked up and after collecting the rest of the group and a cooler full of water and pop, off we go.

I've made arrangements to go on a tour of caves, waterfalls,

towns, etc., about hundred and fifty miles north of Manaus. The major village is Presidente Figueiredo. This village is very close to the area of the protected environmental lakes, now a reserve. There is also a large hydro dam at Balbina, about fifty miles away.

There are a few other people on the tour with me today. There's a husband and wife and their two young teenagers, an older couple closer to my age, and my friend Harashi, and of course, the driver. I

SOUTH AMERICA
ENCHANTMENT

asked if there was somebody who spoke English and the answer is "no."

On our way to the waterfalls, we pass the *Encontro das Águas*, or Meeting of the Waters. This is the section of the river where the Rio Negro joins up with the Rio Solimões. When they say "Negro", referring to black water, it is really black, especially seen alongside the light sandy waters of the Solimões. The color distinctions run for quite a distance alongside each other, without mingling.

I suppose everybody has his or her own impressions on what the jungle will be, regardless where it is in the world and I was no exception to the Amazon jungle. I somehow had this idea that I'd have to use a machete to cut my way through the vines that have grown up during the night and the vegetation that enclose the paths. I'm sure that this is not entirely out of the question when a path or a route has been neglected for a good many years. But, the jungle area we were in was very similar to what in my country would be called "dense forest".

Obviously different vegetation than the pine and cedar forests of my region, but trees are the order of the day in this jungle. Yes, there are some big ferns and an abundance of fruit-bearing trees. The soil here is very sandy and a reddish color. I'm told that the soil only bears about two or three crops before it is depleted of nutrients to produce any further crops. This kept the original Indian natives, whom Manaus is named after, on the move, due to the fact that the soil just does not produce any long-term agriculture.

267

Robert F. Edwards

The Brazilian government in the seventies encouraged a lot of people from the south and other parts of Brazil to open up these areas primarily so that they wouldn't lose the lands to both foreigners and encroachment from other countries. This is similar to what North America tried to do with the far north: that if it isn't occupied, it's fair game to be taken. Brazil was trying to open up agricultural areas and increase the population. This road is quite remarkable, to think that it's in the middle of the jungle. Excellent condition and I have no idea what the cost to maintain such a remote area of a highway would be, but I give them full compliments for the fine job and the quality of this two-lane highway.

We walk a short distance in to see the waterfalls, *Cachoeira do Paricatuba*, and spend some time taking pictures and telling each other how beautiful it is. There is a young man who speaks some English. His name is (believe it or not!) Gerald Edwards. Besides the scenery, I've taken some pictures of lizards, in all sizes. Their colors are magnificent, such different shades. And do these little devils ever move! It's so funny. They obviously blend in with the environment and then when you do spot one, and I think he probably hears you rather than sees you, he starts to get up on his hind legs and moves in a jerky motion. But, if you don't think lizards can move, you've never seen one in action. These critters really know how to run and I don't think a fast dog could catch one of these guys. I see some very interesting mushrooms and flowers that I take pictures of also. Oh, we did see one wild boar, and I spot a monkey in the tree. It's not what Hollywood produces as the chattering noise in the jungle, for it quite quiet and very peaceful.

We make our way down to the next port of entry, to see the caves and grottos at *Refúgio Maroaga* and waterfalls of *Cachoeira da Iracema*. We walk about a good kilometer or so in and quite steep, which brings back memories of the Inca trail, going down ladders and railings. By no means is this to be considered a remote area of the jungle; it's definitely *turista* stuff. Even the walkways are elevated and there are board-

SOUTH AMERICA
ENCHANTMENT

walks to make it easy for the city-dweller to enjoy some of the beauty of this part of the world without the challenges of the jungle.

The first cave we get to is very large and majestic. Without too much encouragement, a bunch of us start to walk into the cave. It's got water running out of it, not too deep, six inches at the most. It depends on what time of the year you are there, otherwise it fluctuates considerably. The driver has a large torch and as we enter and turn a bend we start to see some bats. The two women are quite apprehensive about this and I must admit that the gravel bed is quite sharp, so I was thinking, "Geez, I wish I'd worn my sandals rather than my boots, and I would have left my sandals on as I walk through this water." However, shoes off, socks off, and bare feet tickling the stones as I wade further and further into the cave. We walk in the better part of half a kilometer, and there's a lot to see in this cave and it's not all bats. There are some very interesting formations, and one section is shaped almost like a grand tiara, with different types of stone or lime deposits on it.

Robert F. Edwards

Also, there are huge caverns high up that have been gouged out by erosion. Our guide turns his torch off two or three times to give us the full effect of total darkness. I have experi-ences in caverns and underground mining, but there is nothing like a black hole, being totally devoid of light. I couldn't help myself, and made an eerie noise to enhance the uncertainty of the group everyone has a good laugh about it and we proceed further. Of course, the timid at heart prefer that we turn around and go back, but we continue on, and see some more cave-life. There are spiders that are about the size of my small fingers. They're blind because they live in total darkness, but just the same, between them and fleas and other insects in here, I wish the bats had a bigger appetite. After everybody's more than satisfied and the cave is becoming uncomfortable, we wade our way back to the entrance. It's nice to be back out in daylight. I wouldn't want to be a cave dweller, now or in prehistoric times.

I am glad to get my boots back on and it is time to hit the big metropolis of Presidente Figueiredo. I had originally been considering staying here for about a week and hiring a guide to work my way inland through the jungles. I'm grateful that I have chosen the other itinerary due to the fact that this town is quite touristy. It's got a sandy beach by the river, plus the restaurants and hotels, but not much else. I am still looking for a bank to try and get money out of, but no bank here. It's not crowded, although there are a few tourists that are enjoying the facilities by the river in the off-season. The town has a large statue of the native Indian with the huge bow and arrow.

In reality, these arrows are about a meter in length, and the range is quite extensive when drawn with a bow.

We stop for our lunch break, and one of the gentlemen in our group orders a beer. He tells me some of the history of this Bohemian beer. A German plantation baron missed his beer, which is more than understandable, and had it brought over for him. It ended up that an Italian created the Bohemian brand, which is the oldest brand of beer in Brazil, dating back to 1853. I've been on tours where food is included and I can honestly say without any hesitation I really wished that it hadn't been, but this a real exception. If this is Brazilian hospitality, it's the best-kept secret. It's an absolute feast. There are about four or five different types of fish. They asked me what I would like to eat and I said, "Well, you know, I prefer fish." Everybody was in agreement and ordered the same with again, the beans and rice, and salads, with chili peppers, sliced tomatoes and onions. One of the items that I am going to try when I get home is these fried bananas. They deep fry the banana and then roll it in sugar and cinnamon. If you really want to be a pig you can pour cream on it or even ice cream, if you so desire. Or, you can eat it along with the other part of the meal, as a vegetable. Also, the famous *papa fritas*, not the recycled mash, but real potato and then deep-fried. The crowning glory to finishing this meal was ice cream and believe me, it was real cream. It just melted in my mouth and left a silk coat. No matter what the price is in North America, we do not have access to this quality.

Everybody's motivated to get on to the next stop, and we head on to the next place, where a couple of parrots are sitting on the fence. I think they're quite tame to be very candid. Talk about security getting in! I couldn't help but say to Gerald, sitting beside me, "Geez, you'd think this was a real border that has a conflict with each other." First, we go through a gate with a big restriction, then over a speed bump that would knock the wheels off an eighteen-wheeler, and then through a huge dip, which might not have sunk the Titanic but would have put a dent in any keel. After this torture test for any vehicle, we manage to go up a small roadway and now have to pay quite an exorbitant price per head to get in. We stop along the way and the driver shows us some of the Granada fruit lying on the ground. As we work our way further in, we come to another huge waterfall, and a few of the group go for a swim in the river. It's quite swift, but there's a little pool off the current and the water's warm. I said to Harashi that I don't swim, so no point in me trying to prove anything.

Further down is a cave that has the appearance of a cathedral entrance and, of course, we take lots of pictures of that. Harashi mentions that about a kilometer or so down the river, there's another waterfall. Without too much encouragement, I thought, "Well, I'll take a walk down the trail, for at least a little bit." So, by now we are at least a good four kilometers from the vehicle, and half of them are real jungle trails, not these pre-made tourist sites. Still, I set off, and this gentleman and his two sons decide to take part also. I was only going down as far as I felt comfortable, but now that there's four strong, I decided, "Well, if we're gonna see a waterfall, let's get going." I find walking through the jungle similar to many forests. There are the trees that have fallen over across paths, and roots sticking out exposed from erosion, and the usual leaves and debris that make the weaving and twisting of a trail in the jungle the same. I found it easy to adapt to the walking, and whether I'm on an Inca trail or a climb in Africa or I'm walking the streets of Vancouver, I've got a fairly fast clip. Once I get the feel of the terrain, it's quite easy to judge where to put my next footstep, so I start to really pick up the pace.

We've gone the better part of half-an-hour and the three others are asking me (in Portuguese) how much further. I

SOUTH AMERICA
ENCHANTMENT

keep on saying, "Well, you know, another ten minutes. It's a kilometer and we haven't gone that far yet." Finally, I can see one little fall. Well, it's not what I would consider much of a fall, but probably would have sufficed them. I said, "No, no, the trail isn't finished." So we agree to walk at least for another ten minutes and if nothing materializes, then we'll turn back. I'm boogying pretty darn fast, sort of running through the jungle more out of curiosity and actually enjoying the walk. It's not a *turista* trail but a natural path in a jungle. I really feel in tune with nature, and my other companions, I think, are enjoying it but nowhere near as enthusiastically.

Believe it or not, I think the young men are worried about danger more than us two older men. Anyway, close to the time permitted me to find the falls, lo and behold, almost like Christopher Columbus, I'm saved by the sound. He was able to have somebody spot land; I'm able to hear a real roar. We have gone over the ten minutes, but now my companions are as enthusiastic as I am. Of all the falls that we've seen today, it was well worth it. This one is the most challenging to get to, but it's broken into two parts and it's difficult to see. We have to work our way down to the riverbank. As luck will have it,

273

there's a tree that's toppled over and we are able to scramble out on it to get a view. We feel that we have just discovered a very remote falls. Like a couple of happy children all dancing with glee, we spend some time congratulating each other.

The young man, Gerald, is interested in taking quite a few pictures. I'm ready to return and start walking back, only to hear, "Mr. Bob, Mr. Bob". I stop and Gerald's brother comes running up, "Please, please, wait. We all want to stay together." And I realized for the first time that I'm their guide (Leave it to a crazy Canadian!) These people have trusted me now in finding their way back in the jungle. I am somewhat surprised because, although I probably have more experience in outdoor living than these three put together, but I just think that when it's your own terrain, you know a lot more than a foreigner. However, this was not the case. Being quite conversant with trails in general, I have no problem returning to the first waterfall and keep stopping to make sure that the others are within sight, and that they haven't lost sight of me, or vice versa.

The mother of these two guys is anxiously waiting for our return. I think she is of Japanese descent. She shakes her finger at me and I guess she was very concerned and worried. Of course, when you walk two kilometers in a city park, it takes some time. When you're walking two kilometers in a forest or jungle, it takes longer because the paths are very uneven; you're climbing over fallen tree stumps, and the protruding roots of trees. You have to be very sure-footed and take your time. I guess every one, including the driver, was somewhat concerned about Jungle Bob and his expedition. Now that we have arrived back safe and sound, and Mom is assured that her family hasn't been gobbled up by wild beasts or squeezed to death by pythons, she is a happy little person again.

We get back in the van and head back to Manaus, arriving about 7:00 p.m. It's been a full day and an enjoyable one, as they are nice people to be with. The couples with their sons are going to the tree house also, so I will be able to meet up with them on Monday to spend a day or two with them. I enjoyed being with both sons, though Gerald speaks more English, and is a camera buff, so we have that in common.

Harashi gets out, and says he'll see me tomorrow and I'm dropped off at the hotel. I spend a little time with the Internet, sending off an e-mail to Marietta, reading some of news and so forth. It's not that late, it's only about 8:30 p.m., but I am really tired! I probably walked the better part of fifteen kilometers today and a lot of it is heavy terrain. For whatever reason, my knee is still aching. It's odd, it doesn't seem to bother me too much when I'm walking or climbing, but when I'm lying in bed, it sure seems to hurt.

As much as I'd like to take part, or at least witness some of the events of the carnival, I'm just too tired. I have full intentions of resting for an hour or two and then getting up to see what's happening. It doesn't happen. I spend the entire night staying in bed.

Robert F. Edwards

Once again, little honey-bun, I miss you very much and no, I didn't really get to see any critters, did see a few birds and got a picture of them, so you can see those. Who knows? Maybe the next few days will produce some of the little critters that you really wanna see and I'll keep my eyes open for it. Wendy and Cole, I hope you're looking after Marietta. She sounds a little sad these days with her e-mails. Love you all very dearly and miss you a lot. For the rest of you people, I hope that you've enjoyed today in your mind's eye as much as I've enjoyed it with my two eyes. It's a beautiful part of the world and I hope that some of you will be able to see it with your eyes. Goodnight, one and all.

SOUTH AMERICA
ENCHANTMENT

February 9, Saturday

Manaus, Brazil

For all practical purposes, it's a day off. The big event that I'm counting on is the parade of the carnival, which is tonight. To the best of my knowledge, this starts around 8:00 this evening and goes right up until 7:00 Sunday morning. So, I am going to take it easy today, catch up on some zzzz's and conserve all the energy for the long night, which I'm hoping is going to be fulfilled.

Still, I am an early riser and at 7:00 a.m., I've finished my breakfast. This is probably one of the best breakfast facilities I've been in. A real Continental spread, different types of fruit, papaya and even watermelon as far as that goes, to cheeses, eggs, meats and fresh buns. Also, a delightful bunch of pastries, each one has its own surprise, some have a little bit of sauce in it, others have a piece of meat, and a choice of four or five different juices; and of course, coffee.

I still have this quest to get the credit card to work, and have given it a considerable amount of thought. I do have sufficient U.S. funds to meet the two other excursions. Unfortunately, if I did do this, I would leave myself extremely vulnerable to cash flow, with less than a hundred dollars U.S. total. To try and get passage on a boat for the rest of the journey and just hoping that I would get into a place where a bank was available is too much uncertainty. The other alternative is to stay another day in Manaus, but I'm going to be returning Friday night. There's a good possibility I would be three days behind just because of bank problems, or access to money through my Visa card.

I've chosen a plan of action: number one, to do another reconnaissance on trying to secure funds through the automatic banking system. Number two, is to have the travel agent phone these places and ask if they take Visa and if they do, then there's no problem; if they don't, then I'm obligated to cancel. With this decision reached, I take a stroll down through the different areas of town. I've been told that grocery stores have ATM machines, which is what I need, but also one that has international acceptance.

I do find a large grocery store, and ask the young lady at the information desk. She doesn't speak English but she seems to know what I want, takes the credit card, and walks with me through this mammoth store. The size of this place would give any of the box stores in North America a challenge. When we reach the other end of the store, there is a machine and my heart jumps forward. We try it, it still won't accept it. Not discouraged, this young lady motions me to come with her. We're back on the street and she takes me to another grocery store. She talks to the manager about it and he's nodding, but "No, this machine won't take it either." What I need is an international machine and he writes down for me 'the Amazona Shopping Center' which has one. I asked if I could walk there. And he said, "No, you need to take a bus or a taxi." I seem to be slowly closing in on the net of achievement.

I get back to my friend, the travel agent, and we make a bit of small talk and greetings of the day. I explained the situation to him the best I can and he phones the Green Planet. The gentleman says, "No, he doesn't take credit cards, but takes *real* or cash." I explained to him that I don't have either, due to the fact that my credit card is not being accepted. He assures me that he can do it, that he has done it even yesterday, for foreigners. He assures me that if I show up about fifteen minutes earlier at the lobby, he'll take me to one of the places and get me the money; and if he can't, so be it. He'll still take me on the tour and he says he just wants me to have a good time. I'm sure that he is more than confident that he is going to achieve cash return, and he seems like an interesting person to meet, I'm looking forward to it. With the other place, the Tree House Hotel, absolutely no problem. The hotel takes Visa and that's fine with them.

SOUTH AMERICA
ENCHANTMENT

So, that problem seems somewhat resolved, and everything is status quo. My wife often says that I have a lot of tenacity or determination and I'm sure that she's got a proper assessment. I have a philosophy in life, if you don't succeed the first time, try and try again. My credo is that if the job's worth doing, it's worth doing right. The difficult can be done at once and the impossible takes a little longer. Never use your friends and you'll always have lots of friends. I live by this credo and as I get older and more determined, these rules have fared well in my life. So, I haven't actually accomplished the impossible, but I have got the difficult behind me now.

Relieved of that pressure, I catch up on the Internet and to my pleasure; my wife's e-mails are waiting for me. I'm very grateful to have them and it's a wonderful way of keeping in touch. I find that tomorrow, Sunday, is a day of rest in the city and just about everything that commands trade and commerce is going to take a day off, including this place with the internet. My lines of communication will be severed.

Harashi, my travel agent, *amigo* and friend, has told me that he's going to take me to the carnival. This is the last thing this man likes doing. He's a quiet person and crowds and a parade is not something that he cherishes, but because he knows that it's a real quest with me, he's going to do it. He's done his homework and the seats fluctuate anywhere from a hundred and fifty *real*, to free. The hundred and fifty gives you not only a chair but also a little table, sitting at ground level with the parade. The other prices fluctuate on the location of the tiers in the Community Center. So, I said to him, "Well, you know, go ahead." He said, "It's gonna cost about ten *real* each." I said, "No problem. You know if you wanna bring your girlfriend or some friends, let me know and I'll pay for them as well." When I returned from the e-mail, he informs me that he's phoned up some person at the Convention Center and no, we don't have to pay. He's looking after my money better than I can get it out of the bank. That's for sure.

Robert F. Edwards

Harashi tells me he's going home around noon to get some rest, and he'll be back around 8:00 p.m. to pick me up and then we'll go to the Community Center. I find a lunch spot for myself, and yes, I have fish and oh, what a terrible disappointment. I've been spoiled by Harashi's restaurant. This one, I pay as much for my meal as I did for three of us at the other restaurant. Not that the money is the point, it was the quality of the food. A heavy white cheese is melted over the entire portion of fish that I've got, and the fish itself is tucked inside a thick batter and deep-fried. If there is fish in there, it passed through very quickly.

I wish now, (and of course hindsight makes no mistakes) that I'd chosen the buffet. In this particular restaurant, you can either order off the menu like I have, a fatal mistake; or, you can go to the buffet and take what portions you want and they weigh the amount. So, I would have been far better off, but it's done and I've begrudgingly paid the money, not because of the price, but with a disappointment in the quality of food.

I return to my room, and spend a little time reading the Lonely Planet book. My travel bible confirms that the Bank of Brazil is the one that I should go to, which I have, and that all the major outlets have a twenty-four hour service. Still determined, at least in my own mind, to find out if the information is correct or inadequate, I get back to the Bank of Brazil. Yes, there is a twenty-four hour automatic machine. I remember a young man telling me that he was able to get some money out of it. So, when the third machine became vacant, I tried it. Unbelievable! After two attempts, I have five hundred *real*, cash. Mission accomplished. The impossible done. My piggy bank is full. Now I have cash to suffice me till the end of this trip, or at least until I get to Rio de Janeiro, but will still use the convenience of a credit card.

As I'm walking back, I pass by some street vendors. They are more in the line of hippies or flower children of a by-gone period, with their jewelry and trinkets and self-made artistic designs. One that attracted my notice was some drawing on a turtle's back. I have mixed feelings about animals that are deceased, and hope this turtle served its time before the shell was used to create art. She wants seventy *real* for it and that's a lot of money. A year's wage down here is probably on a national basis around two thousand five hundred *real*. So, she'd be asking for a week's salary. Plus the fact that it's extremely heavy and I almost need a crane now to lift my backpack, let alone carry it. So, although it is an artistic piece of work, I have to consider the weight factor, rather than the financial amount.

Back at the hotel, about 5:00 p.m., I decide to send my ever-loving wife another e-mail, as we're not going to be able to communicate for the next two or three days. I think that she's getting extremely lonely and even the new little dog, Pepper, has not taken her mind off her isolation. She's not going to welcome this last e-mail due to the fact that I've told her that Sunday is null and void and there's the possibility Monday also, with Tuesday night being my first access to the Internet.

I start to prepare for the carnival parade at the community center. Sure enough, about 8:00 p.m., Harashi shows up with a friend, with a car, and we stop to get some gas. It is rather interesting, the gas prices per liter are about twice as much as in Canada and I thought we're expensive on transportation cost. I guess I would have a motorcycle, or be forced into what I'm doing right now, walking, if I was a permanent resident. We pick up a couple more guys, and I've got my small pack full of juice and some cookies, the camera, and some extra rolls of film. With supplies well in hand and enthusiasm at an all time high, the five of us head towards the community center.

What a difference compared to the first time when I went with Harashi to do a reconnaissance. This is wall-to-wall people and the mood is electrifying. Kiosks are lining every major artery to the community center, plus men are blowing whistles to get you into their parking spots, at an exorbitant price. We park the car and start our trek into the community center. By the time we weave in and out from where the car's parked to the entrance, it's close to a kilometer away. It's very difficult walking because the crowd is massive and swelling the closer we get to the community center. But, we get in and Harashi says, "Right, we don't pay anything, we get some really good seats, and let the parade begin."

This is not the first carnival I've been to and I hope it's not going to be the last. There is something about the carnivals in Brazil that draw global attention, but are unique to themselves. This will be the third one I have been to, but they all have a similar theme, in that the group numbering from fifty and up are all dressed in a similar costume. Then, there are also individuals dressed in their own creation. Of course, some of the women don't wear much of a costume. They believe that skin is the best costume of all and anything from tiny patches on the breast to bare breasts can be the ingredients of their costume. One of the things that is very popular is that they oil their bodies and decorate the skin with sparkles or body paint. Usually, the most fabric is in the headpiece.

The floats are remarkable. Not only are they huge, but also they are pushed by hand, and they can be anything from mystical figures to politicians, and impressions. Whatever the imagination can conjure up and the artistic abilities can produce, is acceptable with these floats. They are usually two levels high and people are precariously dancing on platforms staged on different levels - a feat of engineering just in its own right. After the parade, I got to see some of the inner construction of the floats. The inside supports are made out of half-inch angle iron at various angles to support the physical structure of the float. The exterior structure is made out of tubing and then covered with a rubbery-type of texture, painted. The details, when you get up close to these, are works of art. I understand whether it's the costumes or floats, that as soon as the carnival is over, they start working on the next one. The detail work takes many hours of dedicated enthusiastic commitment.

SOUTH AMERICA
ENCHANTMENT

The community center is filled with music, and I have no idea of how many people. From where I'm standing, it looks like ants unlimited. With the magnitude of activity that's going on and the music, the dancing, and the continuity of these performances, I can't help but get into the mood. In some of the bleachers, there are people waving balloons of one distinct color. The bands in the parade at the end of a column play and beat their drums, and the crowd responds with roars of enthusiasm. It's party time, there's no other word for it. The colors of these costumes and the huge lights beaming down, it's better than any street performance. It's very well organized.

There must be thousands of people that are taking part in the parade itself. To have a parade go for ten, eleven hours, there has to be a lot of people involved. I'm hoping some of my pictures will turn out to demonstrate the groups, they're all in different costumes, and some of them are very creative. One group is dressed like bishops and they carry huge platforms around their bodies, stopping periodically to put them down on the ground and do a performance of different dances, then they go back and put these arches on their shoulders, carry them another distance, stop, and do the same thing. Another group is dressed as the Centaur of Greek mythology, they put the horse down, do a dance and go back and attach their horse body to their Homo sapiens one and off they go again.

A word of caution; because the crowd of spectators is massive and there's a large consumption of beer, there is pushing and shoving and before long, in our particular section, two men decided to fight it out. I have to give the police full points. Within a matter of seconds, before we actually realized what was happening, the police were there and apprehended the two people involved and curtly scurried them off. I can now understand, when you read about people being killed at soccer games in Britain and in Europe. It is a concern and you do have to be cautious on what's happening around you, because if there were some kind of hysteria or even heavy movement of people in one direction, somebody

283

would get trampled to death or seriously injured, just by the sheer numbers of people around. But, I don't want to put a wet blanket on this remarkable evening that I'm having.

An amazing thing that I'm experiencing, is these costumes are just discarded afterwards, and the same with a lot of the floats, just thrown away. I guess it's my Scottish heritage that would have kept it for another event, but no, for these people, it's "I've made it all year, I've worn it for the parade, and I've had enough of it."

There are many schools and universities that take part in the parades, with their own bands. The people in our group have a particular color, red and white, representing their sect or school participants. I get a flag to wave (and probably the oldest student here) and keep it as a souvenir. By 2:00 a.m., I think Harashi has probably had as much as he can endure. The other two men don't seem to be motivated one way or the other. The driver seems to be enjoying himself as much as myself.

I've shared my juices and cookies with all of them. It's rather odd, that as the foreigner, I don't know the rules of what's transpiring, but I always seem to have the food chain in hand. I'm always glad that people take some and appreciate it, but I would have thought that they would have brought something or been prepared for such a long evening. Not that you can't get food. A lot of the fried banana chips that are quite popular in this area are being served and something that looks like cheese on very small shish-kebab sticks is available, and water. If you venture down into the mayhem you can secure beer and bring it up, which a lot of young people are doing.

We are starting to feel carnivaled out. I probably could have stayed longer, but I'm becoming a bit uneasy. A lot of people are moving from one area to the other. Then, two young guys that are just goofing around, but got some beer on one of the fellows and they started pushing and shoving, which is the type of thing that can create a very serious danger. About half an hour ago, somebody pushed a girl behind me and she fell against my shoulders. It just happened that I was the stabilizing wall in her case, but if we'd both gone forward, it would have been the dominoes effect. I'm quite content that I've enjoyed a good portion, at least five or six hours of the festivities, so I decide it's time to leave.

I meet up with one of Harashi's friend who is a doctor, and was in the parade. He is still in really good spirits, and we play around, taking pictures of ourselves putting on some of the costumes and hats. I tried to get Harashi to participate, but he doesn't like that type of thing. I was probably more into the carnival spirit than the other four, but we make our way back to the vehicle and drop the other two fellows off, then it's my turn to get back to the hotel. Harashi asked me if I'm doing anything tomorrow for lunch and I said "no". He says, "My friend is a good cook. We'd like you to come for lunch."

With that, I'm back in my room with my souvenir hat and flag, and a memory that will last a lifetime. Marietta, I can honestly say without any hesitation, this would not have been a night for you. Just the sheer number of the crowd, even if they'd sat there like mannequins, would have been more than you could have endured. However, my dearest little wife, I hope that some of the descriptions and pictures I've taken will be the next best thing for you to being there. And that goes for you, Wendy and little Cole. To each and everyone,goodnight.

Robert F. Edwards

February 10, Sunday

Manaus, Brazil

As usual, the early bird is up and I've put some of my thoughts down from the previous days. By now it's clean-up time and surprisingly, I have hot water. It's rather a funny little machine. On top, there's the showerhead, but on top of that, there is a small white cone and some bare wires running into it from the wall, which, I guess, generates the instant hot water. You don't have to worry about it being scalding, but it's not cold, at least. Pleasant enough for this guy, I'll vouch for that.

I go down for breakfast and, again, a much more elaborate breakfast than anything I've had on this trip for Continental breakfasts, and I've got into the habit of taking a couple of extra bottles of juice to suffice my needs along the day. With that behind me, I'm on another quest today, now that I did mission impossible yesterday with the money. I'm now going to see if I can find an Internet to send my beloved little wife an e-mail and, just maybe she has returned some of the ones I've sent her.

With that in mind, I start my quest. The streets are deserted. It isn't a case of being empty. They're not quite as deserted as the streets in Iquitos when the protest was on, but it is Sunday and the day after the big parade. I'm sure that if you attended the parade or some discotheque and danced the night away until the wee hours of the morning, either you're staggering home by now or you're face down in your bed. Whatever the case is, you're not on the streets.

Just the odd shop is open and I've asked two or three places about an Internet and they just shake their heads. So, it doesn't look too promising. I work my way back up to both the theater and the cathedral in the central *piazza*. I see a woman breast-feeding her child and begging at the same time. I passed her before I realized what she was really asking me for, and go into the church. It's a beautiful church. The inside consists mostly of marble. Not overly large, but very majestic. The dome above the altar has frescoes on it and there are alcoves, one for the confessional and another one for baptism. The cathedral has pews that are made of a very hard redwood, probably mahogany. It's not full yet, but the Mass service is still forthcoming. I kneel and pray, then realizing what the woman outside wanted, I went back to give her a small portion of money, and returned.

By now, the priest is commencing with the service and he walks down the aisles blessing the people with holy water before the mass commences. A fairly modern rock band is playing, and the lay people are very active. They say the Epistle and women are serving as 'altar boys'. Latin may still be spoken in the Vatican, but that's about the only place that still uses the language. I find the service is uplifting and this particular priest is about my age. I think they retire at sixty, so I guess he's a little younger, but white hair and beard, and an inspiration in himself. He involves the congregation when he asks them questions, he gets them to answer; and he is patient and he's got humor. In a lot of ways, he's the priest that I've always hoped that I would be, if I had the vocation, to communicate with the congregation on a very one-to-one basis and not be remote. It's rather unique to be in a country that maybe I have access to less than half a dozen of their words, and yet feel I understand. When this priest delivers his sermon, I'm inspired by his body language and the pitch in his voice. Many times I have been to a service that I've fully heard, comprehended, but was not inspired.

I guess you can spot me in a crowd. Just as communion is taking place, a young man comes over to sit down beside me. I recognize him; he'd been on the boat coming down from Iquitos. We renewed our friendship and he was sincerely glad to see me and asked me if I like Manaus. I say, "Oh, yes, I really do and I'm having a good time." This is where he lives and only speaks a little English, and I have no capability in any other language.

287

Robert F. Edwards

It's been a very moving moment in this journey and I'm grateful to be able to take part in this service, and to have experienced the warmth of Mother Church to its people. The good Father, at the end of the Mass, congratulates some people on their achievements, and the congregation even sings "Happy Birthday" to one of the parishioners. A much closer tie of community and church to each other, and I'm very moved by the whole service and the people that attended it.

After leaving, I return to the hotel. It's only about 10:30 a.m., so I stroll down to where the docks are. Yes, some people never do sleep, for the need of trade and commerce and I end up buying a pair of shorts (for fifteen *real*) just because my shorts are getting very dirty. I'll probably need them once I get to Rio and also for the journey down the river again.

It's extremely hot and humid. I've gotten used to perspiring. I notice that the locals do also, maybe not quite the excessiveness that I am, but this still shows that no matter how long you've been here, you're not immune to the high humidity and heat of the rainy season.

I am just enjoying the day, and sure enough, at 12:00 noon my *amigo* shows up with his friend that I met at the carnival last night. Harashi tells me that we're going to have lunch and then we're going to the zoo. We head over to Roberto's house. (I think there's an awful lot of Robertos in this neighborhood). I find out that he's a professor of Portuguese at a university in Manaus. A quiet man, and with his slender appearance and studious glasses he fits the perfect mold of a teacher.

When we drive up to his home, it's in a secured area and we have to go through a guard premise. Then there are small homes, single storey, but very nice, and they're all unique in design. Here, I guess you just do additions as you're motivated to, or that your pocketbook provides. Some people have put on attached garages; others add another building to the back, and so forth. These are all made out of brick and cement, mortar put on top of them, and then painted according to the taste of the people. In the rainforest, if the tree doesn't grow it rots, and wood is not the best construction material if you want it to last any length of time, and here, they've already learned the lesson.

Inside the house, there's a small living room, two small bedrooms, a bathroom, some storage areas, and then we go where most Westerners would say "into the backyard." This is where the kitchen is; it's an open-aired kitchen with a canopy on top. Even the shower is back here. It's very private because of the high walls. He's got a nice little flower garden and there is lots of working space for the kitchen. Just an ideal way of enjoying the outdoors and it reflects the open-air lifestyle of these people. This area lends itself to outdoor living, probably for most of the year round. Even in the rainy season, when the rains are torrential, it only lasts half an hour, an hour at the most.

In Canada and the rest of North America, we are starting to adopt the idea of large kitchens and family rooms sitting off the kitchen so that people can be more communal. These people just take it as a way of life and don't think that the *hacienda* has been rediscovered by the great minds of architectural ingenuity.

289

Robert F. Edwards

They're just starting to prepare the meal. I ask if I can help and it is "no, no" at first; but then I start chopping up the onions and the garlic, my favorite ingredient as any basic substance of the meal. Harashi is the number one cook. The other fellow, even though it's his house, Harashi takes over in the kitchen preparing pasta and hamburger and some mammoth steaks. While I'm cutting up the onions, two other gentlemen I met the previous night show up. Harashi tells me that this is a regular thing; that these four men get together on Sundays and have lunch together. They all prepare a big meal and just sit around, eat lots, drink lots of pop, and just enjoy each other's company and socialize. I'm always grateful wherever I'm able to visit, when somebody adopts me and integrates me into their lifestyle, and today is no exception.

The older gentleman is preparing the olives and the other two are making conversation while the owner of the house, Roberto, is scurrying around providing things that are required. Harashi is, boy! He is Mr. Cook Unlimited. He's got lots of pots and pans going, and he knows exactly what he wants to do. And he's very particular, I'll tell you. I asked him, "Do you want the onions diced?" And he thinks for a minute, "yes" "garlic" "Yes." When it comes to the olives, the other gentleman left one of the pits in the chopped-up olives. Sure enough, Harashi spotted it and started giving him a bit of razzmatazz about it. He says, "Mr. Bob (that's what they call me) is a good cook and you're not." It is nice to be part of this camaraderie.

I've always enjoyed the female companionship and still enjoy meeting and talking to women, but these last years that I've traveled extensively throughout different parts of the world where women go their way and men go other ways, I feel I have gained the true enjoyment and camaraderie of just men being with men. Mixed groups take on a different protocol and air about them, than when men are just with men. When I was a boy growing up in the Catholic faith and being educated by priests and nuns, once we reached our teenage years, we were separated and boys were taught by the priests

SOUTH AMERICA
ENCHANTMENT

and the girls were taught by the nuns. Now that I'm considerably well seasoned in years, I can understand the advantage. It seems a more carefree, less peer-pressured environment to work in, and I'm experiencing that again today. Just men being with men, nobody's trying to prove anything except being themselves.

Harashi and the other two men (father and son) are Arabs, from Lebanon by origin. Harashi still has relatives in Lebanon and this man's wife has gone back there. One of the men has a job in the administration of education. They all have good professions, and well above the average income of most Brazilians. They don't speak any English, though. Harashi is the only one, and has to be the interpreter. Surprising enough, this older Arabic gentleman and I communicate relatively well. We both have a common feeling about the abusive behavior that the Americans are imposing throughout the world, as well as their total lack of respect for the Islamic and Arabic needs and contributions to the global community.

The meal is now prepared and what a feast it is! Humungous amounts of pasta with this wonderful meat sauce on it. I'm sure the Italians would crave to have this recipe. Some of the ingredients that I'm aware of to enhance the flavor are garlic, onions, hamburger, tomato sauce, some corn, and olives. The steaks are equally well done. I would have never thought to have a rich pasta meat dish with steak on the side, but I've ravished this food as if I'd been deprived of nourishment for days. It's absolutely delicious. I tell Harashi, "You should be a cook rather than a travel agent," and everybody laughs. After we've completely gorged ourselves, I brought a chocolate bar and we have that for dessert. These men are very grateful when I give any kind of contribution, and even Harashi (when I bought a little bit of pop and stuff) says, "Why do you spend your money? Why are you buying things?" And I said, "Because I want to be equal." He says, "Oh, okay." It's funny, I'm the only person that has not been able to communicate as well as the others, but I sure feel part of this group.

291

Robert F. Edwards

After lunch, the man and his son depart as they have their own agenda. Harashi, Roberto, and I go to the zoo. I've taken as many pictures as possible of the animals for Marietta; they range from monkeys to cobras, turtles to zebras, panthers and crocodiles, parrots and parakeets, and so forth. The zoo itself is quite large. I wouldn't say well maintained, that would give it too much credit; but the newer sections, housing the larger cats, meet any modern zoo requirements. The rest of the zoo is contained in the small restrictive cages that are so well known

292

SOUTH AMERICA
ENCHANTMENT

as what zoos used to be, with caged animals in stressful situations.

From here, we get in the car and Harashi tells me we're going to go to a very nice five-star hotel, the Tropical Hotel.

To my surprise, it's the one that was just mentioned in "The Lonely Planet" and I had wanted to go and visit it. It has its own zoo as well. Once we get there, it's definitely a five-star hotel. It's like a giant oasis in the middle of the jungle. You have all the atmosphere of jungle surroundings with this metro scene. On their board, a single room is three hundred and eighty-three *real*, but after a discussion with the front desk, she said that they could give it to a person without paying the travel agent's fee for two hundred and eighty-four. She gives me a phone number and says that often they have specials or deals below that. And when I asked her, she says, "Our particular agency has a special arrangement with them and I get it for a hundred and ninety-two *real*." You may say almost fifty percent off. Yes, this is where the rich, and not necessarily famous, hang out, but a whole different category of people in here.

We sit by the pool and enjoy a Pepsi and just laugh like a bunch of schoolboys being where we shouldn't be. I keep on

Robert F. Edwards

saying to them, "Well, we'll pretend that we belong here, and so forth, and so on," and we're giggling and laughing about it. Afterwards, we go through the zoo here. Yes, money does have its advantages; this is much better than the zoo in Manaus itself. I don't know how they've attracted the birds, but even the birds are chirping in here and you really feel like you're in a jungle paradise.

The main buildings are about three storey's high and whitewashed. Outside are the swimming pool and waterfalls. If you can think of what you want to do, they've got the facilities waiting for you. This is one place that I would feel comfortable in taking Marietta. I think she would enjoy the atmosphere of the jungle at its best. I've taken some pictures of the huge lily pads, which are famous in this area and big turtles. You'd probably be able to stay here and feel you have experienced the jungle of Brazil.

We're just about ready to depart, only for the torrential rains to start. Again, I don't know why, but people here sure don't like it. In Vancouver, where it rains a lot, people can only get up in the mornings and say, "Oh, goody, it's raining." But here, they find it quite offensive, even though it doesn't last very long. Even during this period, it isn't like they last forever and ever, amen. It's just a good cloudburst, but boy! This one's filling up gutters and it has such flooding effects when it does come down. So, we're sitting, waiting it out until the rain subsides.

I say to Harashi, "Look, I'm just gonna go and check and see if they have an e-mail." And of course, they have a whole room for that facility alone and twinkle fingers here jumps in, has an e-mail from his beloved, reads it, sends her an e-mail, and mission impossible accomplished as this enjoyable day is ending on another high note.

We get back into the car and by now it's about 7:00 p.m. this evening. The Merry Men head back to town and they asked me if I'd like to go shopping. I said, "No, I really would like to get everything ready for tomorrow." We say our good-byes and I return to my room and start rearranging my baggage. I've now taken my sleeping bag and my compressed pack out of the main bag and attached it to the main bag. I've seen sherpas in the Himalayas with packs this size, but I never thought I would join their ranks. No matter how much in shape I feel, I could not carry this up the Inca trail, let alone to the base camps of Mt. Everest. However, I am able to carry it short distances.

I watch a bit of the carnival parades throughout Brazil on television before it's goodnight one and all. Goodnight, my little beautiful wife, and I'm glad I was able to read your e-mail as well as get one off to you and I hope that just by sheer curiosity or hopefulness that you might check the internet and spot mine before Tuesday night. If not, it will be waiting for you, along with one on Tuesday. I love you very dearly and miss you immensely. Wendy and Cole, thank you both for looking after Marietta and God bless you. To one and all, goodnight and let the journey continue.

Robert F. Edwards

February 11, Monday

Manaus, Brazil

I get up, and make the final preparations for my next stop, the tree house hotel. I have a quick breakfast, check out, and leave the humungous bag at the hotel desk. I am waiting patiently for the journey to continue. A matter of ten minutes after the designated time of 7:00 a.m., a young lady and gentleman arrive and say, "Mr. Robert Edwards?" And I said, "Yes." They said, "Please come with us." A nice modern bus is waiting to take us to the *Ariaú Amazon Towers* .

I board the bus with some other people already onboard, and we start heading off out of the city. Our first port of call is the Tropical Hotel and my heart drops for a minute thinking that, "Oh, no, maybe this is just an extension of the hotel which I'd been at yesterday." Not that I would have been devastated, because it is a five-star hotel and the facilities would make anyone happy who's in their right mind. However, it wasn't what I had in mind.

SOUTH AMERICA
ENCHANTMENT

To my relief, this is just where we board the boat that is going to take us to this remote area of the Rio Negro. The boat holds about a hundred people and it looks like a little ferry, round at both ends, and quite colorful. We cast off in good time and start making our way up the river. Of course, forms have to be filled out, and information has to be given, but other than that, I enjoy a Coke. About two hours later, we start to get the first sight of this complex as we're entering the inner harbor. It's a multitude of single standing towers and they're all on high stilts, to allow for how high the river rises.

These towers all provide different accommodations. I've chosen to stay in The Tree House which is exactly what it is. It's a huge Brazilian nut tree and this building is prefabricated around it. As we get off the boat, we're escorted to the reception area, where we are offered a drink, even a T-shirt. Two young people are dressed up in native attire (quite skimpy) one being a boy and the other a girl, and they give us shell necklaces as a welcoming.

At the Registration desk, they're saying, "Okay, Visa, that's fine; but the exchange rate on a hundred and thirteen dollars is two fifty, rather than two thirty-five." I just drew a line in the sand at this point and said, "No, all the banks are giving two point three five, why should you charge a fifteen percent premium?" They go in to some detail about hotel policy, but after some discussion, sure enough, I get the two point three five. It's only about twenty-five *real* differences, but still fifteen dollars U.S. means a lot to us poor Canadians. I'm very pleased to say that they accommodated the true rate of exchange rather than the premium.

With that out of the way, they show me where my new dwelling is going to be, The Tree House. It is the furthest part of the complex and there are catwalks throughout the whole area so that, I guess, your feet never really have to touch the jungle ground. There are a lot of reasons for this, and one being the depth of the river. The river swells on an average of about eighteen meters (over fifty feet). I believe the record was set somewhere in the 70's and it rose twenty-eight meters.

297

Robert F. Edwards

When you're traveling down these narrow waterways, you see the dark lines on the trees that indicate how high the water actually goes. For the average person not from the Amazon area, it's hard to comprehend that the rising of this water is so exorbitant during the rainy season and this goes right up until June.

Many of the fish move inland when the waters rise and they eat mostly vegetation and berries. However, when the waters recede, the fish return to being carnivorous, eating other little fish and bugs. Also, the insects and animals move further in to the interior as the waters rise. So it is a unique ecosystem.

As I walk along these catwalks, I can see the variation of vegetation, anything from small ferns and water grass to humungous trees. In the short time that I've been here, there are three different types of monkeys. I'm no monkey expert, (except in monkey business) but I know one of them is a spider monkey. They're just running wild and I soon become aware that these little guys like to pick up your glasses or your beer (they really like drinking beer) and other little knick-knack things, including jewelry if you're foolish enough to leave it lying around.

This place is *turista* orientated, and a different type of clientele from the conventional backpacker. However, not to say anything against it, just more affluent than the people I normally travel with. Quite surprisingly, about eighty, maybe even as high as ninety percent, are Brazilians that are taking part in this. Very few Europeans, some Orientals, but I find they're business people that are working in Brazil rather than visiting.

I'm being escorted along

SOUTH AMERICA
ENCHANTMENT

these catwalks and as I go further in, there are different facilities and accommodations. Obviously, the majority of the people stay in cabins and I notice a lot of them do have air-conditioning facilities, somewhat on the lines of a Club Med idea. As we reach the pyramid, the young lady escorting me explains that this pyramid is air-conditioned, and some people even sleep in there during the night. There are plants and vines growing up around it, and when I entered, there's a mini pyramid in the middle. I wouldn't say it was cold; but it's cooler by comparison to outside. There are little mats, with pillows and cushions, so you can lie in there and listen to New Age music and meditate.

We continue onward and not a great distance away is a little helipad. There is also an observatory, which looks like a big dome made out of fiberglass with little windows in it. Not a great distance from this is my new residence. It's a huge tree; it would have to be three hundred feet in height. The tree house itself is starting at the base. There is a little shrine off to the side of it with a waterfall. Then there is the main

floor, with two stairways leading up that are very steep. On the next floor there are the facilities for people sleeping (or

hammocking) and then another floor. There is, for some unknown reason, a little screen door on the stairs. This leads
out on another catwalk, to the toilet facilities.

By the fourth or fifth floor, that's the one they've chosen for
me. I have no reason to know why one floor is better than the
other, but I'm very near the top. There are about two more
floors and they become more consolidated as you go higher
up. My escort puts a hammock up, shows me where there's

shampoo, toilet paper and
soaps available, and even pulls
out blankets and a sheet for
the hammock. There's even a
fan. After he shows me how to
put it on and so forth, I give
him a tip and he leaves.

Alone now in my new Tarzan
dwelling, I decide to change
into the T-shirt and little beads
that they've given me, and
start checking out the rest of
the complex. It's very close to
lunchtime and the main
restaurant is (in my particular
case) a good fifteen-minute
walk to the main complex, that
is, if you don't take any long routes. I check out the toilet facilities and to my amazement, they're actually flush toilets. I
just took for granted that they'd be dry toilets or, at very best,
chemical ones, but no, they're flush toilets; and they even
have showers and civilization in the jungle. I am sure the
Swiss Family Robinsons would have never left their tree house
if they've had all the facilities that this one has.

I make my way back down to the reception area, and on the
third floor is where the restaurant is. My guide's name, I was
told, is Michael; and I look for the sign indicating his table,
which I do find, and start to eat the mid-day meal. It's the
standard type of buffet; three or four different types of salads;

SOUTH AMERICA
ENCHANTMENT

and the ever-present rice and pastas. Today, there are three or four different types of vegetables; and a selection of fish, meat and buns or *pan;* and along with that, tea or coffee or water. The desserts are pretty modest, two types of puddings.

I meet Michael. He is in his early fifties, speaks English well, and is from what used to be British Ghana. The most ironical thing is my traveling companions are going to be three Japanese. Two of them work for the embassy here. This is going to be the English expedition into the jungle. Michael tells me that at 2:00 p.m., we're going to take a boat up a narrow channel and cross over it to one of the points of Rio Negro, to visit a small village. Then, we will do piranha fishing; and after we return, have supper and we might do some alligator search and find missions.

Right at tow o'clock, we all pile into a fairly large boat. It's not anywhere near the capacity of the one I came on, but with only four people and our guide, plus a Korean group and their guide, we toddle off to this village. It takes us the better part of an hour to get there, but in the interim, Michael tells us a little bit about the river, and before long, we end up in this village. There are two hundred and fifty people. It was founded by a young woman in her early twenties and she's now in her mid-forties. The main source of income or lifestyle here is fishing, with a bit of agriculture. The buildings are wood construction and there's a neat little school. Michael tells me that the school accommodates only the children that are here. Just like the old days in Canada, when you graduated from one grade to another, you just moved from one chair to another in the same classroom and the same school. Also, there are two churches and there's even a little restaurant which, of course, we end up going to and needless to say, have something to drink.

At least for me, the highlight is a bird, the toucan, famous for its huge colorful beak. This bird is tame and a young lady there is picking the bird up on her arm. I think that it would be a great photo op.; so after taking a few pictures of it sitting on the veranda, I asked if I could have it done. Well, there's an old saying, "Monkey see, monkey do," and of course, all the

Oriental people want to do the same thing. By this time the bird is getting pretty tired of going from one arm to another, but I do get a picture of him on my arm. I think it will be rather a unique picture, especially for those who know that I'm not very fond of having birds near me, let alone perched on me.

Michael shows us how to identify the famous Brazilian nut trees. They have a huge seedpod that holds up to eighteen Brazilian nuts. I asked if I could buy one, as a souvenir, and paid one *real* for it. I'm not going to open it up and find out how many nuts are in it, but I can hear them rattling in there, and it's fairly heavy. We start looking around and for five *real*, I can get a blowgun. It's just a hollow tube, like a bamboo cane, that you shoot small arrows with feathers through. The natives use different types of poison to bring down their prey.

As we walk around the area, I see some interesting cone shapes, upside down. They're nests of some beautiful black and yellow birds. In many cases, the hornets share these nests and protect the young from unpleasant intruders and the hornets are rewarded by having the nectars and droppings that the birds have provided for the young. Co-existence, I think you'd call it.

We continue looking around the village, and come to a football field. No matter what size the community is or how isolated, they still have fields for the new soccer champions of Brazil coming up through the ranks. The houses are on stilts, even though they are a considerable distance from the river. There is a very steep staircase going up from the riverbank at the present time. I guess forewarned is forearmed, and these people have experienced enough to realize that Mother Nature in some years gets very aggressive with coming inland, so these houses will withstand the rise of twenty or thirty meters, which sounds horrendous. It is hard to believe that this river floods its banks to that extent, but it does and these people live with it.

As we see inside some of the homes, Michael explains that these people don't have any water facilities inside, or any electricity. They either use a kerosene lamp, or the poorer ones just use fat from the animals that they kill in the forest. This part of the world is very self-sufficient, if you know what's available in the jungle. Generation after generation, these people have lived here and they know how to exist. They trade, rather than use money, for goods that are essential.

We continued down this river and Michael signals the driver to pull in to some side pools of calmer water. He brings out these sticks with about two meters of line on them and one little bare fishhook. He then provides us with some meat and we go fishing. The Japanese gentleman caught the first fish. It looks like a good size sardine and then it happens. We are really pulling in the fish and the majority of them are piranhas, and one of them is larger in size than my hand. I could feel the fish  biting, but they must be the smartest fish in the world. Or, maybe because I am a novice fisherman, but they got the meat and I was left with the bare hook, only to repeat the task of putting another piece of meat on. I continued to do this right throughout the duration of the fishing expedition. With having the experience of getting a nibble on a line, that's the closest I got to the success of pulling in my meal. I lost track of how many fishes were caught, at least ten or fifteen fishes and probably twelve of them were piranhas of different sizes.

303

Robert F. Edwards

The body of these ferocious little fishes is very attractive, but boy, their mouth sure shows what their intent is.

We start up the motor again and make our way back to the village of the *turistas* in the jungle. Supper's waiting. It is a repeat of the menu from lunch. About 8:00 p.m., we start heading out on the Rockville adventure. I get into a very small dugout canoe with a little motor, and start working the shorelines of a narrow tributary, looking for crocodiles. Ironically, I was the first one to see this *jacaré*. We were scanning the riverbanks with torches, eventually; we do find a small one. It's a little over two feet, and Michael tells us that these are unique to the Amazon. They're not really a true crocodile. They have a gizzard and this is how they digest their food. They heat their body, like other cold-water animals by basking in the sun and when they get enough heat, this is how the blood circulates throughout their body. However, once they're back into the water, the blood only goes to the brain, conserving on energy. They also back into the water rather than go face forward into the water. Michael' s showing us the different parts of this little crocodile and the membrane over the eyes that it has for water submergible operations. He taps on the snout, and it opens up the mouth. This is more like a holding area for the animal; rather than swallowing it in the water; it comes back up to the surface before opening a passage down to the stomach. An interesting factor about this animal is that it dates back two and a half million years. I feel sorry for the little crocodile. It's just a baby and this has got to be a hair-raising experience, to be pulled out of its natural environment and be mauled by the most dangerous specie in the world, Man. But, it's still a lucky day in his life. It's going back into its natural environment, probably scared to death, but at least alive.

Back in the village, when we went into the small restaurant, there was a skin of a boa constrictor, the large snake that wraps itself around you. This had to be in excess of ten, twelve meters and it obviously was skinned and they put varnish on it. The width of it would have had to be about a third

of a meter. So, huge! This particular snake that I looked at
was in the process of consuming a six-year-old boy when his
father came running with a gun and shot it in the head.
These snakes are dangerous and prefer to be in areas where
water exists. They wrap their body around your legs and by
the time they get to the middle part of your body, you're finished. When they get to the head of the victim, they just wrap
it with their body and put it into a semi-conscious state and
continually squeeze until all the bones are crushed in the victim. Once this process is finished, the snake then has a
hinge-type mouth and regurgitates a foamy slime over the victim and starts to consume it by pushing the victim into its
body. The teeth are all pointing backwards so it just keeps on
chunking it down with its muscles as it is consuming portions. Also, it has a metabolism that relaxes so that it can
expand its body to consume the mass that it's taking on.
Once it does this, it becomes very docile and will float in the
water to aid the digestive system. This skin of the snake that
I was viewing was a female and it had sixteen young that it
was preparing to increase the population of their specie.

Michael tells us that this event took place three months ago;
and I guess about six months ago, a man was fishing and he
wasn't as fortunate. He lost his life and when they found the
snake floating docile, they killed it, dragged it ashore and
opened up the snake, and the crushed body of the man was
still in there. These snakes are capable of taking down a cow.

When we do return to our village, there's a cultural event-
taking place at 9:30 p.m. in the auditorium. Though I'm quite
tired and we have to be up at 4:30 a.m. tomorrow, I would like
to see it. So, I go upstairs and have a Coke. There was a Brazilian lady from Saint Paolo who spoke very good English, and
I join her group, waiting for the cultural event to take place.
She and her husband are in their early fifties, just exceptionally nice people! I guess her mother liked to travel with her
father when they were younger, but she was like myself and
we only speak one language. In her case, it was Portuguese.
They asked me how I could possibly travel to the extent I do

Robert F. Edwards

and not have command of more than one language. Then they relayed this story to me. For this Portuguese lady, her favorite spot in the world was Frankfurt; and on more than one occasion, they would go to Germany for a visit. There was a shop which had porcelain and she liked to purchase different collectibles. The proprietor of this shop was a German lady, only speak German. However, over the years, they seemed to be able to converse, or make each other's wishes known. On this particular visit, this woman was going to the shop, and she said to her husband, "Well, you'll meet me there later", which he did. Upon arriving, he finds both women just crying and holding each other and sobbing and the Portuguese woman says to her husband, "This poor, poor woman, her husband is very sick and he's dying in the hospital and she's very emotionally upset." And the husband said, "Well, how do you possibly know that that's what's happening, you don't speak German." And sure enough, that's exactly what happened. So, we had a good laugh about it.

Then, this Portuguese daughter's husband tells of a situation that he had with his mother-in-law, when he was in Washington, D.C. getting some gas in a black neighborhood. This black guy drove up in front of his car and pinned him in, so that he couldn't get out after he was finished getting the gas. He said he was quite prepared just to sit there and wait until the fellow finished his transaction, but his mother-in-law was not putting up with this kind of nonsense, got out, and she's a small woman and this black American was very big. She starts just chewing him out left, front, and center. He said he couldn't believe it, and was very concerned about what was going to happen. But the guy got back in his car and moved the car forward. So, a person doesn't always need to speak the same language to get the message across.

By the time we leave to go over to the cultural center, we're a little late and actually, there's only about ten minutes left of the actual costumes and regatta of the event. Then, they want everybody to get up and do some dancing which I do a few numbers, before excusing myself to go back to my tree house.

SOUTH AMERICA
ENCHANTMENT

On my way back, I've mislaid my directions after the better part of half-an-hour; I'm just not finding my hammock. With that, I'm thinking, "I'll probably take the young lady's advice and just sleep in the pyramid."

Earlier today, in the afternoon I had gone into the pyramid. It was full of people and the only place left was the floor with no mats. A young girl, probably seventeen at the very most, gives up hers and insists on me taking it, and I said, "Well, at least have the pillow that goes with your feet." Kindness, and throughout this journey, it's not just a pleasure, it's an honor of experiencing kindness. Something that seems to have been null and void in many parts of the world are these deeds of kindness. For the rest of my life, in my mind, will be these unique people that would renew your faith in humanity for the future.

I'm in the pyramid now, and there's absolutely no one in here, so I have as many pillows as I wish. There are about forty mats with two pillows each. You lie on these rectangular type of pillows with your head and support your legs with the other one, which is softer, and listen to the tranquil music for meditation. I'm going to do a little something different and try and sleep. I start to gather three or four of the foot cushions together to make a mattress and lie there. I can't turn the lights off, or the air-conditioning and I am still wearing shorts and the T-shirt that was given at the presentation. I'm not in here more than about three-quarters of an hour, before I'm actually cold. You wouldn't think, with all the heat and the high humidity, that anybody would want anything but a chilled room to sleep in. However, I really do wish I had a blanket or at least something to put over my shoulders. The next fifteen minutes has convinced me that I should try another reconnaissance to find the tree house.

It is just too cold to be in this pyramid all night; and to be outside, there are just too many lively things going on. As I was walking down one of the walkways, some kind of moth or flying creature (about the size of my hand) just about flew into my head, plus salamanders and other things running across

Robert F. Edwards

the deck, and bugs. I try to collect my thoughts and get my bearings a little bit more, and to my delight I'm successful. I get back to the tree house and I'm still the only one in this whole complex. By now, it's about 12:30 p.m. and as I'm lying in the hammock, I can't help but think of that large boa constrictor that consumed that man in the boat, especially when I look at the massive tree trunk sticking out of the wall. I'm wondering if it isn't a support beam for something that keeps awake while I'm dozing. Not pleasant thoughts to go to sleep with. At least I am not turning and tossing in the hammock. I'm trying to position myself accordingly, as my left knee still seems to be feeling the effects of a cramp or pain that is persistent. I must have stretched a muscle somewhere and it's not getting the tender loving care it deserves.

With all this whining and complaining, I will say goodnight to my beautiful wife and no, I know you wouldn't want to be in one of the rooms tonight, even if we had the whole floor to ourselves. With that, I love you very, very much, and I miss you a lot. Wendy, I hope you and little Cole are doing well and everything is moving along in an orderly fashion in your life. Goodnight one and all and God bless.

SOUTH AMERICA ENCHANTMENT

February 12, Tuesday

Amazon River, Brazil

I can't say that I got up with the birds. I have to say I got up before the birds. At 4:30 a.m., I swung out of my hammock and got myself ready to trek back down to the reception desk where we're all meeting before going out for the sunrise tour. Sure enough, I have one cup of lukewarm strong coffee and my Japanese partners are ready. Off we go in a small, glorified dugout canoe to the designated spot to see the sunrise. Not that Jungle Jim here is taking over the expedition by any stretch of the imagination, but I'm the first one to see the break of dawn against the horizon. Enjoyable! It's an over-cast day, so the clouds provide a multitude of shades on the sunrise. We're only three degrees south of the equator, so the sun doesn't pop up with that same demanding presence as when you're further from the center of the planet. I tell the Japanese men that some of the most breath-taking sunrises that I've ever witnessed were down in the Ushuaia and sailing through the Beagle Channel at Puerto Williams.

Robert F. Edwards

We return for breakfast and have a good variety of food to choose from. My choice is a rice cereal, which I thoroughly enjoy, and a couple of cups of coffee. I'm ready for adventure now, and this morning we're going to be taking part in a jungle trek through another part of the shoreline. We get in the boat and start heading to the designated spot that we're looking for, which actually starts with the pig farm. The hotel complex owns the pig farm and any of the food that isn't consumed by the other pigs called *turistas* is then transported up here to feed the animals. There are parrots and I get a picture of a huge boar and a few other animals.

Again, back in the boat and we head onwards for the trek through the jungle. When we get there, this particular place is owned by a man who has had it in his family for four, five generations. To give you an idea of some of the sizes of the families, this man has thirty children (yes, thirty), and his father had more and God knows, I guess they lost count on the grandchildren. Michael, the guide, has eight children. This part of the world loves to make babies and of course, the women are extremely young when they start bearing children and so have the better part of twenty years of being fertile. So, this is one of the problems; because of the amount of young children for a considerable length of time being produced, there's a population explosion that's taking place in Brazil. And even on the streets, I notice that there are very few old people, like me. The age spectrum seems to be like about thirty and under, an advantage in some ways to have a very young nation being produced. On the downside, to have these children educated is a mammoth task that the government is faced with. I have been told that a lot of children are abandoned and there are even terrorist groups that hunt down these children and kill them, saying that they're doing Brazil a favor because these children only have the capabilities of becoming hardened criminals if they did grow up. This is the dark side of these beautiful people.

This farmer (with the thirty children) takes us through the jungle with his machete, and he starts to explain some of the

SOUTH AMERICA
ENCHANTMENT

things which Michael translates for the rest of us. The first things we come across are large black ants, about the size of a fingernail. We're told that if these ants bite you, you are violently sick for twenty-four hours, throwing up, fevers, and convulsions. There is no antidote or remedy to ease the suffering, other than putting you out of your misery. The Indians do this as a ritual to prove manhood. When a young man reaches puberty, they put one of these ants on his chest, his hands and his feet, and if he can endure the pain, then he's going through the transition of manhood. The more excruciating effect is when they prepare to get married. They fill a bag with these ants, and you have to put your hand in this sack twenty times and let as many of the ants bite as they see fit. This must be one of the most painful experiences these men have in their lifetime and this is to prove that they have the stamina to look after a family. It is quite a marriage ceremony. I am sure more people in North America would avoid marriage if they had this kind of initiation. However different regions have different customs.

We go a little further on and see these brown ants feeding on vegetation and anything else that's acceptable. These ants are marching through and they're aggressive. There are literally hundreds, if not thousands, that we're watching beat their way through.

The jungle has hundreds of different types of palm trees and there is really only one palm tree that was introduced here. All the rest are native to the region. The palm tree, like in so many other parts of the world, fulfills so many needs and requirements of the people. It is often used for thatched roofs and the man shows us how they take a young succulent branch and shred it, then make the foliage for a thatched roof. If these thatched roofs have enough pitch in them, they can last up to seven years, even in this rainy climate, before they need to be replaced.

An interesting plant that we come across is one that has roots that look like vines. They chop it with the machete, and the vine carries water up to the branches high above and you

311

can actually drink the water. I drank some, and it tastes a lot better than some of the water I've drank out of taps. It's got a  bit of a woody taste to it, but if you needed some water, it does quench the thirst. There are many different plants that are used for ointments and medication. He showed us the bark of a plant that if you have a wound, all you have to do is shave this and make it into a powder. It not only clots the wound, but you won't get any infection in it. There is another plant, important in this part of the world. You can smear its bark on your skin and it acts as an insect repellant, especially against mosquitoes.

Michael shows us a leaf that has quinine in it. He said when he was working in the mines in British Ghana, he got malaria and he was so sick he could hardly move. An old Indian told him to take this leaf and make a tea out of it and drink it. He said the first couple of times he drank it, he just threw up profusely, but then after that he started keeping it down. He drank it once a day for three months and it not only cured the malaria, it never returned.

There is a nut that a beetle bores a hole in and then plants its eggs, and if you crack it open, the larva is in there. No, I didn't eat it, but I did watch Michael eat two of them. So, if you're a little down on protein and you don't mind eating a live larva, there is always food available where you least expect it. I did take a couple of the nuts as memorabilia of this trip through an exotic wonderland of plants and animals. I've seen quite a few birds. No snakes, I've seen them in cages where I prefer to have them.

I'm thoroughly enjoying this walk through nature's paradise. Once you do get off the trails, you can easily get misplaced. The foliage is dense and it's confusing amidst the vines and trees. It feels like you've been just dropped in to a plant kingdom with no routes out. A person could easily think that they were walking in one direction, only to be going in the opposite. You really have to stay on the trail, and need to have a machete if that trail had not been used for some time. A lot of the trees' roots are not only due to heavy rains, but also because the soil is very sandy and has few nutrients left in it. So, when the leaves fall and start to decompose, that's where the tree gets its nutrition. In a sense it's feeding itself or replenishing its own food supply.

We come across a large tree where I've taken a picture of myself, beating it. It has the same effect as a drum. You can hear it a great distance away by hitting it. It's got a hollow sound, so that provides a noise. As our farmer-guide is walking through the forest with us, he's busy weaving different little things out of bamboo shoots. The first one is a grasshopper, which he gives to me. He gives a bow and arrow to one of the Japanese fellows. He makes a whistle out of another one, makes a Roman leaf headdress out of another, all while he's walking through the jungle, weaving these remarkable pieces of art.

Also, we come across a termite mound. Big black mounds, and when you cut a chunk off, the termites are alive and well, just struggling to find out what happened to their dwelling.

This whole morning is just one piece of knowledge after another and each one is equally as interesting as the other. Michael tells me that shortly after he'd been divorced, he was very emotionally upset about it and he went into the jungle for six months. He had a shotgun and foraged in the jungle and lived off the land. Once you know what you're looking for in the jungle, there's very little else you need.

There's a plant Michael showed us from which they take the leaf and put it in water. It kills the fish by clogging up their gills so they can't breathe and they come to the surface as they die of suffocation. This toxic poison is not fatal to human beings so people can eat the fish. The bad part is that it will poison the waters for many years and the Brazilian government is educating these people that if they want to have fish forever, it's better to use nets and hooks and more conventional methods of fishing rather than poisoning the waters. So, not all practices of natives are ecologically sound either.

We return to the farm, and like every family in this area, they strongly wish to have the tourists buy as much as they can and leave as much money behind as possible. I buy a stuffed piranha, not an overly large fish, but one I think I can get back into Canada without having a crane lift my backpack.

Also, I bought a mask, made from wood, with piranha teeth on it, and bones from other animals. In art that is regional, they use the materials that are available, and it is amazing what kind of artistic ability comes out of a person or society.

I decide to give this man a tip, for the knowledge that he has provided for us, to say nothing of all the gifts that he has handed out with these palm leaves. One of the Japanese fellows asks, "What are you going to give?" I said, "Well, I think two *real*," At first, they're saying "Oh, that's too much" or "Well, I think it wasn't worth anything." But, they're not cheap, and I've always enjoyed being with Japanese people. They have a collective attitude. If one sets the pace, all of the rest fall into line. I've enjoyed being with these men very much. The oldest gentleman had spent some time in the Japanese Consulate in Edmonton, Alberta, and he's seriously thinking of retiring there. I said, "You're a braver man than I am when it comes to winters."

We head back to the hotel, and have about an hour before lunch. Then two hours later, we will start heading back to Manaus. We get a diploma for our trek and achievements of participating in the ecosystem of the jungles of the Amazon. I'm going to frame mine and hang it alongside my Kilimanjaro diploma. I thoroughly enjoyed sharing the experience with these people. I get on the boat to depart; a fellow comes running after me and says, "If there's anything we can do for you at any other time, please give us an opportunity." He's the general manager of the complex. I've really enjoyed myself here and I would strongly recommend it. It has lived up to its brochures, if not more, and when I filled out the questionnaires on good, bad, or indifferent, mine was thumbs up.

When we return to the hotel, I'm deeply touched. The girl at the reception desk welcomes me back, and when I collect my big luggage backpack, I notice a package on it. I'm curious as to what it is, but decide to check in first. I'm tired and haven't shaved today, plus I have a few extra mosquito bites from the jungle. When I get up to my room, I open it up and one of the ladies from the reception had bought me a carnival T-shirt and a bandanna. It's the maraschino cherry on top of a great experience.

315

Robert F. Edwards

I've been talking to everybody about the carnival and my enthusiasm for it. This kind woman has bought me these accessories to go boogying on the streets and clubs in. I'm very emotional about this kindness. This is the way Brazilians act and think, and it's very difficult not to want to stay and be a part of their life. They're just wonderful people, period, and dot, COM. I wasn't planning to go out discoing. In fact, I wanted to get ready for the adventure tomorrow, but after what this young lady has done, I take a different stance on it.

I went down to check the e-mail, but to my dismay the Internet is closed. I've been to carnivals before and know that Brazil literally shuts down when it gets into the carnival mood. As this is the last day of the carnival, it'll be the grand finale. But, since I'm leaving tomorrow, I'm more than a little motivated to find some place that will let me use an internet, almost at any price, just to get one small message to my beautiful wife.

With that in mind, I go to the Holiday Inn. Last time I checked there, their Internet was down but I talked to the same gentleman, believe it or not. He remembers me, tells me that I need a card, and I said, "Look, I know I'm not a resident here but I really do just want to let my wife know I'm okay and everything else." He says, "Go ahead. You'll have to buy the card which is ten *real* for one hour."

I know I'm not getting the best rate at this place to send messages out. My regular spot is only three *real* for an hour. This is three times and then some of the price. Mind you, I would have paid a hundred times more just to use the facilities. I've used a lot of computers now and I've used a lot of systems through my travels. This one is both unique and difficult. You place the card in, which is fine, but it's got a round ball and it's supposed to be a modern space look. I think that if it were just the conventional keyboard and a mouse, people would know what they were doing. However, with help from one of the people in the restaurant, I get the thing up. My beautiful wife sent me a couple of e-mails and a

SOUTH AMERICA
ENCHANTMENT

wonderful card, and I got some e-mails from my friends and just a bit of junk mail too.

Now, I feel so much more relieved. Earlier, I was asking a person at the hotel if he was going to go to the carnival or the disco, and he said, "It's just up the street." Sure enough, about three blocks further up is the disco, just in the open street. I walk up there and everybody's in a real party mood and it's only about 7:00 p.m. I return to the hotel and shave, shower, and put on my carnival gear, which is just great. Up the street I go to join the rest of the people that are in a party mood. We dance the hours away.

Now I'm starting to understand about the carnival and the things that take place. For the *turistas* and for people that are very dedicated to the parades, the parade itself is a major event. But for the average Brazilian, it's the free open bands that play on the streets that they congregate to and dance the night away. Beer is a *real* and a half, and food is available, and it's a party. That's the bottom line and it's free. There are always little kiosks all over the places that are serving different types of food or beer or beverages, whatever the crowd demands or wishes; and the bands vary from ones that are brought in from Rio de Janeiro, El Salvador, and in this particular case to Manaus.

This is an easy-going lifestyle of the moment, what the rest of the world would call "letting their hair down." I think that Brazilians don't have any problem doing that at the best of times; they're very easy-going and exceptionally friendly. It doesn't take much to get them to play some music and start singing and dancing at a whim. I gather in some of the cities, especially El Salvador, that you don't have to have the word

317

carnival attached. It can be just somebody gets started in the street; before long the same type of atmosphere persists on the week-ends or even in mid-week. The crowd soon becomes one mass of bouncing, yelling and happy faces. I'm no musician to start with, but even I understand that the theme is quite repetitious. When the band blares out one particular theme or word, it's then repeated by the crowd, your hands are going up, your body's swaying and young and old are dancing.

I'm getting a bit of the perspective of what a woman at the Internet was trying to explain when she said, "It's also boys' night." For the average person in North America, transsexuals exist and we accept them as a way of life these days. But here, I don't think it's just that they're transsexuals. I believe boys actually like, once in a while, dressing up as girls and going out dancing, in this particular case. This is the period in which they do so.

Thanks to my wonderful little friend at the reception, I'm one of the better dressed party animals here and in full regalia. With my hands going up and down, and my feet bouncing around, people want to dance with me from all ages and I gather sexes too. There's one guy that has this mammoth flag. It must be at least two meters long and one meter high, on a large pole. He lets me wave it into the crowd and I'm perspiring heavily, there's no two ways about it. This is a warm wonderful night and even at 10:00 p.m. at night, I'm most reluctant to leave. I have a few shish kebabs with an older lady and buy her one, along with one or two beers. I thoroughly enjoy a carnival, and now I really understand what the locals were trying to describe. Street dancing is in and is going to last forever, while one Brazilian has music in their veins.

With a reluctant heart, I start heading back to the hotel and bump into the young lady that provided me with all this attire, as she is picking up some of her friends to go out carnivaling.

SOUTH AMERICA
ENCHANTMENT

I get a picture with her just to cap off this remarkable evening. In my room, I get ready for bed. This whole day has been a prelude to a tightening in my throat and I hope I'm not getting a cold. Over and above that, I'm having second

thoughts about going on another jungle expedition. I had a remarkable time in the jungle, but looking over the brochure, it's pretty well a repetition with just the different group of faces. However, no use trying to figure out what's going to happen, I'm just going to take one day at a time and I've enjoyed all the days that have taken place.

So, with that, my beautiful little wife, I'm trying to be able to get one more e-mail off to you and I miss you very much and I'm looking forward to taking part in some adventures with you. No, they'll never be quite as extravagant or as grandiose or as enduring as this, but it will be fully as enjoyable. Well, Wendy, I hope that little Cole man is giving you a little bit of rest and now that you're back into the routine, you can reflect on the times you've had and the enjoyment that you took part in. Goodnight one and all and think carnival, if you're thinking of having a party. With that, I'd like to say goodnight.

Robert F. Edwards

I got up at 6:00 a.m. and started my routine. Unfortunately, that tightness and tickling in my throat has developed into all the markings of a cold and without any other forewarning or stubbornness. I've started to take some penicillin and aspirin. I just don't feel like the mighty Jungle Bob today. I shave and shower and prepare myself to be ready by 8:00 a.m. for another excursion in the jungle. If I had reservations yesterday, I have some regrets today about doing this, but I'll take one step at a time and maybe after having coffee and some juices, hopefully this tightness in my throat will go away and I'll be feeling more like my dynamic self.

With my packing completed and the expedition now ready to be in full swing, I go down for a modest breakfast and have a little bit of eggs and bread, a couple of glasses of juice and coffee. No, all this extra nourishment hasn't encouraged any feeling of well-being. As I'm sitting in the lobby trying to decide, to make matters more discouraging, it's coming down in a torrential rain. It's not letting the rainy season down by being limited in amounts. So, jungle in the rain, that's about the sum of it, with a cold as a backpack. By now, my nose is running like two taps both running cold and continuous. I can't find a faucet to tighten them up at all. Even the young girls at the desk are remarking that I have a bad cold and that my cough is something that I'm not just aware of, but other people are aware of.

As 8:00 a.m. finds 9:00 a.m., my guide still hasn't arrived, and by 9:30, I've reached the point where I know that I'm sick. I know that three days in the jungle, lying in a hammock, is not going to be inducive to my well-being whatsoever. Rather than try to make a lot of conversation and excuses and compromises, I am going to vamoose.

SOUTH AMERICA
ENCHANTMENT

So, I put on my poncho and off into the rain I go. One thing I found about this poncho, it might be great for the military and it's absolutely waterproof beyond any stretch of the imagination. The only bad part about it is if you're perspiring, you get just as wet from your own perspiration. I am literally soaking wet. My shirt, I can literally wring out with my own perspiration. I've probably got a fever, but to wrap myself in a rubber poncho is not going to enhance circulation.

I do some extensive walking and to add more to my feeling of being downright miserable, nothing's open, including my essential Internet and I wanted to send an e-mail to my wife. I am feeling disillusioned as last night was the end of the carnival period.

I continue to make my way along to the wharf to try and find what accommodations there are on ships that are leaving in the future for Belém. Between my nose running and these Nike shorts with the pockets full, Jungle Bob is not feeling too good in the rural jungle today. I make my way along the shoreline, and find the entrance to where the ferries leave for Belém. I am told that there's one leaving today. This is very good because it's a metal boat versus a wooden one tomorrow.

I ask if I could see the boat, which is not quite as easy a task as it sounds like. You don't just walk down the wharf and climb on board and check out the facilities. Border patrol is extremely tight. First of all, I have to show my passport, I have to get a certificate stamped by an official; and then after three different inspections of both my passport and the special certificate, I'm permitted to get on board the boat. The boat is not quite as modern as the one that I had to come down on, but would suffice. The prices are within range of the ones that I've previously paid. I am feeling by now that there's no point wimping around and saying that I'm going to overcome this. Today, I'm either going to be forced to stay in bed at the hotel or get on this boat going somewhere, so that I can at least be making progress while I'm sick. I let the people know that I've got to go back to the hotel and make arrangements to notify people.

Robert F. Edwards

As I work my way back to the hotel, I am somewhat surprised at myself. I'm getting to know this city fairly well, with all its different angles and corners I wouldn't be able to do a guided tour of it, but I could find my way back without being intimidated.

Once at the front desk, I explain to the young lady that I'm going to Belém rather than on the jungle tour. Sure enough, they phone the fellow and I explained to him that I'd waited an hour and a half. He said that his vehicle had problems and he had to pick up all the other people first, and when he got to my hotel I wasn't there. I said, "No, I wasn't, because after an hour and a half of waiting, I thought you had given up; and it was raining, so I thought you weren't going and I'd made other arrangements to go to Belém." He was very nice about it. He said he was sorry and it was his fault, and I got out of that situation better than I anticipated. I then phoned Harashi, the travel agent, and explained I was going on to Belém instead of hanging around. I wished that I could have seen him in person, but it was continually raining, and it didn't make any sense for him to come down to the hotel just to shake hands and say goodbye.

I asked the girls at the front desk if they could get my laundry. I'll be honest, at this point I was quite prepared to forfeit the laundry if worse came to worst and I'd leave it behind. Again, I went up to the Holiday Inn to send an e-mail to my beloved wife, only to find out that their e-mail was down and of course all the other places are closed. I was more than just concerned about this and I racked my brain for many moments to try and think of how I could overcome the situation. However, the decision was made and ninety percent of it completed. I completed the last ten percent by going back to the hotel to find the young girl that had given me the bandanna and T-shirt to participate in the parade. I'd bought a CD of the carnival music of this year for ten *real* and I'd written a little letter of thanks and gave it to her.

To my amazement, my laundry was done. I can't believe it. In a matter of hours, they'd washed it, dried it, and ironed it.

SOUTH AMERICA
ENCHANTMENT

So now I'm complete and without any further ado, I head back down, this time in a taxi with my humungous backpack. It isn't filled with stones but it might as well be, and every God-forsaken thing that I have accumulated during this trip is now in my possession. I can tell its heavy when these men make expressions like "Boy, this is not exactly a piece of luggage; this is a piece of cargo."

The cab is able to get right down to the dock where the boat is and I get on board. I'm not going to be penny-wise and pound-foolish. For a hundred and sixty *real*, I get a hammock; for two hundred, I get a share of cabin. I need a bed. When I see the wall-to-wall hammocks, I'm sure that I would have been wrapped in mine and set out to sea, with stones attached, after continually coughing all night.

As I get to my room, I'm still coughing, sputtering, and my nose is continually running. I'm so glad that I have two rolls of toilet paper, and not for the lower extremities of my body. It'll be consumed by these two flowing taps. After the better part of an hour, I'm sweating and feeling more than uncomfortable. I realize that I'm going to require more than just the aspirins that I have in my facility to stop coughing.

The boat doesn't leave until 4:00 p.m. but I have to be back on board by 3:00 p.m. It's about 1:00 p.m. now. I am hoping I can make a reconnaissance to the downtown core to pick up some Vick's Vaporub and anything else that might suppress some of this incessant coughing. The more you travel, the more you become experienced in figuring out what to ask. I check to make sure I can get back on board with the certificate of paper they'd given me. I do have the key to the cabin which is fine, but that's not the thing I'm concerned about.

When I get to the first major obstacle of immigration, I say, "Well, I wanna assure the passport." By this time, we're close friends; she has seen me that many times. But no, I have to get my ticket transferred into a computer strip so I can get access in and out of the system. Good thing I'd asked, otherwise I would have been freaking out about not getting back on the ship with all my stuff on it. When I was in Russia, I learned something that I use often now, and think of many times, and that is ask, ask, ask, and then ask again. It's not a bad rule of thumb, no matter where you are in the world, to ask the same question over and over again, and if you get the same answer, chances are it's the right answer.

With that procedure out of the way, I toddle off to find a pharmacy and get some Vicks, cough syrup, cough drops, and a bottle of pop, some cookies and chocolate bars. It's nice to carry a bit of extra food aboard these ships, because it becomes pretty mundane when you get rice, spaghetti, and beans as your main course, for days on end. For whatever reason, this ship is going to take four to five days to get to Belém, a little longer than the one I've taken from Santa Rosa.

Now, I am feeling cocky enough to see if I can get an e-mail off to my wife. The stores are open by now and since Tuesday night was the grand finale of the carnival, nobody had opened their stores until at least noon to recover from the night of feasting and whatever else. So, with luck, I get a small e-mail off to Marietta explaining to her the change of plans, still heading in a progressive direction towards my beloved wife and my homeland.

Now, with all that accomplished and behind me, the only thing on my mind was to take this coughing sick little body back to its holding tank in the boat and just wait my turn. As I work my way back through the streets of Manaus, I have a feeling of satisfaction that I know this place like the back of my hand. I just wish I were feeling better. To add to my day of aggravation, the Nike pants that I bought don't have much quality. Both the pockets have torn themselves free on the inner lining and I've been holding on to my precious documents, my passport, and the ticket back to the boat.

After I've completed buying a big liter of Coca-Cola, a few chocolate bars and biscuits for this boat trip, I start to make my way back to the docks. Still coughing and sputtering like a broken down John Deere tractor that is firing on one of its diesel engine pistons, I'm always amazed that when I do get some germ, that it doesn't come on gradually, it comes on like a storm.

I get through the gates and see lines of people still waiting to buy tickets for departure, but I have no confusion or realignment this time. I sweep through the procedure and I have to give these people full points. The United States, especially after September 11th, has put security as top priority. But these people have procedures that are congenial, functional, and highly efficient. You go through three security stops before you actually get to the dock and they check your passport and documents, and they're polite about it. The most amazing part is there are no queues or huge line-ups.

I go up the gangplank, open the door to my cabin, and lay down after taking some cough medicine and a cough drop. The cough medicine is disappointing. It's nice tasting, but I was hoping it would have more effect on the aggravating tickle in my throat. I am in cabin number 17 and very grateful that I've chosen the cabin. The short reconnaissance that I've done on board, this boat is an older vintage than the one that I took down to Manaus. I've seen on the sign that its capacity is for 300 passengers, but it seems more adapted to carrying cargo than humans. Already the centre deck is just a maze of hammocks.

I know that with my continuing coughing, congestion, and running nose, that if I didn't annoy my fellow passengers beyond their tolerance by throwing me overboard, that I probably would have spent the larger portion of my time sitting in an upright position on some bench, coughing continuously, rather than lying in a hammock.

I made a wise choice by being in a cabin even though there will (probably) be another person sharing it. Also, it gives me a great deal of comfort to know all my gear's stored before my watering little eyes and everything is accounted for. In the cabin, there's a ventilation shaft that seems to be blowing in some cooler air. I am still coughing and blowing my nose, and just hoping that whatever I got is as unhappy with my presence, as I am with it.

Robert F. Edwards

The ship doesn't actually leave at 4:00 p.m. Like so many vessels, they always seem to take off in the evening hours, somewhere between 5:00 and 6:00. At 4:00 p.m., I'm just resting and somebody starts knocking. I've now got my new roommate. A young man in his mid-twenties; doesn't speak  any English, and you know where I stand on Portuguese. After the brief introduction, and getting his luggage in, it's remarkable but we still have enough room for both the passengers that are going to take part in this storage area.

I am then approached by a person that wants to sell me a pan of food. I'm anything but hungry, and I've not been able to do my homework on board the ship I had the previous one, so I don't know whether I have to pay for the food or not. I'm thinking, "Well, I guess, maybe I'd better," and ended up paying five *real* for rice, cold spaghetti and some kind of meat that I couldn't identify.

Soon, I'm listening to the preparation for departure. At about five- thirty, our ship breaks away from the shoreline and starts its journey with us all waving good-bye to the people on shore.

I wish I were feeling much better. Manaus has been a wonderful and rewarding experience in my life, but I'm grateful that I'm on board this boat completing another leg of my adventure. There is another knock on the door, and the steward indicates that dinner is being served, which I graciously pass over.

Now in the cabin I find it actually quite chilly, but I'm too sick to take the sleeping bag out. I grab a large towel, and some of the clothes that I've been wearing earlier that day and put it over me. That is my blanket. There's only a sheet that covers the bed, and there's no extra sheet on top. I'm taking penicillin and aspirin and I'm sure that I'm fighting not only the cold, but probably my body is fighting a fever also.

My little treasure bee, I'd like to say good night and I love you dearly and I miss you a lot. I do hope that you've got my e-mail by now and that you realize that I will be taking the better part of five days to get another one off to you. Wendy, I love you dearly and my little Coleman. I hope everyone is having a better night's sleep than I am.

Good night, one and all.

Robert F. Edwards

February 14, Thursday

On Board to Belém, Brazil

I've already labeled one day back in Cuzco a "lost day". This must be a shadow. This is going to be one of those days that I have nothing much to do. I've had a very restless night. My nose is still running like the fountain that's overflowing. My cough has not caused a murder on the river Amazon, and luckily I have a very congenial roommate.

He's already gone for breakfast, which, for some strange reason, they decided it has to be at five o'clock in the morning. This is the least of the things that I have on my mind at that time.

By nine o'clock, I take some more medication and make my way to the washroom. I have to say I'm sick. There's a lot of ways of being polite about things, but this isn't one of them. Even the very smell of the latrine has brought on an almost uncontrollable desire to throw up. I managed to get back to the cot. While strength and persistence are in full unity, I pull out my sleeping bag and crawl into it. What a difference it makes. I feel very warm and cozy.

With the additional medication, I've indulged myself in a sleeping pill as well. I feel that the more sleep I can get, the better I will be. With the loud music that's being played just a couple of doors away, the sleeping pill will probably aid and assist my slumber.

The day moves on without me. I do get up periodically. The shoreline looks similar to what I've experienced on the journey down to Manaus. Even though it's rather a shame that here I am being stuck in the cabin, I'm not overly distraught by it.

We do stop in a small port. The cities here appear more modern, with bricks and stones, compared to the wooden shacks that persist up the Amazon. As I get closer to Belém, civilization is catching up and settlements are far more predominant. If I was in better spirits, I would have been more interested in exploring it.

Lunch is being served. More out of curiosity than hunger, I go down to participate. Would you believe it, rice, pasta and some meat? It seems to be the meal of choice on board these types of transports that, if you're not going to have rice, beans and pasta, then you're not traveling with the locals. Still, I managed to eat a little bit of it, before going back to my cabin. The Bear of the North will hibernate.

The day continues as non-eventful. My amiable cabin companion tries to make a bit of conversation with me, but realizes that I'm not 'up to the mound' by any stretch of the imagination.

The only break in the monotony of the day was around ten o'clock at night. A border patrol boarded our ship and decided that it was time to take a count of passports, documents and boarding paraphernalia. In my sort of stupor state, I've qualified on all accounts. That was the beginning and end of that event during the night.

I would like to say good night, Honey Bun. I sure wish I were at home, beside you and listening to all the things that happened in your day. I love you very much. Well, Wendy, I understand you keep looking for houses. Like anything, if you look long enough and hard enough, you'll find something that will meet your wishes. Good night, little Coleman .God bless each and every one of you.

Robert F. Edwards

February 15, Friday

On Board to Belém, Brazil

I get up. Yes, I am feeling better! Although, not the 'Robust Rapid Robert' that is world-renowned for being active, at least not the 'hibernating bear from the North' either.

I go down and have two cups of coffee, which seem to brighten my spirits. My cough does seem to be loosening and though my nose is still running, it doesn't seem to be the cascade of waterfalls.   Penicillin is still the wonder drug of the Amazon.

I spend a lot of time resting. The passengers on this particular vessel are nowhere near as party-orientated, now that the carnival is over. It's very crowded with people returning to work. We are lazily chugging along, when I hear a commotion outside my door. I'm not overly motivated to get out of my sleeping bag to see what's happening. But, upon opening the door, I find out that a Colombian family had their cabin broken into, their passports, all their money and valuables stolen.

There's quite a scurry of activity when we get to the next port. The police come aboard to search all the cabins, include mine, which they're welcome to. They look like they're ready for a SWAT operation rather than an investigation into a robbery; bulletproof vests, machine guns and full battle gear. Nobody seems to be the wiser. I do feel sorry for the Colombian couple; they have to leave the ship because they don't have the documents to continue.

While we're detained at this small place, hoards of small children are buzzing around. They are selling little Dixie cups from the ice cream wagons on the dock. They literally jump over, and it has to be a good two meters' on this plank to get to the ship. I'm thinking, "Boy, oh boy!" This is entrepreneurship at its height. In North America, you wouldn't find any kid thinking of doing it because it would be far too dangerous.

330

SOUTH AMERICA
ENCHANTMENT

Parents would be just mortified if their children were jumping and scrambling, just to sell Dixie cups.

A fellow was selling coconuts, and the one that I've managed to get has quite a bit of juice in it. It's just so, so good going down my sore throat. I'm also watching women selling fresh

shrimp. They don't seem to be using the weights and measure systems, but just take a big plateful and put it into a plastic bag. They look quite delicious, to say the least.

I get off and walk through a little gift shop. There's nothing there that I would have bought, maybe a basket, or some straw hats for Marietta and Wendy. But, my luggage is becoming too heavy, it's not a lack of wanting, it's just a lack of not being able to carry them.

I get back on board the ship, and I happen to meet, over lunch, a charming young lady. She's in her late twenties, early thirties, from Hamburg, and her name's Christine. I can't believe it. I've met two Christines, nurses, one from Berlin and now one from Hamburg.

She's telling me that two or three other people down in the hammock area have been robbed. There seems to be a real insurgence of theft going on. Again, I'm more than grateful

Robert F. Edwards

that I've chosen the cabin for more than obvious reasons now. I have read in "the Lonely Planet" book and have been told by other people about thefts on boats. I am so grateful to have all my gear in one place, and still intact.

I am enjoying a bit of the outdoors today and the weather is very hot. I'm having a beer for the first time in a long while at this complex on the dock. If I had known how long the ship was going to be unloading here, I would have gone in to town and looked around. Since I have no idea, I finish my beer and I go lay down, before the ship casts off.

We haven't gone a great distance and I hear the ship stopped again. I'm thinking, "Well, gosh, what's happening?" There's a real commotion going on. Somebody's jumped overboard. There are TV cameras and people being interviewed; this ship is not exactly dull. We have to turn around and go back, and spend some time picking up the culprit. They think he might be the robber, and opinions are running rampart. My interpreter, Christine, speaks five languages fluently. Two of them happen to be Portuguese and English, which is most rewarding in my particular case.

Once we return to the port, the police board again. They come to my cabin and ask me very politely if I speak Portuguese and I say only English. They soon realize that they're not going to get any information from me, and I go back to bed. Amongst all this commotion, I am starting to feel better. I guess the medication is kicking in. My cold is losing the battle and I'm winning. So, that's an important part of my criteria.

In general, there's uneasiness about robbers and thieves on board the boat. It's like lost luggage in an airport. When one person has experienced loss, others come out of the woodwork and tell about their misfortunes. There's a Belgian fellow that's been traveling by bicycle and lost seventy *real*.

I don't believe that this ship is full of pirates and plunderers of wealth; it's just very crowded. In the hammock area, your luggage is exposed to anybody that wishes to rummage through it. Now, not being quite as naive, I realize that people

332

SOUTH AMERICA
ENCHANTMENT

slept in their hammocks for more reasons than one. I was fortunate enough, and had the presence of mind, to have my luggage strapped with a security cable to a pole on my last boat trip.

The day wears on and I go for a modest supper, which is the basic rice and spaghetti with a bit of a potato salad and meat. In the cafeteria are these massive sides of beef, still dripping with blood as we were eating our food.

Christine and my roommate now join up to make a trio again. Christine is our translator, so he has a chance now to ask questions about myself. I learn that he does repairs on engines of Honda, and he's taking courses through work-to-learn programs.

The roar of the engine in the hull below is almost deafening. I couldn't help but think that this is not the Love Boat that I'm on. Some of the cruises that my beloved and I have taken have been upgrades even though we've gone the most economical way possible.

However, I still am enjoying it. One thing I'm aware of is the size of populations on the sides of the rivers now. Not only are the cities much larger, but also the foliage is sparser. It must be cattle ranching country, not the large pampas of the Argentine, but small mixed ranching.

The houses are not much different than they have been throughout; still wooden homes on stilts. There seems to be a general appearance of not only more people, but also a better standard of life that they have. When I see a satellite dish, I can't help but chuckle and think that they might not have microwave ovens at their disposal, but they do have TV and as many channels as developed countries.

The river widens to a width (I've been told) of 325 kilometers at the estuary. In some cases, I can barely see the foliage on the other side. Then in other cases, the river narrows and breaks up around deltas. This is what we're coming into now, some large tracts of land that are in between. The foliage is breathtaking with huge ferns, and everything looks so lush.

Robert F. Edwards

With the speed that the boat is traveling, there is a pleasant breeze flowing that takes the heat and the humidity out of the air. I'm not so sure that it would be as comfortable if you're paddling one of the numerous little wooden dugouts that I see on the waterways as we're passing by. Like many countries with large landmasses, you see children riding bicycles. Here, you see young children rowing these little dugouts.

The wooden paddles are made out of a heavy wood, not exceptionally long. It's just a deep stroke isn't required. These boats would be quite interesting to paddle like canoes, they're shallow and so you'd have to be quite agile. I see them scattered at all times of day and night for different errands that are being done.

The evening is upon us. The dancing and the huge speakers blaring music on the back part of the deck keep conversation to a minimum. It's a pleasant night. I'm feeling much better. So, like everybody else, I'm participating in the events, and having a beer with the rest of the locals. Brazilian people are very friendly and fun loving and just love dancing. Some of them keep on asking me if I would dance. I'm saying "no", but eventually I get up and dance a few numbers.

SOUTH AMERICA ENCHANTMENT

Christine tells me that they really like the way I dance. It's one of the few countries that people have ever commented on my dancing ability. It's quite an honor. These people always have their feet moving in a rhythmic mode.

By nine-thirty, I've decided that this convalescing person has had enough activity for the night, and I say my good nights and return to my room. Off to bed I go. It's probably about eleven p.m., when suddenly, we have a military patrol come aboard to check our passports and make sure our documents are in order. Efficient, pleasant, and I've been cleared again for another leg on my journey down the mighty river of the Amazon.

I would like to say good night to my beloved wife. I'm one day closer to you, my beautiful, wonderful person. I miss you immensely. With Wendy and Cole, I hope that all is going well with you two. And to each and every one of you, have a wonderful evening.

Good night.

Robert F. Edwards

February 16, Saturday

Onboard, Amazon, Brazil

I've had another pleasant night's sleep. I am feeling much better. I'm still coughing, but I think it's due to the cold air blowing in and the extreme changes of weather in the rooms versus the outside.

I manage to miss breakfast again, being too late, and several different people are giving me the high sign and best wishes of the day. I start to enjoy the warm weather, as more people join my time frame, now about eight o'clock.

The foliage along the sides of the rivers is changing, as we're getting further into the delta. Grasses appear more than the dense forest of a jungle. There's a lot more boats and activity on the water. I watch many of these 'entrepreneurs, at they're very best; row their boats towards the ship. The ship doesn't reduce speed, and continues its course.

These small dugouts are rowed frantically at an angle that's appropriate and then they throw a gaffing hook on to one of the tires and rope themselves on to the boat. Usually there's

336

SOUTH AMERICA
ENCHANTMENT

two to three in the dugout and obviously the man is the one that throws the hook. But, the other two often are young women. Once they've secured the dugout to the boat, they ride high out of the water. Just the stern of the dugout is left in the water. Gingerly, they jump aboard and sell their goods.

One of them is a fruit that they put in a jar with liquid. Thinking it over, it may well be sugar cane they're putting in the jars, with probably river water, and letting it soften. Maybe not quite as good as a licorice sticks, but welcomed. I marvel at the ingenuity and precision that they use in securing their position to the ship. They've got this procedure down to an art, and the dugout is tied so that when they want to release themselves from the ship, they just let the rope down gradually. Once the bow is in the water and they've made sure that the person in the stern is in control, they release the rope.

At lunchtime, I go down below and have my regular quantity of rice, spaghetti and meat. I remarked to Christine that it would be rather easy to be the supply master along this trade route. You'd never have to really worry too much about the selection. You just have to make sure the quantity was there, because every ship has the same menu. With all my coughing and sputtering, and even the sore muscle in my knee, I'm in good physical shape. As far as digestion-wise, you can't knock the diet.

I happen to meet a young fellow called Guy. He is a vegetarian and has a young woman accompanying him. I find out that he's born in Israel, has lived in Britain, has an American passport, and is now spending a great deal of time in Brazil. He's a musician, and teaches music in Rio de Janeiro. He is not sure if he will have a position waiting for him, due to the enrollment. If there's enough in the classes, then the teacher has a job. If they don't have enough in the class, then you're without a job. Keep it simple, make it work.

He said very candidly, when Christine asked about which passport he used the most, "I'm using the British one." He says, "You know, the Israelis aren't very popular or Americans aren't much better off." There are very few Americans that I've seen on any of my trips to South America. Like so many other parts of the world, the Americans are not held in great respect, and they realize that they may control things but people don't enjoy having them around. They always correct themselves and say that obviously, the individual is different than the country. But as far as Americans in general, they are not particularly well-liked. This man has reconfirmed so many other people's opinions.

As the day wears on, more young men venture up to the top deck. They do like to drink their beer. Many are coming up to me and asking, "Well, you know, you go discoing and dancing tonight. We want to see you dance." Christine being the interpreter at all times is telling me that, "Yes, they really want me to dance." The ham in this old body tells everybody that because their demand is so great, the request is going to be granted, and I'll not only do some discoing tonight, but I will put on my carnival T-shirt and bandanna. This adds to the excitement of our last night on board.

I don't know how these people do it, staying happy, as the two other levels of the ship are packed. When I said to Christine that it was like a refugee ship down there, she didn't say anything the first time. Now on three or four occasions, when she's returned from these other decks, she said, "You know, you've just described it very adequately." There's just no room. These people, between their luggage and the hammock, that's all their space that is allocated for the better part of five days on the water. The only time they venture in any direction is to relieve themselves, or to take on some food. If everybody got up, there wouldn't be enough standing room to accommodate them. The men are leaning over the railing. Then you have to push some hammock out of the way to get by them, and usually there's a body in it. But, everybody seems to be surviving, and tolerating the conditions with a congenial attitude.

The coastline just drifts along on both sides, and sometimes we come very close. There are two or three little buildings together, then a vast void and then another village. In a small boat, you could probably go up and down the waterways and enjoy a year or two of just being a vagabond in these tranquil waters. In the delta, the water doesn't rise as much, as it's able to drain huge amounts of water into the ocean. I've been told how many metric tons of water go per day into the ocean, enough to supposedly be able to give everybody water in the world. This is not only the second longest river in the world; it's the widest river and produces the most amount of water. The Amazon has many things over the Nile. It is a remarkable piece of nature. I am very grateful to have fulfilled this dream of mine. It is much more magnificent and rewarding than what my imagination provided.

The afternoon is well intact and I'm beginning to fall into the lifestyle that seems to exist here. If you're not perspiring or it's not raining, you're having a *siesta.* I'm no exception to the rule. Back on deck, around five o'clock, the heat of the day has dissipated and sitting around is a lot more comfortable.

The landscape is repetitious, and so is dinner. The menu has not fluctuated whatsoever; it is consistent and plentiful. Some of the procedures are peculiar. We've been dining at our designated times, without any hesitation. But this eve-

339

ning, we had to produce our ticket to show that our meals were included. I don't know what would have happened if there had been no money available. I'm sure you wouldn't have been able to regurgitate three or four days' worth of rice. The more I understand the things they do, their systems do work. I'm sure that this one is no exception to the rule.

After my meal, I head upstairs, and the music is blaring. Of course, the young people want me to take part. As I promised, I wore my T-shirt and my bandanna, so let the party roll. A woman in her late thirties comes up and asks me to dance with her. I must have the Swing, and be a Brazilian at heart. The body movements are the same. It's open dancing, not close-quarter or structured dancing. It's just bobbing along. It's so different from my lifestyle that I grew up with. I'd no more think of dancing near a guy, let alone with a guy. But here we've even got them organized that we're all in a lineup dancing. There's a young lady that does a belly dance with a lot of skill, and I thoroughly enjoyed her performance.

With all the robberies and events that have taken place, including the man jumping overboard, on this particular boat, people now have their own stories and their own paranoia. People start rumors, and then they expand as their imagination permits them to exaggerate. One woman told Christine to tell me to watch our drinks, that people are spiking them with drugs, and then they get robbed.

There was one fellow that was on drugs but they were prescription drugs, for a mental disorder. He, for whatever reason, seemed to have taken a very close interest in me. Finally, I asked Christine to request a ship's personnel to have him stay away from me. There are two types of people that I always am very cautious with. One is somebody that's mentally deranged and the other is somebody that is doing heavy drugs. Both these types are unpredictable. When you're in a situation that you can't communicate with rational people, it's prudent to avoid them, which I've done.

We dance the night away. By nine-thirty, I excuse myself. There are a few people that are getting intoxicated. I don't

SOUTH AMERICA
ENCHANTMENT

have to worry. I'm an old guy so nobody is too interested in accosting me. There are a few that are leaning on me to buy them a drink, but a couple of *real* is no big deal in my life.

I return to my cabin and lie down for a while. I was going to call it a night but I can't sleep with the continual sounds coming out. It's a relatively nice night, so I return and sit up a little longer and just enjoy the fun and the sheer happiness of these people in their last night on board the boat. By eleven-thirty, I'm getting ready to say "Good night, folks!" again. I can still hear the music blaring through these steel walls as the party continues. I can only hope to get some more rest and wait until tomorrow to see what transpires.

Good night, my little beautiful wife. I'm a lot closer to you today than I was so many days ago. I love you very, very much. I'm looking forward to being back with you and spending time together.

Wendy, you're always on my mind. I always hope that things are going well for you. I hope little Cole is healthy and robust as always.

With that, I would wish one and all a good night.

Robert F. Edwards

February 17, Sunday

On Board, Amazon, Brazil

I get up with a continual banging on the door, which indicates that breakfast is being served in the halls below. Somehow I'm not motivated to get up at five-thirty in the morning to go down for a cup of coffee, even though I would enjoy one. By eight-thirty, I'm hoping that I can still obtain a cup of coffee. Once I get down there, I'm late again. I've been on this ship now the better part of five days, and I've yet to experience what's being served for breakfast. Christine did tell me that on one occasion there was quite an elaborate breakfast. They had bread, buns, cheese, meat, coffee and juice. Most of the time it is just bread and coffee. However, I will just have to take other people's word for it.

The day is very pleasant. People are starting to stir in the lower hulls and on the upper deck. As I'm sitting, trying to collect my thoughts, more and more people arrive on deck, and they give me the high sign. The friendliness and the camaraderie are intact. Shortly thereafter, my roommate and Christine join me. Amidst our conversation, we notice the increasing traffic. There is a certain excitement about seeing more of these little riverboats going up and down the river. It's different from the tranquil *feluccas* of the Nile, as these are like miniature tugboats scurrying to points unknown.

I start to prepare myself for the horrific task of trying to get this mammoth piece of luggage in some kind of conformity so that I might be able to take it off the ship. By ten o'clock, everybody seems to be in the same general consensus that dismantling is the order of the day. With myself, I stuff my sleeping bag in my bag and miraculously managed to get everything else put in it, which amazes me.

The weight becomes more of the problem than actually the size. My roommate has volunteered to help me lift it down through these very narrow passages to the decks below.

342

SOUTH AMERICA ENCHANTMENT

We start to see our first glimpse of Belém, and the time now is about eleven o'clock. Even off in this distance, I can see that there are many high-rises. It's the largest city I've seen probably since Lima, and very modern. As we watch this city become more a reality in our sight, we start to prepare for departure. Now, I've forfeited my ticket as the purser has reclaimed it. I won't have this small piece of memorabilia to paste in my scrapbook, but I have enough pictures to justify that I was present on this voyage.

This completes the "three wishes" that I had for this adventure. One was seeing *Machu Picchu*. Number two is seeing the *Nazca Lines*. And number three was sailing down the entire Amazon River. With every passing kilometer, my dream has now become reality.

We dock by one o'clock, and with my roommate's help, I managed to get down the three levels. I told Christine and Marcus that I would be more than happy to pay for a taxi, if they want to come with me.

Christine and I managed to get through the security checks very quickly. We wait about ten to fifteen minutes for Marcus, but he never does materialize. I don't know what happened to him. It's going to be one of the mysteries of this adventure, as he was right behind us. So we never even got to say good-bye.

Christine and I share a taxi, and she's chosen two or three hotels that are within a given area. The first one is completely unacceptable. It's moldy and smelly, and they want forty *real*. She would feel more comfortable paying around twenty or twenty-five. I'm quite prepared to spend even more just to have a nice room.

I suggest that I stay with the luggage and, because she's fluent with Portuguese, that she go up and down this particular street. There are hotels available on either side. After fifteen minutes, she finds one that looks quite nice, but they want forty-five *real*. She's not prepared to pay that much even though the room is very nice and the building is exceptionally clean. I'm more than satisfied with the price, so she asked if she could leave her gear in my room while she does a reconnaissance to find some place more in her price range.

My first challenge of the day has been fulfilled. I've got a nice room, and my gear is safe. Now, the second challenge, which is always on my mind, is to get to an Internet. It happens to be Sunday and even in this large city, it's a day of rest. There are very few places that are open.

I seem to have blind luck. I asked the lady at the front desk about an Internet and she gives me some directions. Once I get to the main artery a gentleman asks me, "Can I help you?" in English, believe it or not. I said, "Yes, I'm looking for the Internet." He says, "Oh, just go up two blocks and the telephone place will have one."

Yes, success was mine! My beloved wife had a few little e-mails for me. Life is good. God is great. Belém is treating me right.

Afterwards, I stroll around the *piazza*. On Sundays, they put up small kiosks that are easy to assemble to display their

goods, anything from Chiclets to jewelry to thongs and every other conceivable consumer good that you could possibly imagine. Also, there's produce and I enjoy a coconut for half a *real*, which quenched my thirst.

Belém is not an overly attractive city, but it's modern. Some of the streets are cobble-stoned. The sidewalks are similar to what I've seen in Spain and Portugal; the little blocks of stones arranged in mosaic patterns. The only disadvantage to this is that they often get dislodged, so these sidewalks are always in dire need of repair.

SOUTH AMERICA
ENCHANTMENT

Today being a day of rest, the streets are sparsely populated. With not much to interest me, I make my way back to the room. I am expecting, in the next half hour, for Christine to return and, hopefully for her sake, to have found accommodations both price-wise and sufficient for her requirements.

I am enjoying a good floor under my feet, and a nice double bed to lie on, when she shows up. She has been successful in finding a place for about half the price of what I'm paying, not a lot of value but her budget requires the reduction in rent. She takes her gear and we make arrangements to meet at seven o'clock for dinner.

Belém is known in Brazil as probably one of the rainiest cities in the world. There's a standing quotation here is that "I'll meet you right after the rain," because it rains pretty well everyday. The humidity is very intense. You can stand still and watch your body start to glisten. It's not just foreigners, its residents alike. It's a climate that produces a tremendous amount of perspiration. I blame my lack of getting rid of this cold on the air-conditioning. Going from hot outdoors with perspiration-soaked clothes into cold surroundings, if it isn't the torture test to see how your immune system is, I'd sure like to know what is.

It doesn't seem that long before Christine's arrived and the adventure begins. She's easy to get along with, outgoing, and very independent. Off we go, like a couple of buccaneers that have just landed on the Barbary Coast, and start heading down towards the wharves. She's told me that there's a row of different types of cuisine along the docks. We made our way down to the wharf and it is exceptionally well done. They've converted old ships, still with the rails and the old cranes themselves used for destuffing, and built this magnificent mezzanine with restaurants, facilities, and a museum of artifacts from a by-gone era of the rubber boom period and other prosperous times of this city.

In the city's history, Belém has been attempted to be taken over by the French, the British, and the Dutch, but nobody

345

Robert F. Edwards

has been successful in taking any landmass from the Portuguese or the Brazilians. The old story is 'what I have, I hold'; and this city, though it has been under different sieges, has always remained in the long term Portuguese; and then when it got its independence, Brazilian.

These wharfs reflect the history and it's creative, ultramodern, and inside you'd think you were in an icebox. The air-conditioning is exceptionally strong, but they also have seating arrangements outside of each designated area of the restaurants and they range anywhere from Italian cuisine to fish specialty restaurants, and so forth. I've made my mark in the sand and said to Christine, (knowing that she's on a limited budget), that I would be more than happy to treat her to a decent meal as well as myself.

I've been reading in "The Lonely Planet" about certain types of food and we're going to take part in a restaurant that has authentic cuisine. After discussing with the maitre d' what was available, he said yes, they have this particular dish, *Manicoba,* which is a stew using the ground up shoots of the *Maniva* plant, and cooked for at least four days, then combined with beef jerky, cast offs like hooves, bacon and God knows what other parts. He says, "Yes, we have that," but he strongly recommends that we take the combination dish which consists of *pato no tucupi.* It's a lean duck cooked in a *tucupi* sauce. It's a yellow liquid extraction from the *manico* or the *cassava root,* poisonous if in its raw form. In its cooked form, it is absolutely delicious and the yellow sauce accompanying it makes this one of my new favorites. Also, there's a unique crab dish. It's called *unhas de caranguejo,* it is crab claws and these are, in our particular case, served deep-fried. They are very small compared to the Dungeness crab that we have on the West Coast and are a different shape and size from the ones that I'm used to. Also, we have *casquinha de caranguejo* and this is stuffed crabs. It's equally as good and I thoroughly enjoyed it. To give a perspective of what this particular crab looks like, it is the size of a large egg. I have the *manicoba* roots, and thank goodness that I didn't just settle

346

SOUTH AMERICA
ENCHANTMENT

for that. Out of all the dishes that I ordered, this is the one that I was determined to take part in, but it is not something that I will ever order again. I said to Christine that it's like black mud and there's a corn grain that the Indians and Brazilians use just about on everything. To me, it tastes almost like gravel, and I said, "Gosh, I don't know which is the most distasteful, to be eating this mud plain or to mix it with the gravel." Out of all the dishes, that's the only one that I really don't have a liking for.

We also have some different fruit drinks and they're quite tangy. With a bit of sugar in mine, it is pleasant and enjoyable, and juices are very prevalent in these parts. Of course, fruit is available everywhere, but they have made some very interesting drinks from them. Some are very pulpy and thick, while others are a clear liquid, and sometimes they're chilled with crushed ice; others are just an extraction and poured in to a glass. After enjoying these unique, exotic dishes, we also have the special type of ice cream made from some of the fruits that are available.

It is a pleasant evening to be sitting out. However, the rains come and go, like people passing on the street. We are in a sheltered area with a canopy and we've enjoyed the meal while watching the torrential rains pouring down. I make a few comments that I wonder if we're going to have to spend the night here. Just as we've completed our ice cream, the rain is over and as they say in Belém, "Meet you after the rain."

We start walking back and pass by a microbrewery, making different ales and beers. Christine says, "At least let me treat you to a beer." So, we order, and she said it's the first time she's ever had any dark beer, which was very pleasant. No, it was not Guinness, but still, a fine dark beer. We stroll back to the main street and it's not that late, only about 10:00 p.m. But, for me it's time to say, "Goodnight, folks" and she makes her way to her hotel. Back in my room, I enjoy reading a bit of my favorite book on the road, "The Lonely Planet", and flick through the channels to see if there's anything that I might be able to comprehend.

Robert F. Edwards

With that, I'd like to say goodnight to my beautiful wife and I'm one day closer to you, my dearest, and my love. Wendy, I hope you and Cole are having a good time, and I will be looking forward to being with you. To the rest of you, I hope your day has had some adventure in it as well. Goodnight, one and all.

SOUTH AMERICA ENCHANTMENT

February 18, Monday

Belém, Brazil

I've got up, still got a bit of coughing and sputtering, but went down to a very delightful breakfast, a full complement of fruits, juices, buns and meats. I enjoyed having a leisurely breakfast before going to meet Christine. We're planning to see a bit of the wharfs and the market place around 10:00 a.m. and then we'll see how things progress. I also want to get to the Internet and also check out the possibilities of moving on to either Salvador or heading towards my final destination of Rio de Janeiro.

Now that I am back out on the streets, what an amazement! Where there was barely anybody participating yesterday, it is mayhem today. Monday morning has produced the 'back to work, get on with life' crowd.

I start to assess my priorities. It's approximately 9:00 a.m., and one is to find a bank that will take my trusty Royal Bank Visa card, and also use the Internet. I find the Internet, but it isn't working and after the better part of fifteen minutes, it doesn't look like success is going to be there. They tell me that at the Hilton Hotel up the street, the rates are the same, and I can go there. Yes, much better equipment and facilities. I have about thirty-nine e-mails waiting, some of them just the regular business, and a few personal ones which I'm always grateful to receive. I write off a few quick ones and advise my wife that I'm going to be investigating the possibilities of moving on and will advise her accordingly.

Back out on the street, the activity is immense and people are scurrying back and forth. I don't think the buses are quite as aggressive on the streets of Belém as they were in Manaus, but I wouldn't want to challenge them. Here, there seems to be a bit of respect that pedestrians do exist. I pass by a man begging, and my God, I don't know what must have happened to him. He has nothing below a belly button, as far as the

349

body, and his arms are amputated to stumps. But he's smiling, as he is sitting/perched on a little wooden deck in the middle of the traffic flow of pedestrians. This is one time I wish I could speak Portuguese, so as to find out what terrible event must have taken place to reduce him to a portion of what he was. Who knows, maybe an alligator, just really hard to say? You do see beggars here and people that are deformed, but not in any great extent. I recall his pleasant face and his gratitude, when I gave him some money.

I mention to Christine that the other day I saw a fellow, whose legs were mangled, begging in the middle of the road. Somebody was throwing some coinage to him and it landed in the gutter, close to where I was. I managed to pick it up and add a *real* to it before passing it on to him. These people inspire me to appreciate and be grateful for all the gifts and the abundance of life itself that I've been blessed with. I am always very grateful that I've had good fortune in my life, and today is no exception.

I start my second quest of the day: to 'rob' a bank of some *real* in exchange for plastic credits (my Visa card). For some unknown reason, Brazil is a difficult place, not just with Visa but also MasterCard, to get money as a foreigner. After about three or four attempts, I am told the Bank of Brazil is the only one that's going to accommodate us Canadians. When I get there, it is very well organized. A fellow is directing traffic, asking people what they need, and then directing them to these instant tellers. There must be a good twenty of these ATM's. He makes any traffic cop look like he could take a lesson from him in directing. When I get to him and I show my plastic, it's no problem. He's pointing to the one I need, and out of all of them, there's only one that takes foreign cards. After two or three attempts, I'm five hundred *real* better off, and my credit card is the worst for it.

Now, with money in my pocket and most of my quest behind me, the time is fast approaching to rendezvous with Christine. She arrives and we start strolling down to the docks and to the common market. I have been to many open markets and

SOUTH AMERICA
ENCHANTMENT

this is standard to ones throughout the world, with produce, the meats, fish and poultry inside a large housing area for butchering purposes.

We go to a spot that specializes in herbal remedies, and I buy Marietta and Wendy some perfume. There aren't great deals of things that are unique to the area, some straw hats and weaving products; but this is not a city with much consideration for tourists or artisan work. This is a  working city and these malls concentrate on anything from clothes to shoes to hammocks, even some plumbing accessories.

We work our way down along the wharf and see some of the old sections of the city. They're in the process of getting these buildings restored. You still see some of the old blue Portuguese tiles on the external walls. I said to Christine, "If it had been in my country, they would have opened up this wharf area to the yuppies." It's just ideal for a bohemian setting. With all of the fishing boats, it is an interesting part of Belém to be in. Just above it is the fortress that protected the harbor in days gone by, and a couple of cathedrals. This is about all of the colonial part of Belém that anybody will see.

We then returned towards the core of the city, in full glorious swing, now that the carnival's over and the weekend is finished. People are scurrying around in their daily routines. The thing that still confuses me is the small kiosks that fill the secondary streets. They have somebody sewing shoes in a kiosk just outside the premises of a place that has a large display of shoes. I would think there's a conflict of interest.

351

However, everybody seems to get along relatively well in these congested markets.

We stop and have a coconut, which I am finding to be an addictive drink, no two ways about it. I thoroughly enjoyed the fluid and they seem to have a lot more here than in some countries that also grow coconuts. The vendor uses a machete to open them up, and there's just the beginning of the actual pulp, which is easily scraped out. It's more a skin of very soft texture. Anyway it is a good quencher.

The afternoon is well in hand and I'm feeling the effects of it. The heat is oppressive. I still have to get a couple of e-mails off to Marietta, and do a few personal errands. Christine and I have agreed that we'll meet for dinner around 7:00 p.m. We both decided that we're going to have fish, and then see how the evening takes us from there.

I do the errands that I have in mind and check my luggage, make sure that I've got everything packed for tomorrow and just relax a little bit preparing myself for the days that lie ahead. This is a nice room and I'm going to take full advantage of not just the showers but the facilities also. After I catch up on a bit of everything that requires my immediate attention, I am back on the street. I do one last reconnaissance to pick up some pop and chocolate bars and biscuits for the trip ahead. I've found from past experience that buses, in this part of the world, all have their own rules and regulations. So, trying to be a little more prepared than the average guy, I make my purchases for this journey. Also, I'm really enjoying these milky yogurts, good thirst quenchers and quite filling at the same time.

The magic hour fast approaches and my traveling companion shows up right on time. We start to walk down to where we were the previous night, but take a different route. Brazilians seem to make their midday meal one of the largest, and the cheap restaurants either have the food left over from the midday meal, or are closed. Whatever we did wrong, we weren't able to find the restaurant of last night.

We end back up into the old market square, and by now, it's totally deserted. There's an uneasy feeling in this area and I expressed my concerns to Christine. She agrees it's just devoid of people. It's not really that late, only about 8:30 p.m., but the only people here are of shabby appearance and unsavory character. We are convinced to return to the more populated areas when we see four men, sitting on a dirty street, with four bottles of hard liquor as their companions. Not a place you really want to test your ability on the martial arts or see if benevolence and good nature persists in a den of inequity.

We head back to the main area, but it feels like somebody has given an evacuation notice and exercised it. When I said to Christine that maybe people leave the core of the city to go to the suburbs to enjoy their rest, she reminded me that in Vancouver and other large cities, the downtown core is where elegant restaurants and all the night life is. It is rather peculiar here; that the streets become very sparse of people and the city locks itself up. With the heavy metal grates down, you sure don't do any window-shopping. Even the small kiosks have now been dismantled and taken away.

Robert F. Edwards

We are really having a difficult time finding a nice place to eat. When all else fails, I suggest that we go to the Hilton Hotel. So, the two weary travelers that have covered who know how many kilometers to find a restaurant end up eating in a five-star hotel. To my surprise, the menu has a great variety, plus there's a huge buffet. But the prices are relatively inexpensive and in line with the cuisine we had the night before. Christine orders a bouillabaisse fish soup, and I order a local fish with the yellow sauce I enjoyed the night before. Done differently, but then no two chefs prepare food the same way, but equally as spicy and delicious.

We decide to share some red wine. Chileans and Argentineans have remarkable wines, but Brazilians seem to be more beer drinkers. I sampled three different bottles before we found one that was acceptable, and this is the Hilton.

It's interesting, when people meet under different conditions from these their normal lifestyles and find a common bond, their friendship and camaraderie strengthens on a continual basis. This is what happened with Christine and me. She has a different background from me, and she's thirty-four years of age, but very sure-footed and independent. She laughs and says that might be part of her problem, why she hasn't secured a long-term relationship. She tells me that her younger sister has gone through a bad marriage, and is having emotional problems, as well as trouble adjusting to life in general. Her mother had the misfortune of getting diabetes, but has handled it with determination and is doing well. Her father taught music in the University of Hertzberg, a very accomplished pianist and composer. He was asked to compose a work that would complement the great masters like Mozart and Beethoven on their anniversary. He is an exceptionally talented man, and Christine said that she would send me a CD of his music.

In the course of the evening, we talked about many things; just an easy conversation between two friends, only to find the hours had danced away. The maitre d' and waiter are hoping that we will end, not only the conversation but also the meal, and settle up accordingly, which we do, now its 11:30. We quickly walk back to the street that parts our ways, my hotel is one way, and hers is the other. We hug each other a couple of times and wish each other well in our journeys. She is a fine young lady and an enjoyable traveling companion. I do hope that our conversation isn't the last and time will prove what course will be taken.

With that, I get back to the hotel and to my room, and prepare for a final good-night's rest before the journey that lies ahead. Goodnight, my beautiful wonderful wife. I miss you very much and I just hope everything is going well. Wendy, I hope the same for you and Cole. To all of you, I wish you well and hope your day has had its rewards as well.

Robert F. Edwards

Yes, I get up and do my usual toiletries and go down to have a very good breakfast. The spread these people put on for breakfast is more than commendable. I have some water-melon (which I don't normally have at home), some bread, meats and cakes, also some juice and a couple of cups of coffee. This is the second morning that I have been watching this cartoon playing on the television, and it looks like a little leopard with an exceptionally long tail. I'm even starting to remember his "gubba, gubba " probably one of the few words that I'll ever remember in Portuguese, only to find out that it doesn't have any meaning to it.

I settle up with the hotel and it's ironic, you can barter for a discount and get it, only to find out that there's always a hitch. In this particular case, when I produced my Visa, the girl was very nice about it, but said, "Oh, no, no, we don't give discounts if you pay by Visa." So to stand my ground, I tell her that it wasn't part of the negotiation; it wasn't mentioned at the time, and when she checked it on the card, I've put forty *real* instead of forty-five. She is good-natured enough to say yes, that she'll honor it. That's one thing I do find here, that they are not as hard-nosed as North Americans and more accommodating, and will give quarter on issues, which is nice compared to the attitudes that we've become accustomed to, especially where I live.

It's time to get to the bus terminal, and everything goes very well. It's much easier to find the platform. The bus is right on time, our luggage is loaded, and to my delight, the space allocated for each seat is very large. They issue blankets, which I am grateful for, as I really do need them with the amount of air-conditioning that is in full force. The bus leaves on time, and we even get a little bag of snack foods to enhance the relationship of the bus line and the passengers.

SOUTH AMERICA
ENCHANTMENT

My bus trip is going to take me twenty-seven hours, heading to Fortaleza. It's also in the province or state of Ceara and this particular part of Brazil's pride and glory are the coast-lines, which consist of over six hundred kilometers. The Brazilian government is trying to develop the area for tourism.

This is my first opportunity to get outside of Belém, and the terrain is completely different from the jungle. It's much more open and inducive to farming and agriculture. It is still very lush and green, but not the dense, impregnable growth of the jungle. It's also more populated, and the buildings in the small communities are now adobe, brick, and stones rather than wood. So, we've gone back to mortar and cement again.

The roads are exceptionally poor compared to what I remember in other parts of Brazil. Also, they have large speed bumps that this mighty piece of transport has to slow down and hobble over as we go through the small communities, and there are many throughout this artery of transportation. The scenery is repetitious until we start to see the first hint of mountain ranges. These are really just large hills, but different than what I've been used to, in the previous weeks spent

Robert F. Edwards

in the Amazon, where everything was at water level, depending on what level the water was.

From what I've read, the main industry is cattle-raising. They seem to use the cattle for everything, from food to leather goods; even the hoofs have a purpose in their existence. This is the poor part of Brazil and as we pass from one village to the other, the buildings reflect this. Even though Brazil claims that they run about eighty percent literacy in their country, they say that probably less than forty percent can actually read a newspaper or have much writing and reading ability.

I am lucky to be able to sleep on the bus; and to my amazement, I sleep relatively well. I'm blessed by having both seats, so I spend considerable time being spread out at different angles, securing catnaps here and there.

And with that, I'm going to conclude tonight, for it doesn't really stop or end. And I would like to say goodnight, Marietta and Wendy and Cole and everyone else.

SOUTH AMERICA
ENCHANTMENT

February 20, Wednesday

Enroute to Fortaleza, Brazil

It's all in the eyes of the beholder as to when the morning happens. I start my day looking out the window on the bus at 6:00 a.m., and the scenery hasn't changed much. With six hundred miles of coastline, I am still just far enough away that the coast is evading me. However, I am heading in the right direction and we keep going on our marathon. We do stop at one place and now I don't have the paranoia that I did last year when we all get off the bus and the bus takes off and I'm standing there with nothing but my clothes on. I realize that this is a chance for the people on the bus to relieve themselves in toilets and take on a bit of nourishment in the facilities that are available, and for the bus to get fuel and swept out.

This particular place actually doesn't do too badly for a quick snack. They give us an egg, some bread, and a couple of pieces of raw onion and a tomato and a cup of coffee. It's welcomed by all, and then we get back on the bus. It's non-eventful, until we arrive in Fortaleza, shortly after two. My first quest is to find out when the next bus leaves for Salvador. To my delight, it leaves at 10:00 p.m. tonight, so I get another night's sleep on the bus. Soon, I'll have difficulty sleeping in a bed. I can't remember how many other modes of transportation that I've taken, as well as slept in different positions, with different apparatuses. However, now that I'm in Fortaleza, with the better part of eight hours to take care of, I decide that I'm going to see what the city has to offer.

My first challenge, as always, is to try and find an Internet, but I have to get rid of the luggage first. There is no conceivable way that I can drag this backpack around. To my good fortune, yes, there is a big storage department and for five *real* I get rid of the entire luggage, except my camera and my waist

Robert F. Edwards

pack. Of course, now that I have a ticket to Salvador and my luggage out of the way, my quest is to get to an Internet.

I find the information desk very helpful, but no English. They give me a map of the city and try to explain, to the best of their ability and to the best of my comprehension, where an Internet might be secured. However, it's going to take a cab to get there. This bus terminal is very modern, and also the city with high-rises is a new-looking city. The bus terminal, though, is not in the downtown core. If anything, it's close to the airport and that general vicinity.

I can't remember when I've had a meal actually. I've had some yogurt, a cookie and even a chocolate bar. That is it, as far as a meal goes, in probably the better part of a day. So, I'm quite motivated to have something to eat, and as odd as it sounds, I'm really hoping for some French fries and a nice bowl of soup.

I make my way through some large expressways, and it's a spread-out, cosmopolitan city. I find a park and even a pet store, but no restaurant. However, after a couple of kilometers, I do find a large ultra modern supermarket that any North American or European country would be proud to support. All very helpful people, but the language of Brazil is Portuguese and not much else is spoken. I have a general idea of where this Internet is, so I continue along.

It's extremely hot, a sign says thirty-seven degrees Celsius, so not exactly a day in Canada for sure. For whatever reason, I have lost or misplaced the photocopy of my passport, so I see a photocopy machine and get that done as well, along with my little errands. I finally see a restaurant and make my way over. They have everything - pizzas, sandwiches, hamburgers, spaghetti, but no soup or French fries. So, with a large beer and a hamburger, I have the meal of the day. The hamburger is so good; I indulge myself in a second one as well.

The map I was given is well done, but not very accurate to scale. I get a taxi to take me towards the church and the historical parts of the city. Now, I realize how spread out the city is, and how far the bus terminal really is from the core. After

SOUTH AMERICA
ENCHANTMENT

I am dropped off at the cathedral, and take a few pictures, I then go around the marketplace, asking like a beggar for the Internet. Every conceivable thing you could possibly want is here and the mall itself is ultra-modern. In the general vicinity is also the old market place, with a hodge-podge of different things. It's an interesting place to walk around in, and the mall is about six storeys high with kiosks of every description, one giant flea market.

Again, I ask about the Internet and am given a direction to head in. After three or four kilometers, I enter a part of the city that is more dedicated to tourists, along the beach, and I find an Internet. After a good four hours, my quest has been fulfilled. With communication now complete, I start to walk around this interesting part of town. It's the old section of Fortaleza and they restored it exceptionally well. The *turista* boardwalk is about two or three kilometers long, lined with a lot of clothing and bathing suit shops. It is a beautiful sandy beach. Very picturesque and there are open-air restaurants and musical bands.

I notice an old Volkswagen van that has been redone to the hippie standards of the sixties. A policeman happens to be nearby and I take a picture for the fun of it and he indicates that he'll do likewise. So, he takes the picture of me standing beside the Volkswagen van in its colorful appearance. It really indicates throughout this trip, the openness and frankness of the police, and the good nature of them. They have a much better attitude than a lot of police in other parts of the world.

I actually make my way over to a car dealership and boy, Land Rover, watch out! This jeep looks like a really tough machine and if I hadn't been quite so tired, I probably would have stopped to get some more information on this. I then work my way back to this mecca of kiosks and spend a little time looking around. There is really nothing in there that appeals to my eye and so I get a taxi back to the bus terminal.

Once I'm back there, I grab a *suco*, one of the enjoyable fruit juices, and they come in all different shapes, sizes, and flavors. Now at the bus terminal, I collect my mammoth amount of luggage and make my way to the platform where I meet up with a man. His name is Roberto. I can't believe I met more men with my name here than I have in Canada for years. He is seeing his sister off and he works for the Tourist Department. So we have a nice long talk, as he speaks very good English. We actually say a prayer together, all three of us, and he wishes us a very safe journey. And, yes you guessed it; I'm back on the bus.

It is pretty well the same standard bus, just a different serial number. I learned last year that it's very important (especially to somebody like myself that has little or no knowledge of which bus is which, since they're all the same) to remember which number the bus has. Off we go right on schedule. Its 10:30 p.m. and without too much effort, I go to sleep.

I'd like to say goodnight, one and all. Goodnight my beloved little wife. I am hoping that Buttons and Pepper will give you a better night's sleep than I'm going to have. And Wendy, Cole, I hope that you, too, are sleeping in normal positions in a normal manner. Goodnight one and all, God bless.

Robert F. Edwards

February 21, Thursday

Fortaleza, Brazil

Yes, good morning one and all. It is about 6:00 a.m. All I had to do was straighten up my seat and I'm looking out the window. Most people are still sleeping. This seems to be a national pastime when traveling on the bus or at least these long extended jaunts that I'm doing. This trip will be another twenty-six hours before I get to Salvador. The scenery is similar to yesterday, but more farms and larger cities that we're going through.

I'm really getting the feeling of how vast Brazil is, and how diversified it is. It's got to be one of the greenest and warmest countries that I've been in for many years. There are cactuses, so it's fairly arid in this area, but there are also many trees. Cactuses are blooming now, with beautiful red blossoms, and there are fields filled with lilac colored flowers. It must be a good agricultural belt, judging from the large tractors for farming that I have seen.

The day just wears on, from one scenic view to another. We stop to relieve ourselves and take on a little bit of nourishment, and the bus rolls on. The roads are in rough conditions in these areas. Just washboards and a lot of puddles and in one particular case, we didn't lose a wheel, but I'm sure we must have destroyed our shock because what we hit felt like a crater. Just a little surprised, because in the southern parts of Brazil, the roads have been in immaculate condition.

We're making as good a time as possible. We do go through an area of very steep embankments, but once we've completed that, it is a straight way into Salvador. We arrive at the designated time, around six-thirty. Of course, my first quest is to make reservations to Rio de Janeiro for Saturday and I'm very fortunate. There are two buses leaving almost within the hour of each other, one at noon and the other one at one o'clock. However, there is only one space left on either one of them, so

SOUTH AMERICA
ENCHANTMENT

I'm glad that I erred on the side of caution and followed the procedure that I do and that's to get the necessities out of the way before I start taking part in any other activities. With that task out of the way now, I have paid and completed my last leg of trip by land; the next after Rio de Janeiro will be the flight back home.

I've made arrangements to get a taxi to take me down to the old part of the city of Salvador. I'm going to be staying at a hotel suggested by my "Lonely Planet" book. It's called the Hotel Pelourinho and the address is Rua Alfredo de Brito 20. It's right in the heart of the old city, and the Pelourinho (which means whipping post) district is where the site of slave auctions where held. It is a converted old mansion and reputedly the setting for Jorge Amado's novel, *Suor*.

Salvador is in the state of Bahia. It's divided into three distinct areas. The first is *recôncavo*; the next is *sertão*; and the last is *litoral*. The first one is very hot and humid and this area of the Baía de Todos os Santos must be the range of mountains or hills that I've seen. The major cities here are where the wealth of sugar and tobacco centers is. The *sertão* is a dry parched land, with some cattle-raising. Just south of Salvador is the *litoral*, where the beautiful beaches are and tourism is a priority in this area. On one of the islands here, Club Med has bought a large chunk and added its style to this part of the world for people that want everything done for them.

Brazil is Portugal's historical colony and strong ties have remained, including the language that is predominantly spo-

365

Robert F. Edwards

ken here, with dialects of Indian and African blended. When the Portuguese settled here, they had a different attitude from some of the other countries like Britain and France. The Portuguese were not deprived of land in their homeland, so these people weren't being oppressed by religious persecution. They moved to Brazil with dreams of grandeur, great wealth, and opportunities that were not available in the cities where they lived in Portugal.

Settlements were created with full optimism by settlers, priests, and even prostitutes to make life completely acceptable in the region. As the settlers positioned themselves in this part, they found that enslaving the Indians wasn't quite as easy as first anticipated. Unfortunately, the natives that were captured were not as strong for the vigorous work that the Portuguese demanded, and they were afflicted by the European diseases like small pox and tuberculosis and died very quickly. So, the population of the Indian depleted in two ways: one was through death and intolerable working conditions; and the other was to vanish back into the deeper forest and finally into the jungles of the Amazon Basin.

The Jesuits set up missions to convert the Indians, but to also protect them against the slavery that the Portuguese required, in working the sugar canes, which was extremely profitable, and then later the tobacco plantations. With the lack of labor, all eyes turned to Africa, where the Portuguese had already established slave trade areas. They started exporting large numbers of blacks into Salvador, and this proved to be the making of one of the most exciting and multi-ethnic regions of South America.

The Africans proved to be stronger and endured the heavy labor that was required of them. They were not all from one region of Africa either, so there was a multi-tribal connection. They brought their culture, their traditions, and above all, their religious beliefs with them. They stayed very strongly knitted, even though the Portuguese would never let a family of blacks remain in one region. In a family, they would always

366

SOUTH AMERICA
ENCHANTMENT

separate the men, women, and children to protect themselves against black reprisals and uprisings.

Salvador prospered and the wealth of the great land barons controlled both the Parliament and the seat of power, as far reaching as Lisbon in Portugal. Their powerful lobbying was felt, and this was one of the last areas to relinquish slavery, as a viable alternative to paying wages. Salvador also showed great respect and honor to the Roman Catholic Church. The wealthy land barons in the New World gave honor to the Church with altars of gold and silver, which were both plentiful. I suppose, in some ways, given with hopes that their sins will be washed away, or at least painted white as they abused the lives of other humans.

The African history is vibrant. This is really the only place in the New World that the Africans were able to maintain their culture and religion. It was harmonized into a coexistent with the Catholic Church, a remarkable blending of tolerance by the Roman Catholic Church, not only today but also certainly the fifteenth and sixteenth centuries. It showed a strong determination of never leaving their way of life in Africa. Amongst the hardships and the unbearable conditions, these Africans coexisted with the Indian slaves to develop an inter-

Robert F. Edwards

woven culture, along with the Portuguese. The Portuguese intermarried and created a blend of people that exist today of African, Indian, and Portuguese descent. It adds to the flavor of Salvador that you see more African features and culture than you would in the rest of Brazil.

I've not seen a bed, let alone been on one, for a couple of nights, and it's been the third day consecutive without any proper rest. My clothes haven't been changed and I do feel like a true traveler in every respect. I'm tired, as the taxi takes me up a very steep incline where the hotel is situated. As soon as I get there, a woman approached me, probably five to six months pregnant, with another two small children and puts a small band on my wrist. I read this is customary as a welcome, and you're supposed to make three wishes and after two or three days it rots off. If you take it off beforehand, bad luck will come your way.

Anyway, she is trying to sell me jewelry and I'm trying to get this humungous backpack off my back, along with my other belongings, and pay the driver. She's trying to assist me, and in Portuguese, is quite prepared to have one of her children (the oldest can't be more than six years old) lift the smaller pack. With the family accompanying me, ready made and one in the oven, I get to the front desk. The clerk is sort of confused on what I'm trying to ask for, whether a room or maybe the whole floor. However, when he realizes that the three accompanying me are local residents and I'm just looking for a single, we get along very well. She's still quite persistent showing her jewelry and I'm saying *mañana*, so he's wondering if it means that tomorrow I want the room. With total confusion and great exhaustion, I part with my money more than readily for a cheap trinket. I feel it's more of a donation towards the new unborn than a business transaction.

Now, the mother and two children depart and I can get on with the transaction at hand. I'm hoping for a double bed, but he's quite insistent that if I want a double bed, I pay the premium price, even though there's only one body lying in it. With my parsimonious ways, I settle for the small bed, which

SOUTH AMERICA
ENCHANTMENT

is adequate. I also try to bargain for more than one day and that doesn't work either. So, prices are firm and conditions are inflexible. However, I make my way up to the room and am pleased. It's clean, it's got a fan rather than an air-conditioner, and small but more than adequate for all my requirements. I also have (for an extra three *real)* a small safe in the room to put my passport and the small amount of currency that I'm carrying.

Feeling secure and at peace with myself, I am ready to explore this remarkable city. But first, I ask the proprietor if there is hot water and he says "yes". I've got used to these small electrical devices that are attached to showerheads. They produce a minimum amount of hot water, but it takes the chill off coming out of the tap, which is more than adequate for me and in a climate that is in the thirties Celsius. Finally, I can take off these dirty, dirty clothes and shave, shower, brush my teeth, and clean my body. It is wonderful, I'm rejuvenated. With fresh clothes on, I feel like a new person. I even look new, compared to that bedraggled grubby-looking character that waddled through the door under heavy weight. With the new bounce in my sandals, I go downstairs to investigate a C*andomblé* ceremony. I've read that Thursday night, which just so happens to be tonight is the best night to try and see one of these.

When I approached the desk, I found out that they advertised that there's one taking place today, at 7:30 p.m. It's now 7:20 p.m., so I asked if they could make a phone call and see if one more could take part in this ceremony. No problem, instant connection with the powers of tourism, and one more has been added to the list. Its thirty *real,* and I'm not complaining about the price, and luckily I have it at hand, cash. Soon the tour bus shows up and I'm off to the event.

The *Candomblé* is a combination of African traditions, music, dances, language, systems of worship, and enjoyment of life itself. Much of it is still very secretive and it's practiced with the same superstitions and beliefs that these religious cults have passed down from the dawning of their existence.

Robert F. Edwards

The people that participate are the ones that believe more strongly in communicating with the spirits that are beyond. Actually it was prohibited to be practiced as late as 1970, but more and more prominent people (even one politician) professed that they indeed practiced it. In the broadest sense of the term, it's similar to Japan, where you can practice Buddhism and Shintoism as a combination of religions that coexist with each other. Here the *Candomblé* and the Catholic faith coexist with each other. Let there be no mistake, some of these practices are still forbidden, especially the ones that involve blood sacrifices and killing of animals, and those are considered the bad *Candomblé*. It's probably the only place in South America that you could witness anything of this nature.

After being picked up by the bus, my tour guide, her sister and I were taken to a very poor part of Salvador. We entered a room that was plain in structure, with whitewashed walls. There are different ways of getting the women into a trance. The women are the ones that perform the rituals, and work with the music and the beating of the drums to get in a hypnotic trance, and then the spirits enter them and they act accordingly. Also, the men are separated from the women and it's a religious ceremony. I am fortunate that this particular one is more authentic than the ones with the flashy robes in the theaters.

I join the rest of the men on one side, and the women on the other, and tourists are the minority group. We're maybe seven men and eight or nine women. The rest, probably sixty people in this room, are locals. The first part of the ceremony involves leaves from trees. The women beat their heads and whip these leaves all around their bodies. It's to purify the body of evil thoughts and intentions. The tourist guide told us that the women in this ceremony would probably smoke cigars and drink beer to entice the men into a state of trance. Different methods are used to induce a trance, sometimes hallucinating drugs. When I asked the travel agent about it, she curtly said, "Oh, no, no. Not this type of ceremony." In the Amazon Basin, the Indians used very strong narcotic plants to

SOUTH AMERICA
ENCHANTMENT

create a hallucinatory effect to get into their state of trance for communicating with spirits.

The women now have formed a circle and are smoking cigars. There's a fellow beating a drum, and he starts the chant. The women follow, and in a circle, sway to the motion of the chant. It's not quite as exotic as I thought it would be, it's repetitious. At one point, in the beginning of the ceremony, they take a bit of cotton, or sheep's wool, and put some type of powder on it, strike a match to it, and of course, it puffs a smoky odor into the air. I think this is designed for getting into the state of mind.

These women have to go through a considerable amount of preparation and schooling before they take part in the ceremony. The age group seems to be from their fifties right down to the mid-twenties. There is one young lady that has her eyes closed, and I feel that she's deeply in tune with herself, if nothing else. There is also another woman, probably in her fifties, who's small but she has a look about her that would a put a scare in the best of men's souls. All these women continually circle, puff the cigar and sway to the music. Some of them are actually starting to grunt, I guess, part of the ceremony in general. It lasts (and we're all standing, incidentally) for hours. One woman gets down on her knees before the lead chanter and starts to recite something. I'm none the wiser at the end of it; but she gets up, and always holding each other with the right hand, then they hug. After she goes through this ceremony, she then seems to pick people out at random. All the women, one by one, seem to make their own chant and then perform the same ritual. To my surprise, the first one approached me. She was a tall woman, and when I responded, she gave a heavy grunt and then moved on. I was not prepared for it. The one that I was hoping would hug me was the young woman that always had her eyes closed. I felt that if there were going to be any spiritual connection with another entity, she would be the one that I would experience it through.

Robert F. Edwards

Then, she came to me. She's a soft person. As I was watching her, she hugged me gently as she swayed, but she never opened her eyes. It was almost as if she was feeling things rather than seeing them, or maybe seeing them with her inner eye. As she approached me, she reached for my hand and I took hers. Then, with a soft touch, she placed her hand on my shoulder. She leaned back, and I felt she was going to leave, but then she started talking to me, always with her eyes closed. I felt that she wanted to hold me again, so I reached out and again she held me. This continued on for a long time before she left.

Another woman, her features less African than some of the others, had a very beautiful voice and she gave a long repertoire of the chant. When she came to me, she looked deep into my eyes. I couldn't help but feel that she was stripping my mind naked. After the handshake, she held me and again looked straight into my eyes with a piercing effect. When she spoke, I replied that I only knew English, but it didn't seem to have any effect on her, whatsoever. She just kept on talking and then she made a motion of strength, like I was strong. I don't know if the forward arm movement always means (in this part of the world) that you're sexually strong. I don't know whether that's quite the case in my situation or what that interpretation meant.

The small woman that first started the ceremony came over and spoke to me. We did the same ritual, and she had that same piercing look. It was a very commanding ceremony and from this first experience, I know if I had the opportunity, I would want to investigate more of these people's beliefs. After this ceremony, I was interested in the inner teachings of this faith or cult, which had an influence on my being. When I left, I asked the guide about the experience. She told me that what the women were saying was not from them, but from the spirits communicating. So, I got a lot of instructions, but they fell on deaf ears.

On the way back, a young girl in our group said that she was told something to do with flying. Because her Portuguese wasn't that good she didn't understand what was said but she was quite concerned because she was going to have to fly somewhere within the next week or so. So, I quickly said she probably just told you that you don't have to worry about flying. And she said, "I'm really glad you put it in that concept. You make me feel better." I guess I haven't lost my pure optimism in life, in the present or in the hereafter; and in the spiritual world, always looking at the positive side of the message.

Another guide took me back to the general area of my hotel, around 11:00 p.m. I haven't had dinner yet. So, I go to a restaurant and I've been told that one of the dishes that are popular here is ginger chicken. I try to order it and somehow, I ended up with a filet mignon steak. The fellow did admit that it was his mistake, so they adjust the bill accordingly, but I still don't get the meal that I was looking for. The food in Salvador is a blend of Indian, African, and Portuguese food and its dishes are unique to this area of Brazil. A good meal, but not the one that I had hoped for, so I don't eat very much of the meat, just a bit of rice, and had a beer.

On my way back, there is some music still being played in the street. This was one of the things that really motivated me to want to see Salvador. They have the longest carnival period, which lasts for at least seven days. They bring in some of the greatest bands of Brazil to participate, and the streets are congested with people dancing. I had already seen some of the bands on television in Manaus. The music is everywhere and after a while you find yourself listening just for the sheer enjoyment of it. I sat, and had a few more beers. People are trying to talk to me and I really wish I could speak a fragment of Portuguese, just to communicate with these beautiful people. They are friendly and open and throughout my adventure, each moment has been its own reward. The openness and lifestyle of Salvadorians had caught this traveler's taste buds, and I am savoring and relishing these moments.

Robert F. Edwards

With that, I return to my hotel. I would like to say goodnight, my beautiful wife and I'm much closer to you today than I have been in the past weeks. Goodnight, Wendy and Cole. Goodnight, one and all, and I'd like to conclude what a remarkable day this has been.

SOUTH AMERICA
ENCHANTMENT

February 22, Friday

Salvador, Brazil

Good morning, Salvador and friends, Romans, countrymen, and nations of the world. It's a beautiful day and I'm in a beautiful part of the world. Obviously, by this morning's greetings, I can say with all sincerity, I have a good attitude. I go down for breakfast and can't help but be impressed by the spread that's laid out before me, with a selection of fruits, cold cuts, buns, an assortment of juices, a variety of cheeses, and many other delightful tidbits that fill the inner sanctum of man to cope with the challenges of the day that lies ahead.

But it's also the breath-taking view that captures both my imagination and appetite for this city that I have a strong affiliation with. As I gaze through the window, I view some of the remarkable cathedrals in this city that is lying at my feet. The cathedrals are of the sixteenth and seventeenth century and have weathered remarkably well in this humid climate. In

general, they are of stone masonry, which always seems to be in need of repair. These ones are no exception, and also, there is black soot on some of the cathedral peaks. My mind's eye captures some of the bushes and trees that are growing on the steeple tops of these places of worship. My mind reflects that man builds monasteries and temples, only for God to reclaim it in his natural form of trees and vegetation. These cathedrals built by a patronage of the strong religion are now being

375

claimed by the true religion of God, Nature, as these trees and bushes have taken root over man's determination to succeed.

As I gaze upon this harbor, it has a multitude of views. One is the practical; the end that trade and commerce survives on. The large tankers sit anchored at different positions, waiting their turn with cargo laden for points unknown. Further off in the bay is where the rich and famous dock their sailboats and powerboats that make their way to the islands.

To many of the Bahians, they love this large island of Itaparica in the Baiá de Todos os Santos, and the waters are very calm there compared to the open sea. It is a place where you can find tranquility and peace that you wouldn't experience in the heart of two-and-a-half million Salvadorians. In the bay, there is more than one little island, but this is the largest and some of the best beaches are owned by Club Med. The ferries go back and forth and unfortunately, I won't have the time to visit this sanctuary of beautiful beaches and calm waters. However, as I watch sailboats heading towards the island, a tough decision has to be made, whether I visit this or try to absorb as much of the cultural base of this city as I possibly can in the very short period I've allotted. With some moments of consideration, I am chosen the culture for an understanding of the people that I respect and enjoy.

While I finish my breakfast, I take a moment to reflect on last night. Of all the faces and people I've met, I ponder over some of the moments; like the young lady that had her eyes closed in a trance and what the spirit within her had felt towards me. Also, when I was having a beer, a young lady smiled and tried to talk to me. As our smiles and gestures of communication and the salute of the glass of beer became more fragrant, she reached over and touched my white hair with all the gentleness that my grandson first experienced and was fascinated with as a baby. The gentle touch, the curiousness, and the warm smile on a beautiful face are worth a mention in my memory and thoughts. The older woman at the *Candomblé* was a local and I imagine a very frequent participant, as she was welcomed as an old friend. Her warmth, her smile and her remarkably good shape only added to my commitment that old age is just a state of mind.

It has been a remarkable trip and the only reason I wanted to go to Salvador was because of the carnival. How grateful I am today, as I look at the oasis that lies before me. I'm so blessed by being here and I hope with all sincerity that this will not be the only time that my eyes feast upon this city. Even with the disappointment of last night's meal (that I didn't get the chicken that I was hoping for), the food and seasoning blends of African and Brazilian cuisine are the ingredients that make this a culinary mecca. I enjoy different foods of the world and I've always been more adventurous than most, but even the timid of heart and weak of stomach should venture out in this area and take part. The food has distinct flavors. They use coconut cream, a lot of ginger, and my favorite hot peppers, and coriander. Needless to say, with the sea at hand, fish is both abundant and numerous in varieties. Chicken dishes are plentiful in a number of recipes.

Because the region is populated with ranches in the northern parts of this state, meat is plentiful also. It doesn't meet the flavor that I've experienced in Argentina, but it's worth a meat-lover's consideration. One of the most terrific flavors, and it's used in dishes extensively here, is *dendē*. It's an African palm oil and it has a very strong, pleasant smell to it, and is used extensively in cooking. If I wasn't trying to carry the world on my back, I would probably take some of this oil back with me, but the bag is getting heavier everyday.

It's about 9:00 a.m. before I venture out to do some errands. I'm anxious to get an e-mail to my beloved, and see how things are progressing at her end and with life in general in Canada. Also, I do have to get some more money. I ask for the directions of where the Bank of Brazil is and I'm getting better with either listening or comprehending or both. I have little or no problem getting to the bank. Ironically, I am quite proficient in getting money now that this will probably be the last time that I need to take a withdrawal out of my cash reserves.

Robert F. Edwards

At the Internet, I received two e-mails from my wife and one from the chap I traveled with in Manaus, forwarding on a photograph of us posing together outside the theater. My friendships throughout the world are getting more extensive and broadening and I welcome all these newfound friends. I venture out onto the main *piazza* and it's a photographer or painter's paradise. The activities in this square are very numerous, with even more peddlers wishing to put a band on my wrist. The one I received earlier is still on, due to my superstitious nature. I don't want to have any bad luck so close to the end of this remarkable journey. Two women are in the traditional dress, which has huge hoops underneath, and bandannas wrapped around their heads, normally white, but also in multi-colors.

There is a story that I am reminded of, as told to me in my primary grades by a Roman Catholic priest, visiting from East India. He told us young children that East Indians were very proud people and that when God first created man, He didn't bake him long enough and when He took them out, the man was white. So God thought He better have another attempt at His baking skills and this time He left him in considerably

378

SOUTH AMERICA
ENCHANTMENT

longer. When God took him out he was overdone and he was black or the Negro. And God felt lucky, I guess, three times, so He put a third man in the oven and left him about middle of the road, took him out, and of course he was done just perfectly. That's the Indian people, from West Indies and India.

Today, when I gaze upon the interbreeding of the Salvadorians, the bone structure and color composition, I couldn't help but think of that story. They're beautiful-looking people, with many fine characteristics of their Portuguese heritage. They have some of the bone structures of the Indian heritage, along with some of the distinctive features of the African. Like the good Father said, three times lucky, and these people are a lucky race of people. They seem to be just right, both their features and their complexions are good, but it's their attitude that has that perfect blend of contentment; their outward smile, their openness; and their sincere love of life is very contagious.

As I'm in the *piazza* watching, even the peddlers they're po-lite and they're not rude or pushy, but very hopeful, of course. I visit some of the different churches and the frescoes and statues vary, depending on the funds involved. The one that's said to be spectacular, with a notorious amount of gold leaf décor in it, the *Igreja Sao Francisco*, I'll visit that tomorrow.

I can't believe how a day moves on so very quickly, and the heat. In this humid climate, productivity is low. I find, even with myself, just by walking at my normal speed, I look like I've just come out of a sauna with my clothes on. I do see other people with perspiration, and they're local residents. The humidity has a lot to do with the

Robert F. Edwards

lack of productivity, and even the deterioration of the buildings. I see people painting their homes, but probably after a couple of seasons, with the amount of rain and elements continually working against man's proposals God's disposal show that He has a strong upper hand.

As I visited some of the churches, I felt the influence of the African and Indian population on the Roman Catholic religion. Even the statues have a harshness, artistic but not refined. By the expressions, I feel some of the agony depicted, in the saints' statues as well as the frescoes on the ceilings. I read about one of the great artists of the time, "*Manoel Inácio da Costa*", and the painting he had done of *Sao Pedro da Alcantara*. Both the artist and saint suffered from tuberculosis, and the painting give the illusion that, *Sao Pedro* pales or look very ill as you pass the ashen side of the portrait. Tuberculosis was a real plague of the times in the sixteenth to seventeenth century. Even in the nineteenth century, tuberculosis throughout the world was a very serious illness. So, nations that had no immunities, like the Indians of Brazil, must have just felt that the plague of death had arrived with no mercy and a continual vengeance.

As I stroll around the *piazzas* in this old area, it's intoxicating. They have huge animated animals and mannequins in the squares. At first glance, it looks like the carnival's never going. But no, this is just the way they decorate in this region of Salvador. It's probably done both for personal gratification as well as for the motivation of tourism.

I've enjoyed today and thoroughly enjoyed the city with the people and of course the view of the ocean. If I was more motivated to spending time on the beach, this is one of the beaches I would target as a place of commitment to R & R.

Once again, goodnight, my beautiful wife, and I hope your days are having some fulfillment and I'm looking forward to sharing the ones that I've had just like today. Goodnight, Wendy and Cole. Goodnight, one and all.

SOUTH AMERICA
ENCHANTMENT

February 23, Saturday

Salvador, Brazil

Well, as they say in the world of travelers, "The show must move on," and with getting up and doing all the necessary things that are required to start the day off, especially when I'm going to be taking the bus, I have an extra long shower and thoroughly enjoy the warm water that's coming out. I pack all my gear and I'm both physically and mentally ready to leave this remarkable part of Brazil at high noon and head on to, yes, Rio de Janeiro, the city that legends and times are made of and people have a lifestyle that the world envies most of the year.

I head outside, and return to one of the areas where I bought a post card yesterday, a large cross in the square that overlooks the inlets. So, today, Mr. Photographer is going to take pictures of the beautiful view of the harbor. The city has the ever-present little pigeons and I don't know whether they make a bigger mess or clean up a mess, but when people throw garbage or debris, these hungry little feathers consume whatever happens to be in the general vicinity. They follow the saying that birds of a feather flock  together; when one happens to find something, a group of others quickly join the find.

I go to the church that is well known in Salvador, the *Igreja Sao Francisco.* During the successful times of the tobacco and sugar plantation owners, they made huge contributions to exorcise their evil deeds with the slaves and their money-grabbing attitudes. This Roman Catholic Church is covered

Robert F. Edwards

with gold leaf. I have gone into the monastery part as well. Some of the frescoes are hand-painted on blue tiles, lined around the inner courtyard of the cloister. These religious orders, whether it's Franciscan, Dominican or Jesuit, did not appear to be poverty-stricken. The Jesuits were of such a powerful force that they were even expelled from South America by the kings of Portugal and Spain, due to their becoming more powerful than the governments. These religious men were worldly, and it's recorded that they ignored the vow of poverty and they bent the rules of chastity as well. Maybe obedience just automatically failed when it came to the government.

This particular cloister is a prime example of beauty, peace and tranquility. These tiles were brought from Portugal for this monastery. When you see this inner sanctuary, it reflects the decadence of the period and the city. The cathedral is a wonder all of its own. I personally am not spiritually motivated, feeling like I'm in Fort Knox that's spread its' gold everywhere.

The African-Indian culture is reflected in their sculptures. These were not designs of the Portuguese. The architects might have been European but the craftsmen were able to put their own touch of attitudes and beliefs on the subject matter. A lot of the cherubs and small statues that enshrine the pillars at one time had their sex organs exposed with desires. A period of conservatism stood tall and they were covered with plaster; not the cherubs, just the sexual organs. The church itself is a monument to its period and the attitude of the barons, and the richness that these people had, both in Brazil, as well as the influence they had in Portugal itself.

Back out on the streets now, and there are people who are forever hoping that they'll find the *turista* that wants to part with their money and they want to give them something as a remembrance, if nothing else. One fellow approaches me about all the things that he has available and I tell him, "No, I'm not interested." He said, "Ah, English! You like the samba." I said, "Yeah, I like the samba." All of a sudden, he becomes not only an expert in samba, but probably has as good a selection of the top ten as any music shop in the city itself. However, I settle for a coconut, which is always refreshing.

The bewitching hour is fast approaching, time to go down to the bus station. I return to the hotel, thank the fellow at the front desk for all the support he has given me, and order a taxi. The taxi driver takes me to the bus terminal and I'm getting rather proficient in this. I don't want to sound overconfident but, I knew exactly what I wanted and where I should go, and I was the first one there, waiting for the bus. Now, I am looking forward to another twenty-eight hours of transportation in progress.

It's a very diversified city. The part where I spent most of my time and salivated on was the old original city, but there are many parts with high rises and ultra-modern buildings, and even many churches have a modern appearance to them compared to the cathedrals of the by-gone era. The traffic always amazes me in these cities. The speed that even the buses travel, it seems they only know how to adjust the gas pedal to the floor and anything less than that, either the bus is broken or the vehicle hasn't started yet.

But as we leave the city, it also reflects that many residents have a leaner lifestyle, judging by the dwellings that are glued like little blocks of red bricks to the hillside. I settle back into my seat knowing that I have many hours of reflection ahead of me. As we travel out of the city and into the countryside, I recall earlier days in my trip, passing through deserts and areas that have extremely harsh climate conditions most of the year. This seems to be where God must have dropped paradise or at least a big chunk of it fell off as He was passing through. Easy living, that's the word. You can live off the land because the land is full of life and fulfillment.

The bus just keeps rumbling on the hours move and I really am looking forward to going to Rio. It will be my final fulfillment. One, it's a city I've been in before, which is always rewarding. For a traveler that has logged as many new kilometers on this journey, to go back to some place that at least I am familiar with, there's an element of security in remembering what exists, rather than the unexpected.

In the seat beside me is a young man, a very shy person. Even the bus is quiet compared to some of the buses I've been on even in this voyage. It seems that the Amazon Basin of

SOUTH AMERICA
ENCHANTMENT

chirping animals, people and openness has closed its doors and we're now entering the formal southern parts of Brazil where etiquette, reserve, and caution are the ingredients, rather than a smile of openness and curiosity.

This bus line is very comfortable and provides leg room. I wish only that the airlines would remember what it was like, to be able to move your legs and put the seat back more than two degrees. These seats almost lay out and you have a little platform to put your feet on, plus they provide you with a pillow, a blanket and unlimited air-conditioning. It's very inducive to long periods of resting and even as the daylight hours still prevail, this bus has a silence in which only the T.V. monitors are providing any sound. And even with those, we have headsets. So, if you're not looking at T.V. with the headset on, you have only the continual rumbling of the road, beneath the wheels that are continually logging off kilometer after kilometer, towards Rio, my destination.

This concludes today and tonight. I miss you, my little honey bun. I can't help but feel excited that this is my last bus ride before I head home. Goodnight, my beautiful little honey bun, and I'll be looking for an e-mail when I arrive in Rio. Goodnight, Wendy and Cole, and I hope all is well. Goodnight, one and all.

Robert F. Edwards

February 24, Sunday

Enroute to Rio De Janeiro, Brazil

No, I didn't get up and do my toiletries. I just rolled over to another position on the chair. I'm in a reclining position and try to sit through the hours that lie ahead. The time is about 6:00 a.m. and the scenery has now replaced the darkness that prevailed through the long night.

It's somewhat baffling. With buses, even though you travel with the same bus line with the same country and you start to get the same basic concept of what their M.O. is, that there's always something peculiar. One of the great horrors that I had last year was when the bus drove off leaving us at the bus terminal and my total belongings (except my passport and me) left also.

Well, today, I realized that when they do drop you off at one of these feeding locations the general time is about fifteen minutes to give you a break from being on the bus, as well as to allow some people obviously use the toilet facilities and get a hot meal. The bus drives away to get refueled. Actually, they're quite proficient at it. They clean the floors and restock the little canteen of coffee and water at the back. There's a system going and this bus line is no exception to the rule.

When I left Bahia with this bus line, and we did stop at a terminal because of the weather conditions, most of the eating facilities were the open-air type of operations. Even though they have a security system and you don't get a free lunch, they were serviceable but not exceptionally clean or state-of-the-art. As we're getting closer to Rio de Janeiro, not only have the roads improved, but these bus cantinas have taken on a more luxurious décor, from plastic tables to table cloths. The buffet lunches are very numerous in variety and fresh. I noticed, now that I have a little more time to observe, that buses congregate at given periods of time and rightfully so.

SOUTH AMERICA
ENCHANTMENT

This allows the food to be fresh and palatable to the people that are stopping over for a quick meal. To emphasize, it doesn't matter what part of the world you're in, population density and the affluent society demands higher-grade standards. Whether you're in a developed country or developing country, the population is what gives you the highest quality of standards. Today has been the highest quality of standards I've experienced on this trip as I get closer and closer to Rio de Janeiro.

The morning passes on, breakfast is served at 6:00, and at 2:00 p.m., we pull into the next stop for lunch, and the day wears on. As we're getting closer to Rio de Janeiro, about two hundred kilometers from the city itself, you can see the affluence and the money that's in some of the surrounding districts. Some of the homes demand the same admiration, awe, and respect as anywhere else in the world. These communities are collective and when people have things, they want to keep them, so these have a very high grade of security systems. These elaborate homes are probably well into the millions of U.S. dollars.

Robert F. Edwards

The twenty-eight hours finally come to a close; I've arrived at the bus terminal. I am now in Rio. I have completed the last bus program of this remarkable journey that I've experienced. I take a taxi into Copacabana and the hotel that I stayed at last year. When I mentioned people driving fast in the city, Rio is not lagging behind. The taxi driver averaged about eighty kilometers on the expressways, weaving in and out of traffic as if he was in one of the great racing opportunities. The only thing that reminded me that it still was a taxi was that the meter kept ticking as the kilometers kept moving.

At the hotel, I wasn't able to get any kind of discount, and the only room that was available was right across from the elevator. I've traveled most of my life and I can assure anybody that the worst rooms in any hotel are either across from an elevator or beside one. Your adjacent room is going up and down on floors consistently throughout the night. There seem to be a general indifference this time and this hotel was absolutely immobile to a better rate no matter how long I stayed, so I was neither impressed with the room or the people. Probably the only little thing was that the location was still adequate.

After disposing of my luggage in the room and putting my documents in the safety deposit box, I started to relish the feeling of being back in Rio de Janeiro. It's a world-class city; whether you arrive like I do as a backpacker or as a jet setter, it's totally irrelevant. This city has an air about it that you can only appreciate once you've been here and you returned.

The weather is not as humid as Salvador or the Amazon Basin. However, a gentle breeze is blowing off the inlet tonight and déjà vu is in my midst. It's Sunday night, and people put up their little kiosks along the major boulevard at Copacabana. They sell everything that you can possibly think of, from a coconut for refreshment purposes to homemade jewelry to exotic pieces of pottery, and it goes on and on. There are literally thousands of these little kiosks that go a number of kilometers around the curvature of Copacabana.

SOUTH AMERICA
ENCHANTMENT

As I'm walking along, I thought that I would like to do some clubs tonight, in Lapa or Centro, as mentioned in my guide and bible of traveling, "The Lonely Planet". On Friday, Saturday, and Sunday, this area has some remarkable samba, and it's the theater area as well. With that in mind, even though it's going to be an expensive cab fare-wise (about fifteen *real*), I check it out. I meet a nice cab driver and I explain what I want to do and though his language is Brazilian and mine is English (and he's even missing one hand so obviously we have a one-handed conversation) he knows what I want to do.

Off we go. I've never seen a stump shift a gearbox as fast as this man. He's probably in his late forties and goes through traffic like Sterling Moss. Racecar professionals could get their basic training traveling through the streets of Brazil. We arrive in the central area, and it's exactly what it says, the office and business complexes.

He's going to drop me off at the theater area that I've chosen, and fortunately doesn't just abandon me while I try to find the restaurant that I have chosen, with no success. I do see some restaurants, so I thought that I would confident in saying "*Adiós*, amigo!" He drives off, but no, this is not the area of town that I'm glad that I ventured to stay in. Probably a beehive of activity during the daytime, but very sparsely populated and even when it is, the people are not very savory in the area.

I go to a few restaurants and either I am too early or whatever, it's now 8:00 p.m. and restaurants in this one particular area are very sparsely occupied by clients. As I walk up and down the general area and vicinity of the area I mentioned, I just am totally disenchanted and disappointed, not that I wanted to dance the samba in the wee hours of the morning. So, as much as I'm totally in control with the idea of being back in Rio, this is not the area that is of my preference. So, with another cab fare, I return to my haunt of Copacabana, thirty *real* less in my pocket. Much as this town is something that I was looking forward to, it may not be the most expensive place in Brazil, but it sure ranks among the top. I'm not saying that the taxi fares are unreasonable, but the distances are exceptionally long.

So, back in Copacabana and on The Strip I decide to have something to eat in a nice restaurant. I haven't eaten a proper meal for a couple of days now, so I deserve a treat. There's a different atmosphere in Rio de Janeiro and Copacabana. There's obviously a much more *turista* or tourist mood. However, people are friendly and where I happen to be sitting, before very long, it's crowded and I've either been joined by four or five other people. To my pleasant surprise, one of the women speaks relatively fluent English. So, I ask her about the food here and she says, "Well, you know, it's a better drinking hole than it is a food place." I said, "Well, I really like a good meal and I like to enjoy a variety of Brazilian food." She said, "My friends are heading over to eat after we finish having a beer or two." So, I'm enjoying a beer with my new-found acquaintances.

Soon we leave for the restaurant. I've been to this kind of restaurant before and I think it's a really unique idea. They weigh the food and it's a smorgasbord concept but you can choose whatever you want, they weigh it and you pay for the weight. The spread is exactly what these people had bragged about, the variety was unlimited, and I enjoyed three different types of fish dishes, along with a multitude of other foods that would be almost a book in itself on cuisine. There are salads, five or six different types of relishes, to say nothing, of course, of the famous beans, three or more different types of those, and deserts too numerous to mention. It's funny, at home, my sweet teeth number a full set, but here I've had very few desserts and pastries; but the few that I've had are absolutely delicious.

The evening is most enjoyable and these people tell me that they're going to a local bar that they favor and if I want to come, I'm more than welcome to join them. Mr. Fit-in joins the merry little group and is welcomed as somebody that had been away for a while but has returned to this quaint little bar. There is a very small strip of chairs on one side and a bar on the other. It's all local people; I'm the only foreigner that is accounted for here. As one beer follows another and new people coming and going, I'm introduced as some kind of celebrity, it's just a nice homey atmosphere. The only Achilles' heel in this particular evening is that I have to rely on this one lady to continually translate, as questions are being asked and answers are being given on both sides, mine and the other people.

However, an enjoyable evening and they're telling me that if I wish to join them, depending on the weather, they're probably going to either the beach or the botanical gardens tomorrow and we'll continue seeing what the weather is. So I tell them where I'm staying. And when I tell them which hotel I'm staying at, they politely asked me how much I'm paying. I tell them and they said, "Well, you know, you can get a much better hotel down the street. It's going to cost you a little bit more, but it's more central and it's only a block away from the beach. So, I'm considering it, and after saying goodnight to one and all, I return to this dark pit of inequity.

As I enter the room, it's remarkable that I even have enough space. This isn't the crowning glory of my expedition. The room is small, with no windows. It is not the worst place I've stayed on this journey, but it isn't the treat that I was looking forward to when I was enduring some of the trials and tribulations of my adventure. I make up my mind to follow these people's advice and check out the other hotel tomorrow.

So, with that, I would like to say goodnight to my little beautiful wife and I miss you immensely, little honey bun; and this is still one place that I think that you and Wendy and even Cole Man would probably enjoy. It's the crowning glory of this expedition and adventure so with that, goodnight my beautiful wife. Goodnight, my beautiful daughter and my little grandson. Goodnight to one and all of you and goodnight Rio.

Robert F. Edwards

February 25, Monday

Rio de Janeiro, Brazil

Good morning, Rio de Janeiro! As my toiletries are out of the way and I'm getting a late start on the day by sleeping in, I decide that I'm going to take advantage of my new information and go down and check this hotel out. If mine has a star, it must have fallen from the sky compared to this one. No, it's not a five-star hotel but it's just an immensely different one. When I asked for a double bed in the first hotel, they were going to charge me one hundred and eighty *real*. And I said, "No, no. I can probably sleep on the floor to settle that for half price."

This second hotel has the stunning price of one hundred ninety-five *real*. And I said, "Well, if I spend three days or whatever here, or two, can you give me a better rate?" The guy looks at me and says, "Yeah, how about one fifty?" I said, "Yeah, one fifty sounds pretty good. Can I take a look at the double bed?" He says, "Yeah, double bed." Well, I go in and, wow! Not only do I have a double bed, a large room, but a beautiful marble bathroom with a huge shower that you dance in. The place didn't have a fridge, but with one location over another, I'm really happy. The staff here is just great. The more I meet them, the more congenial they are, and a much better situation than I was involved in before.

I do feel that I'm going to need a little more financial clout from the bank, so head off to find one. The banking system is totally antiquated, out of sorts with international markets. My Visa is still the number one credit card in the world, but there is only one bank, the Bank of Brazil, that takes it; and there's only one machine in the bank that has an international capability. Talk about being behind in times, they're not even in the curve. Wouldn't you know it; the one machine that has the international capabilities is broken.

SOUTH AMERICA
ENCHANTMENT

So, they tell me that I have to go to another one that's about four or five blocks up the road, which is not a big thing. I get there and no, they don't even have one, but they have Western Union upstairs. Sometimes traveling is not always a piece of cake. So, with an hour of waiting, this woman starts to process my request, then has to phone to get approval and then she fills out another form along with my passport and my credit card and says to me, "Okay, now you can stand over in the line-up at the counter." So, once I stand in the line-up, which again is about another good half an hour, I manage to get three hundred *real*. I think I could have gone to a printing press and probably done the same thing faster.

The day has now eaten away to lunchtime and I meet up with my new friends. It's a beautiful day, just a little overcast, but they are not really motivated to go to the beach. We go here and there, and the day withers itself away, looking at different things. They're a lot of fun to be around and there's a lot of laughing. I'm not out to achieve much of anything but to try and relax and prepare myself for the long flight that's coming up in a few days, plus all the things that I will have to address once I get back home.

This is really R&R time and I don't have any heavy agendas because I have been to Rio before, and have seen Sugar Loaf Mountain and all the *turista* things. So, I can take part more in typical local flavor. We go into little coffee shops and I now know that I didn't go to the right places the last time. The coffee in Brazil is absolutely out of this world. No wonder it is famous worldwide, when it comes to coffee. They love it strong, and sweet, and one of the things that they're quite notable about is that they use hot milk also.

It's almost a heavy debate on which restaurant we're going to and which one out of the four of them is going to show me what their choice is. We go to another one very similar in style. This seems to be the Brazilian way of doing things. I've also noticed the big meal here seems to be the lunch. There doesn't seem to be any logic to when they eat the evening meal. It's almost the same as their lifestyle, they just seem to do it on an impulse rather than preordained.

For whatever reason, I'm feeling extremely tired. I haven't really slept in a bed for some time other than last night on this narrow strip, but I also had to take a malaria pill again .I do find that air-conditioning is something that does congest me. When I'm on the bus with air-conditioning, I get clogged up. Along with this full medical report, my left knee has its good days and bad days ever since I've done the Inca trail. Maybe it's just old age setting in, but sometimes it has kept me awake at night as well. So, the rest of them are going dis-coing tonight, but this old man is heading home.

With that, I'd like to say goodnight, little honey bun and the days are closing off quickly.

Goodnight, Wendy and Cole. Goodnight one and all. I hope your days have been good ones.

SOUTH AMERICA ENCHANTMENT

February 26, Tuesday

Rio de Janeiro, Brazil

Oh, what a difference a day makes. I slept really well last night in this large playground of a double bed. I do miss the news and this television has CNN and English news so I was able to catch up on the world that spins without my knowledge.

I go down for a very nice breakfast. Once again, the staff here are great. One of the big things on my list to do today is to confirm my flight so that I'm not going to have any hitches tomorrow. The young lady at the front desk says she'll phone and look after all the questions and answers for me. Also, I go to the Internet and this particular one is a bit more expensive but I have my own card to log in and things are working out well. I'm getting my share of e-mails from my little honey bun. To say the least, I am getting anxious to get back and I miss my little true love very much.

Robert F. Edwards

This afternoon I'm going to be a beach bum. Off to the beach I go and wouldn't you know it, the same merry group shows up and they introduce me to the operation of the umbrellas and chairs. I sit there like a big vegetable watching micro-mini bikinis show their cheeky behavior and enjoying a cold beer and the endless soliciting of everything from sun-tan lotion to transistor *radiós* and sunglasses, clothing, pop, water, etc. with this continual stream of entrepreneurs walking the sun-filled beaches selling shrimp on a stick, fried cheese, ice-cream, who needs to travel when you've got a walking mall going in front of you?

I spend the day just observing. There are two young ladies, very attractive and probably in their early twenties whom a fellow with a tattoo book approaches. These young ladies both get one, but these are done with pencil, and last for a day or two, they aren't the ones that you grow old with. There's just a lot of activity going on. When I went up to get a beer, a guy was cooking fish. They were probably ten inches long, and he was frying them in a pan, with onions and other garnishes. I really should have gone over and ordered one of this fish. It is just a really relaxing afternoon. I spent the better part of the afternoon just chilling out, as the Brits say. I'm just sun-baked, relaxed, totally at peace with myself.

I returned to the local watering hole and everybody seems glad to see me. There is a different group, though, and the atmosphere was not the same as the happy-go-lucky ones of the first night when I was doing a bit of dancing. This didn't feel the same mood, so I went back to the hotel.

I have to say goodnight, little honey bun. Goodnight, Wendy and Cole, goodnight, one and all. I'm going to tell you that maybe the early bird does get the worm, but I'm in bed pretty darn early. It's seven p.m. I watch a bit of television. Yeah it is the high life in the big town of Rio. And with that, just have an early night and mentally get geared up for the big event tomorrow, heading on home.

SOUTH AMERICA
ENCHANTMENT

February 27, Wednesday

Rio de Janeiro, Brazil

I got up and checked CNN, and then flicked through the ninety-nine channels to see what the rest of Brazil was doing. I checked with the girl at the front desk, and my flight is on schedule, and there are no hitches on the horizon.

By the time I finished my e-mails and breakfast, it's time to check out. I asked if I could leave the luggage there and they said, "Of course, no problem whatsoever." So, a day in the life of Bob Edwards in Rio de Janeiro, and off I go up and down the streets, even checking out apartments that you could rent by the day, week or month. I am doing a real reconnaissance. It's also just one of those days savoring the last moments of this remarkable city.

It is quite hot, I'm perspiring profusely and I'm sure there isn't one pore in my body that is clogged anymore after the months of perspiration coming out of it. I've found that beer seems to be the best thirst quencher and the Brazilians do make a good beer. So, I have two glasses of beer watching the people on the beach.

Amongst those enjoying the sun, is also the hidden part that the average tourist doesn't notice. I've seen a few beggars and the beach urchins, (the beach pirate children, as they call them) that scurry across the beaches and when you're not looking, they are taking the things that were yours which soon become theirs. These are the homeless children of Brazil. I watch a young mother pull out her breast and feed her child, just a few feet away from me sitting in the shade. Life is everywhere around you. I'm watching a woman walk three dogs; I've read that dog walking is popular in the Copacabana area.

I just try to fill the empty hours ahead. I find with myself, when I'm waiting for something, that time becomes quite tedious. And today, even though the flight doesn't leave until 10:00 p.m., these hours between 12:00 noon and 5:00 p.m. are dragging on me. I have no incentive to get involved in anything other than mentally getting ready for the long flight back to Canada. It is going to be Rio de Janeiro to Miami then Miami to Los Angeles and Los Angeles to Vancouver. So, if nothing else, I'll have my share of airports in the hours ahead.

It's five o'clock, so I've decided "Why not sit it out at the airport?" I go back to the hotel and the new shift of the staff is on, equally as accommodating. When I say that I'm going to take my luggage, the attendant asks me, "What time is your flight?" I said, "At ten." She said, "Well, you're not going now." I said, "Yeah, I might as well." She said, "We do have a driver that's reliable that will take you to the airport for fifty *real*." A little more than what I intended to pay. It's probably about six to seven *real* more and with traffic, it could easily be the same. So, with that, Bob Edwards and his mighty packs are on their way to Rio de Janeiro Airport.

We drive through Copacabana, and then Centro, and other parts as the airport is on the other side of town. So this is not an unreasonable price to pay. I see cruise ships and think that maybe my beloved little wife and I should take a cruise.

398

SOUTH AMERICA
ENCHANTMENT

We haven't been on a cruise ship for a long time and it was something that she enjoyed. I really miss her very much and I'm more than anxious to get home and be with my true love.

On the way out of town, I see some of the famous ghettos, or *favelas*. These are houses that are shoveled up against the mountain. As the story goes, people were allowed to live there for nothing and the state doesn't interfere too much. Now, it's a haven for drug lords and unsavory people, as well as the poor. There is a lot of drug abuse and cocaine in Rio.

However, it's also an area that is very picturesque. A lot of artists have painted this particular sector because it's a very unique part. The backdrop is a very rich neighborhood and the beautiful beach is so near the central part of Rio de Janeiro; it's like having a sore thumb on a much manicured hand.

We continue on our merry way and I'm glad that I did pay the difference. Traffic is very congested and I would have paid more by the meter, watching it tick and the kilometers not going anywhere. We get to the airport and I'm early. Believe it or not, yes, I'm there before United opens up. I wait my turn and the gate finally opens. I explained to the attendant that I'm going to be on the plane for a great length of time and could I possibly have a window seat; and if possible, be situated near a door so I can have a little bit of leg room. He asked me if I'm associated with Air Canada, as he would have tried to give me an upgrade. That's what I found all along down here, that people do things out of kindness. Even when it comes to my walking stick that I've carted throughout South America from the Inca trails, I've taped it with the famous Canadian duct tape to my backpack. He's concerned that it might get damaged and packs it up more securely. On second thought, it might be the other way around, protecting the plane.

Now, I make my way through Immigration. My papers are in order; I have nothing to hide, and so no real hassle going through the Security. I have to admit I was dreading this, as I thought, "Oh my God, with the amount of stuff that I'm carry-

399

ing and the entire luggage probably they'd want to open up something." It wasn't what they were going to see that bothered me, it was being able to pack the bag again so I could be on my merry way. But no, that's fine, keep on moving.

I'm now in the duty-free area and I've got the better part of four hours to get rid of before the first leg of my flight. I've been in my share of airports of the world and Rio de Janeiro's airport doesn't do the city justice. It's not one of the state-of-the-art airports and the area for international flights is quite spartan and the facilities for duty-free shops are adequate but no bargains. I was going to buy a few things which I thought might be unique, but by the time you pay their inflated prices, you might as well go just to an ordinary place, pay the duty and you're dollars and cents better off. All these prices are in U.S. dollars.

But there is one very unique thing and that is they have a free Internet in this one duty-free shop. I send my beloved another e-mail and she has also sent me one, so I'm very happy about that. I do a little wandering around and seem to have a ravishing appetite. There is only one restaurant available and it's really a snack bar.

I go back upstairs and probably time that I should get exchange of the *real*. To my amazement, there is absolutely no exchange area in the international part and I've been told by two people now that there is some kind of federal law that says they're not allowed to take any *real* except at this little snack bar. Not even the duty-free shops. I thought, "Well, I have eighty *real*. I'll spend it on goods rather than have paper money that has little or no value to me." So, to me this is a wake-up call that even though you think you've covered all the events that will take place and that you're global enough that you have the experience to handle them, there's always a curved ball that comes up and now I have eighty *real* that has no place to go.

So, I'm sitting there thinking about it and I thought, "Nothing lost, nothing gained, I'll go down and if those people are still there I'll ask the gentleman if he would be interested in exchanging my *real.*" The fellow lives in Edinburgh, and after we get through the formalities, I said to him, "Would you be interested in exchanging my *real* for U.S. currency? I couldn't help but notice you exchanged some U.S. currency for *real* and I didn't realize that there is no other place available to do it." He said, "Yes, I come here every month so I can always use it. I'll exchange it for you." So, without too much hesitation, I don't think I got the best rate in town but I sure didn't get robbed either. Good Scot, he made the transaction fairly acceptable and I thanked him very much.

I went back upstairs with American money and no *real.* I have about another hour or so before my first leg of the flight commences and with that, the hours on the clock move forward, but the hands that tick the minutes away seem to drag and eventually yes, I can board the first leg of my flight. Wow! I'm on my way. And with that, we leave Rio de Janeiro on time.

The plane isn't a large plane and the fine gentleman did as requested, I'm by the door exit. The fellow that sits beside me, he's literally a giant. He's got to be at least 6'5" and he could have taken up both seats if the bar was movable. He is not talkative. We have a meal, chicken and salad, nice little dessert. In fact, I'm so full I can't eat it all.

With that, I start to bed down for the night and I would like to say goodnight, my little honey bun. I'm on my way home. Wendy and Cole, get ready for Grandpee to return to the nest. For the rest of you, one and all, I hope that you have a much more pleasant place to sleep than I do. Goodnight.

Robert F. Edwards

February 28, Thursday

Miami, Florida.

It's four o'clock, or probably closer to three-thirty in the morning. I've woken up to Miami time. We are served a very modest breakfast and the pilot tells us that soon we'll be on the final approach into Miami.

I don't know how I managed to do it, but I'm about the first person off the flight. The place is packed full of people. Within minutes, the Miami Immigration and Customs places look like a refugee camp. There has to be three to four hundred people. Also, the lucky draw is that the line that I decided to choose is stuck and every other line seems to be moving.

It's just one of those things, and I'm tired. The seats on the aircraft, I don't know why they call it economy; they should just call it poverty. If it goes back a notch, you're lucky. The seat had its own little television and all electronic gadgets. I would have sacrificed everything for about two more notches to move back so that I wasn't in an upright position on a hard bench.   Anyway, I'm tired and grumpy, and a little anti-American, to say the least.

I'm only passing through; I have to pick up my luggage, have them rummage through it; I have to clear their Immigration; and all I am is basically in a holding position. I could see it if I was leaving the airport or the holding area for a flight in and out. But, no, United States always has to do it their way and theirs is the only way. So, now you have to retrieve your luggage; you have to make up your declaration; you have to go through all the same rigmarole as if you were going to stay here for six months or whatever you are permitted on Canadian extension. However, as the hours wear on, it takes over an hour just to get through the Immigration.

Then it is on to Customs. And if they're trying to impress somebody, they managed to do it and it has to be themselves. If this is security, then it is just straight unadulterated hassle,

SOUTH AMERICA
ENCHANTMENT

just to see how much endurance travelers can put up with. They have forms on top of forms; they have agriculture, and they have announcements saying that you must declare everything or you're subject to fines, and it goes on and on. So finally, I get through Customs which, of course, I have nothing to declare because I have no intentions of staying. But I have to be questioned: Where was I, why was I there, who am I, where am I going, why am I a Canadian, and on and on and on and on. But when it comes down to the final crunch of who's right and who's wrong, have a good day, thank you, like what an insult! They're not thanking anybody; it's just a formality.

Then on to the Agriculture Center to go through an x-ray machine to see if you've got anything. If I had any more intentions of flying through the United States, I would put myself in a Glad bag and save them the problem of strip search. Paranoia is one thing; stupidity and paranoia are poor partners at the best of times.

After two-and-a-half hours, I've managed to get my luggage; I managed to get outside the holding area; and now, I'm permitted to go to the other concourse to get on to the other plane. The only thing I can say out of this whole unnecessary crap that everybody has had to endure is it shows two things: the total paranoia that Americans have at this time in their life; and the second is their total indifference to anybody's concerns.

However, when I do get through all this procedure, the attendants are waiting with United and are really trying to aid and assist because they know that the connecting flight happens to be the same flight number but different plane with the same number going on to Los Angeles. They're keeping an eagle eye out for any of us poor people that have managed to go through this horrendous charade of security. So with all the aid and support of the staff from United Airlines guiding us poor befuddled refugees of travel through the maze of security, we are directed to another security check before getting to the holding area before boarding the plane. By some miraculous ingenuity of the airlines co-coordinating what it takes to get from one plane to the other enroute, we arrive and start our boarding procedure. No sitting around now. As we get on to the plane waiting on the tarmac, the only difference is that this plane is enroute to Los Angeles, then on to Vancouver, Canada.

I am sitting in exactly the same seat throughout the duration of the flight, just a different plane. We take off, ironically on time, which is going to be another exceptionally long flight, at least for me. The first leg we barely get to cruising altitude, and a few hours later we are starting the descent into Los Angeles. The passengers, including myself, thank goodness, don't have to get off this plane. We just have to wait until they pack it full of the remaining passengers with tickets for the flight to Vancouver.

Once more we are airborne, and wow, service is absolutely missing. We are served coffee, tea, or water, and reluctantly a juice. Anything else, like alcohol, is $2.00 U.S. and please, you must have the right change. The gourmet meal is a bun, dry, some type of compressed meat, mayonnaise, and oh yes, just what every traveler needs at 3800 feet, a Power Bar. I remember once when airlines served food. This isn't the case now.

As I peer out of the window, I am starting to see some familiar sights, and the landscape through the patches of clouds are the Rocky Mountain ranges, and I know that I am heading back to Canada, my promised land. The flight arrives on time, and what a difference. I am standing in line, waiting to make my declaration to Canadian Immigration and Customs, and when it is my turn, the attendant looks at me, and my passport. The first thing he says is "Welcome back to Canada, where have you been" and I told him. "Have you got anything to declare?" as he looked at my declaration form, and I replied "Yes, just a few things for the family, and the out laws" and he laughed, handed me back the form, and said "Glad you had a good time". That was it.

SOUTH AMERICA ENCHANTMENT

I carried on to collect my luggage, and my wonderful wife was there waiting for me, and so was my beautiful daughter. With all the hugs and kisses, and moments of reunion, somehow this long awesome journey seemed like someone else's memories, rather than my own. We all headed back to the house, and it's a tradition that my wife has always kept, decorating for the homecoming event. This time was no exception, with balloons, streamers, and treats all over. I can say without any hesitation, if I had been an emperor returning with the spoils from a great campaign, I don't think I could have been received any better from my family. They are always in my heart, but it is so much greater when they are in my sight.

And that concludes this journey, this adventure, and this book.

ISBN 142514902-2